Podcasting for Teachers

Using a New Technology to Revolutionize Teaching and Learning

Revised Second Edition

a volume in
Emerging Technologies for Evolving Learners

Series Editors:
Kathleen P. King and Mark Gura
Fordham University

Podcasting for Teachers

Using a New Technology to Revolutionize Teaching and Learning

Revised Second Edition

by

Kathleen P. King and Mark Gura
Fordham University

Information Age Publishing, Inc.
Charlotte, North Carolina • www.infoagepub.com

Library of Congress Cataloging-in-Publication Data

King, Kathleen P., 1958-

Podcasting for teachers : using a new technology to revolutionize teaching and learning / by Kathleen P. King and Mark Gura. — Rev. 2nd ed.

p. cm. — (Emerging technologies for evolving learners)

Includes bibliographical references and index.

ISBN 978-1-60752-023-8 (pbk.) — ISBN 978-1-60752-024-5 (hardcover) 1. Internet in education. 2. Podcasting. I. Gura, Mark. II. Title.

LB1044.87.K57 2008

371.33'44678—dc22

2008043986

Printed in the United States of America

CONTENTS

ACKNOWLEDGMENTS

When you catch the excitement of a vision for a new digital form that can impact education, and you can see a great vision that is open ended, you are at a cross roads. Do you go it alone? Or do you try to find people who are willing to reach out and do the work of stretching toward that vision with you. That latter choice is the one we chose and it has resulted in a glorious collaboration and sharing of skills, creativity, shared knowledge, wars stories, laughter, and frustration, long nights, full-day events, 15 minute sessions, to 3 hour online classes. But the power of all of this excitement and worth has been in what has happened to the people involved.

So first a quick word about what happens through educational podcasting. For us the experience has been overflowing with words that describe excitement and descriptive words for what these encounters mean. Try a few of these descriptors and outcomes on for size thinking of your students in a language arts class or social studies class: Podcasting in education may result in: *building self-confidence, excitement, "can't get enough of collaborative groups," compelling, motivated to attend public speaking classes, and discovering my voice.*

For teachers, parents, and administrators that description has to have your attention and we will lead you through how it happened. But here in the acknowledgments a quick word about who made it happen. First of all, regarding this book, our publisher, George Johnson of Information Age Publishing, having the vision of not only this book but also the series

Podcasting for Teachers: Using a New Technology to Revolutionize Teaching and Learning,
Revised Second Edition, pp. vii–viii

titled Emerging Issues for Evolving Learners. Peter Yanke also created most of the artwork in a simple enough fashion to aid the reader to envision our models and diagrams.

We also want to thank our Teachers' Podcast (SM), and original Podcast for Teachers (SM), family of listeners. They have encouraged us to continue this labor of love and innovation in countless ways. They have expressed their vast appreciation, shared vibrant examples of technology use in their classrooms, provided additional resources with the Teachers Podcast listener, begun and shared the innovative developments of their own podcasts, building astounding numbers of listeners for our series, and being a truly global representation. Without you this experience would not have happened and we could not have realized the revolutionary possibilities of this new media was truly relevant. Thank you and please continue to contribute to our show and contact us—you are the reason we work so hard to create the episodes and the books.

Thank you also to those podcasters, developers, and companies who have allowed us to use images of and references to their work in this book. Among those who have been especially helpful in this respect are Rob Walch of Podcast 411, Steve Ely of Escape Pod, Jeff Bradley of Slauson PodShow and GuyInATie.com, Libsyn.com, Transformation Education LLC, zZounds.com, Wikispaces.com, Radio Owl Podcast of Mansfield CT, Podcast Pickle, Tangient LLC (of phpBB fame), Audacity, and CNET.com. Thank you for your goodwill.

Finally from Kathy—a heartfelt thanks to those who make my days and nights so very bright and remind me why I passionately desire to share for lifelong learning. Thank you for your kind forbearance. My greatest desire is that each of you will have every opportunity to learn, grow, and discover the fullness of your lives and voices for today and into your futures for many years: Sharon, Jim, Bill, Lisa, Chris, and Ruby.

PREFACE

With this book we share our experience and vision of podcasting in education. Based on discovery, work, and development in podcasting since August of 2005, we have not only created eight podcast series, but also advanced resources to broaden the purposes and services included in those podcasts. We have also taught podcasting to many educators both in traditional face-to-face settings, mentoring professional development programs, online, virtual workshops, and through our podcast itself. We have learned much about how to explain what we do and how to help others learn podcasting in education.

This book has three major sections, the first introduces the "revolution" of podcasting and places it in not only the larger societal and cultural context, but also within education. The second section provides the "how to" basics and technical aspects of podcasting, but is not a traditional podcasting how to section. We offer this section from the perspective of educators, for educators, and very much with the slant of making choices among mediums, methods, and equipment, keeping content the primary focus. We also present several models that we have developed and have seen emerge as we have worked in this field. We present models that describe the podcasting process and cost/benefit decisions.

The third part of the book addresses what is involved in becoming a podcasting educator. We discuss curricular applications, resources, and examples. We present a model that demonstrates how educators learn podcasting and we demonstrate uses of podcasting for classroom use and

Podcasting for Teachers: Using a New Technology to Revolutionize Teaching and Learning,
Revised Second Edition, pp. ix–xi

professional development. We finish off the section with a call to use podcasting to expand learning experiences and look beyond traditional uses of new technologies. This book also includes several valuable sections that make it helpful for beginning, intermediate, and advanced podcasting educators. We have included resource lists, key terms sections, and of course ample references and an index.

As we seek to capture this field of new and digital media for our readers, our reference list formatting was challenging. In order to make the book most helpful for you, several chapters' resources listed at the end of the chapter easily list Web sites by their familiar name. In addition, we use the traditional reference list in each chapter where it applies. It is exciting to be in an emergent field!

What is the excitement about? In a nutshell we have come to two major conclusions: first, podcasting is a vital example of technology that can be used by individuals and by our society to revolutionize teaching and learning. We have developed more than 200 hours of podcasting content at this point; we have invested hundreds of hours in development, recording, and production. Why not? Because we continue to see in ourselves and others valuable new developments in teaching and learning happening through podcasting. Introducing current findings and framing and previewing emerging trends are a major focus of this book.

Second, the experience of podcasting can be one which changes those in it: whether you are adults, teachers, or general public involved in podcasting or students using it for class projects; whether you are involved in some aspect with you plan, record, edit, or otherwise produce the podcast episodes, coaching, Web site, or technical support; you are part of a team whose work people hear of and *respond* to. There is a profound experience of hearing the result of that work broadcast globally and then receiving email and written feedback from people you know and DON'T know. It is a revealing experience on many levels. For some people it is a matter of "finding your voice," media literacy, developing research skills, developing motivation to improve research, writing, comprehension, and public speaking. For other participants it might be the first time they overcome public speaking embarrassment and gain confidence.

These are only a few of the changes people may experience and yet, these outcomes can have multiple compounding effects in other dimensions. For example, students who become interested in pursuing research pay attention to comprehension, start to learn how the library reference system works, begin to gain confidence in their academic skills, may build a pattern of success, and even come to class more frequently. Students with increased confidence in public speaking may begin to ask questions in class, and therefore it gets lost in subject study, and improve their grades. The interrelated educational benefits are immeasurable because there are so many and they can extend across such a long period of time.

But on a more personal level, we would encourage you to look at podcasting, digital media production in education, and this book, as a potential journey for yourself. As you explore podcasting for educational purposes you will undoubtedly discover some new academic possibilities, but you will also find some new possibilities for you as a person. We encourage you to take hold of those possibilities. Find your voice, discover your new interests, and explore your different abilities through this medium. The lessons you gain in this context as a learner will deepen your insight as an educator. The enduring model of the reflective practitioner is not just a theory of broad application; it is very important when it is one of personal experience. Let's embark on a journey of understanding, for your students, your classrooms, teaching and learning, and for yourself as a lifelong learner.

What will podcasting in education mean for you? Whether you are a beginner in technology use, intermediate or advanced; Windows or Linux person or Mac aficionado; iPod user or MP3 mystified—you are in the right place to start this journey with us. As an educator you have your experience in education, your understanding of teaching and learning, and your insight into your content and students. We as coauthors of the book want to introduce the world of podcasting in education to you—or for some—show you parts you've yet to explore. We will share our frame and model for podcasting in education and take you on several tours and views of classrooms and podcasting in action. Join us to see what is happening and reflect and determine: What will podcasting in education mean for you?

ADDENDUM 2009 EDITION

"Oh, the places you will go!"

—Dr. Suess (*Oh, The Places You Will Go,* 1990).

Having reached surprising heights of success we made a decision in fall 2007 to redesign the series somewhat launch it independently as The Teachers' Podcast (http://www.teeacherspodcast.org). Transformation Education LLC (http://www.transformationed.com) is our host and producer and holds all rights, and copyright in conjunction with Dr. Kathleen King and Mark Gura. This change provided the opportunity to create a more innovative and "new generation" of the series.

We appreciate the roots of of the original concepts and series, as Kathy returned to faculty status from that of administrator at the university, our work on the podcast has become independent of the institution.

The podcasting work has evolved in additional dimensions. As of 2009, we have developed and produced podcast series for a number of organizations and partners. The work has many forms, however two examples are (1) the grant funded Talking Financial Literacy Podcast (www.talkingfinlit.org), and 2) new media production outsource services for organizations, corporations, government agencies, and schools. Opportunities for presentations and keynotes have also increased and now include new media and podcasting as exciting and valuable topics. Our work of providing professional development services, leadership, innovation, research, and development has been an experience growing out of decades of our collective experience. Still we look forward to many years of pioneering new territory and enjoying the community of our listeners and our colleagues.

What you will find in this 2009 revised and updated edition of the book are many changes. We have included insights and updates related to our additional years of experience in podcasting and new media. We have updated URLs, screenshots, and data tables, added some new curricular examples, and included references to our new series. We have also upgraded statistical information, advancements from the podcasting world, more references, and updated biographical information. In short the book is better than ever, in part because of suggestions from our many readers, students, and listeners, of course!

Your colleagues,

Kathy King and Mark Gura,
Teachers Podcast—A New Generation of
Teacher Professional Development

PART I

REVOLUTION IN OUR POCKETS

CHAPTER 1

FROM THE FRONT LINES

Drafting New Technologies to Revolutionize Education

PUSH-ME PULL-YI PROFESSIONAL DEVELOPMENT DILEMMAS

Walking through the halls of our schools, one can quickly see that life in our schools is always exciting. On the best days classrooms brim over with discovery, enthusiasm, collaboration, teaching, and learning. However in the midst of this positive energy, there is a dilemma when considering teachers' learning. Dr. Doolittle's familiar creature of the Push-Me Pull-Yi (Lofting, 1920) could be used to depict the relationship between professional development and this learning community.

Consider the following statements overheard in many forms throughout schools around the world,

> *"We need all the teachers to have additional professional development time, but we don't have time in the school schedule for additional professional development."*
>
> *"We have this great new software for you to use, but we can't bring in the specialists to lead sessions."*

Podcasting for Teachers: Using a New Technology to Revolutionize Teaching and Learning,
Revised Second Edition, pp. 3–15

> *"We have a training group available to teach this terrific new curriculum approach, but they can only come on Wednesday afternoons, when we are doing our required school assessment meetings for the next 8 months."*
>
> *"There is a valuable conference series on the other side of the country, but the total cost of the event is triple our conference budget."*
>
> *"Some of our teachers need to have the training repeated, or slowed down. Other teachers could really skip some of the sessions. Being able to learn at their own pace would be the best approach. How do we do that with face-to-face sessions?"*

It would seem that many of our teachers, administrators, and staff developers are asking similar questions: Most of the time it seems like our main focus should be teaching our students, but if we don't address the learning needs of our teachers they will not be able to teach effectively. How do we make the choice? Which is the priority? How do we multiply time and space?

We are pressed with the demands for increased student outcomes and additional teacher credentials, but we cannot add hours to the day for the additional training that educators need in order to make both possible. The Push-Me Pull-Yi Professional Development (PD) Dilemma is one which is experienced regardless of national, geographic, socioeconomic status, academic achievement, computer counts, or financial resources. This dilemma is one of time against space; would that we could effectively separate and conquer the needs of teachers and learners.

The good news is that in 2008 and beyond, professional development can be better delivered in a truly on-demand and mobile format than ever before. This solution can help conquer the Push-Me Push-Yi PD Dilemma for many schools and teachers! Based on our experience as educators and working with educators in professional development roles for many years, we understand the pressing needs for quality learning content, of pressing schedules, and varied learning needs. Both on an individual and school level there are variations of all of these issues with which to cope.

At the same time, professional development solutions need to be affordable and accessible. They also need to be related to the teacher's level of application and need. That is, teacher created content is immensely valuable. To only have professional development materials created by professional developers does not always meet the need. Having teachers able to share their experiences *from the trenches* eye-to eye, shoulder to shoulder is a very critical format. Speaking from experience which provides a valuable authentication from which to be heard and also upon to build future opportunities for learning. With this dynamic established teachers have a basis for more fully understanding and appreciating what their colleagues are saying and also to reflect on their own learning. Such learning can easily become mirrorlike.

If technology is intended to be part of their professional development solution it has to be an element with several essential characteristics. It has to be easy to learn and use, accessible and affordable, able to become transparent, and potentially powerful enough to be transformative.

Kathy has been involved in distance education since the early 1990s, and worked with a wide range of technologies. Mark was in the classroom for 18 years and then head of instructional technology for the City of New York. We are accustomed to seeing a wide range of technologies and also to sifting through the good, the bad, and the ugly. When we came together to work with the Fordham University RETC Center for Professional Development (www.retc.fordham.edu) it was to develop and delivery professional development in many forms. When we came across podcasting as a particular form of professional development delivery and development we knew we had found something very different. Podcasting for education could have its roots in the ground of actual experience and daily teachers' needs, something that had potential, and something that might break apart that Push-Me Pull-Yi PD Dilemma and dichotomy.

DISCOVERIES AT 35,000 FEET

It was late July 2005 and I, Kathy, was headed to Alaska to lead sessions about distance learning for a group of educators. It would be an exciting week, with exploring a bit of Alaska as we traveled to our destination, learning more about the indigenous cultures, and reveling in the views of the gorgeous ocean, mountains, and playful sea otters. But most of all I couldn't wait to hear how my work and experiences intersected with those of the adult educators from this frontier. To find this out, I had to endure the long trek from the east coast of the United States to Anchorage, a 5-hour drive down the southwest peninsula of Alaska and then a boat ride out to a remote retreat house island. Endure, yes because of some physical problems I had, however, revel in the gorgeous environment and company, absolutely.

Meanwhile, on a personal and professional level I was frustrated because I had not been able to attend one of my favorite annual conferences that spring. Serious back problems had required another procedure. Well this was later in the summer, and I was able to do the Alaska trip. A small consolation was that with the long flight ahead of us, I had loaded up this new iPod with hours of music and podcasts of all sorts of topics. I guess being captive on a plane for 8 hours provides a good learning and testing lab.

Thirty-five thousand feet over Canada I found myself further *transported, but this time it was* **virtually** and *back in time to the conference I had missed! Through this simple portable audio technology, I had been able to download these recordings off the Web site and load them onto the iPod. Now I was sitting at my convenience (or squashed between two other people in an airplane hurtling through the skies, trying to forget about the hours of traveling captivity) and able to hear the sessions I had wanted to attend!*

The content was one thing. I benefited as an individual and professional for sure. But the potential for this simple technology was terrific! Firsthand, no pun intended with the MP3 player clutched in my fingers, I was experiencing the power of recording quality professional education events, making them freely and publicly available and converting them into a highly mobile format. Each aspect of this podcast production was essential to its success.

The wheels of my mind were turning even while I was listening to the conference sessions. If I could benefit in this way, how could this help other people? How could we plan and design materials to help teachers beyond the constraints of time, space, and location? What were the limitations? What were the benefits? What were the costs and difficulties? Who else was doing this in education? I had not seen much in the listings where I had found the conference podcasts. Still I tried to settle in and enjoy the benefits of the podcasts for myself as an individual without escalating the vision too quickly!

THE VISION

This vision is the one of podcasting as we see it for Teachers' Podcast, Techpod (sm) and in our larger view of podcasting for teaching and learning. There are two prongs to the view, one is the impact of podcasting by providing professional development on demand and the other is the impact for students. One perspective looks at the teacher's side, the other the students' side; altogether one gets a full circle of teaching and learning and learning as *lifelong* learning. As we said before, the podcasting experience is also one of learning new skills and learning about self. This technology is a medium that affords discovery as it can involve a depth of the individual.

As we explore this vision in this chapter, we are drafting this new technology, and potentially other digital media which will emerge, and delve into the details of this unique perspective for professional development for teachers and learning for students. We will also discuss the "what" of podcasting and help explain how it is similar and different from other digital media and it so much more than audio broadcasting.

Along the way we will share some of our podcasting journey as a way to describe how educators can learn. We then briefly depict the cycle by which to try, test, and learn again in our learning of this technology so that you can benefit from our experience and varied expertise. Together this provides a grounded model of theory, action research, and practice that can energize our classrooms and work together.

All together we aim to provide a vision of extending practical application, reaching further, taking our curriculum to new places, and always with constant improvement and change from the experience of ourselves as teachers and learners. Join us for this journey from the front lines.

A View of Podcasting Through Two Lenses

For a vision of podcasting as revolutionizing education we use two lenses. We see (1) the impact of professional development on demand for teachers and (2) the many possibilities for students among the major restrictions educators face with professional development, time, and relevance are close to the top of the list. Podcasting provides professional development that can be accessed when it is needed, so a resource directory of materials can be created and educators can select topics they need at the given time to fit the need of the moment and be able to have access to professional learning. This means professional development is available 24/7, on their schedule, based on their own need and choices.

One of the major inroads in making this possible has been that audio editing has become easier and less expensive. Therefore, very importantly, on the development side, the cost to create these podcast resources does not have to be great.

On the user side, for the teacher, the interface to find, retrieve, carry, and play podcasts is much easier than in the days of such technically heavy technologies as pre-Web bulletin boards, but more powerful than simple Web pages. Teachers are stepping up to experience some of the power of the user-become-creator, Web 2.0, side of the Internet through podcasts. Through finding, listening to, creating play lists, and creating podcasts they become familiar with the technologies that their students use so frequently. Could we even say they become converts? Teachers of all ages and technology expertise are getting "turned on" to the easier customizing and designing "this can be my own" power and perspective of this newer evolution of the Internet.

The possibilities for students learning with podcasts provide an immense vision. At first one might not think this medium and technology is much different than other computer-based formats; however, our experience listening to teachers and students alike is that podcasting can unleash unexpected achievements. Through our podcast listener feedback, professional development sessions, and outreach we have seen a great deal of collaborative, learner-centered projects in K-12 podcasting and the results are that the projects evolve into authentic demonstrations of twenty-first century learning, media literacy, reading, writing, and speaking literacy skills.

What is more, as seen in Table 1.1, the projects develop great motivation for participation, related research, and learning among the students. They provide exposure to different forms of literature and literary forms such as narrative, performances, re-enactments on a wide range of topics, and by their very Internet-based format, they can provide a global perspective and experience of participation. The teacher's role as a facilitator and guide is indispensable in these projects, the time invested undeniable, but the enthusiasm, commitment, and pride of student work are outcomes that will have lifetime benefits.

Realizing the impact that podcasting has already had across teacher and student experiences alike, what shape has this revolutionizing of education taken? In the next sections we review what a podcast is and delve into sharing our experience on the front lines. Our desire is that you will benefit and build on these lessons and advance with us to the further developments that await ahead.

WHAT IS PODCASTING?

A podcast is a series of portable sound files, hosted on the Web, and distributed via a Really Simple Syndication (RSS) feed. There are individual podcast episodes, and there are podcast shows, like the Teachers' Podcast series (aka Podcast for Teachers). As of June 2008 there are 130 episodes to select.

What makes podcasting different from an audio file posted on the Web? It is different because it is part of a series, and the power of a scripting language called XML to have the most recent episode sent to the top of the list. Figure 1.1 briefly illustrates this relationship so that we can see that in order for digital media to be a podcast it has to have the essential elements we named above:

Why bother with the details? Because a podcast is more than an audio file playing on the web. It is portable and it is distributed separate from the individual web page. That is the "magic" of the audio file format-MP3 files. Consider the "Ode to a Podcast" in Figure 1.2

MORE THAN A PODCAST

At the same time, through our experience with Podcast for Teachers, Techpod (PFT) (www.podcastforteachers.org) we are convinced that this

Table 1.1. The Teachers' Podcast's Vision of Podcasting

Impact of Professional Development on Demand	*Possibilities for students*
• As of 2008 an already extensive source of PD resources available. And as teachers build more, they add to the resources that are customized for their specific schools and content needs. Expanding archive of resources	• Learner-centered teaching, classrooms, and projects easy to prepare and transition to
• Just in time availability and 24/7 availability	• Project-based learning
• Interest of students/motivation is a great hook the teachers can use and can encourage them to use this technology platform to research their study units	• Different literacy skills—reading, writing, speaking
• Low-cost development if needed and desired	• Authentic assessment easily accomplished
• Technology has become so much easier than previously (sound editing)	• Twenty-first century learning becomes transparent and highly motivating
• Interfaces to reach the content had become more available and widely adopted)—iTunes for music ... is a parallel that can be captured for the audio podcast	• Research skills embedded in their projects
• Utilizing advances and advantages of Web 2.0 technologies for collaboration, communication, etc.	• Exposure to different forms and genres of literature
	• Collaborative learning teams becomes a natural form to work on tasks
	• Reaching into their areas of motivation and interest
	• Global relationships and communication are much easier
	• Technology learning embedded in the larger projects
	• A variety of media literacy skills are gained
	Visit www.teacherspodcast.org for more ideas and resources!

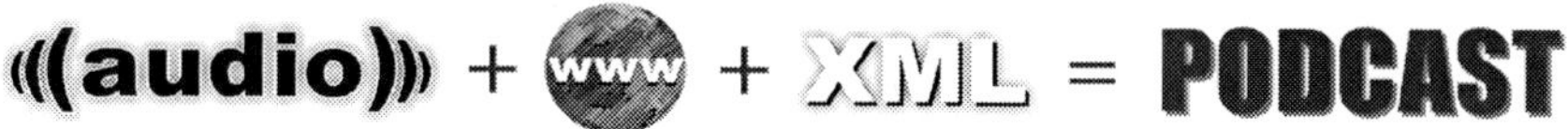

AUDIO file + The Web(Internet host) + XML = Podcast

Figure 1.1. Essential elements of a podcast.

Ode to a Podcast

The podcast is more than an MP3 file posted on the Web, it is a series that is automatically sent to the user's computer—that is the power of the XML program language.

A podcast is portable, personal and powerful.

The MP3 format makes it portable

The XML makes it personal because you select it and it is delivered to your desktop.

The combination makes it *anytime, anywhere* and therefore a powerful combination for teaching and learning

Figure 1.2. Ode to a podcast.

medium has the capability of being much more than the technology of audio broadcasting pushed by XML scripts. Instead we have experienced a growing community and a burgeoning, bursting selection of resources. Our experience has been that our podcast is not only the weekly episode that is delivered to the desktop of our listeners and taken with them to the beach or the gym, wherever and whenever they choose to listen to that episode, but what we point them to is a host of articles, links, and resources with each of those episodes.

And as we have discussed with them, our listeners follow-up on those links and resources and use them with their students. Some have started using wikis; others have developed teacher podcasts, professional development podcasts, and student project podcasts. Still others are engaged in learning about new resources for their content area that they had not known about. And many comment on the news items that we share with them: the perspective that their educational world is much larger than their classroom or their school. It is by so many degrees of connection that some relationships and resources also develop. Our podcast not only brings Teachers' Podcast's cohosts Kathy and Mark into their world, but also the resources, articles, and people we interview. In later chapters we will discuss in detail the specific resources we have developed including, but not limited to: online and virtual workshops, a complete podcast home page or "podcasting repertoire page," online articles, show notes, resources lists for each episode, and our podcast bulletin board.

FROM THE FRONTLINE: NO RISK, NO REVOLUTION

So How Did it Start?

As we undertook the beginning of our podcast series, Kathy now has developed at least nine podcast series, we had behind us experience in education, research, and various types of technology. However neither of us knew anything about sound editing or broadcasting. But as stated, we had seen that this technology was relatively inexpensive, easy to learn, and full of educational potential. Further equipping us for this feat we knew from working together that we were comfortable with "working models." We frequently have taken on the task of discovering innovative solutions, parsing out that dilemma, and creating new options for busy educators. That is to say, to set forth a best premise, work with it, adjust, and try again.

In this same frame of reference we saw potential with podcasting. We hoped to use this same approach to establish a popular mobile learning professional development vehicle; ultimately it became a model of professional development on demand. Such has been our approach of taking risks and riding the rarified air of really no pain, no gain, or perhaps, *no risk, no revolution*.

Thus began the evolution and experience of a successful educational podcast. Who are we? Kathy and Mark, the coauthors of this book are the coproducers/cohosts of the weekly podcast talk show they created as part of their work and extracurricular work at an urban university. Within 6 months these self-taught broadcasters established Podcast for Teachers and attracted over 20,000 listeners; and within 12 months it had reached 600,000.

The details will follow, but fundamental here are the points that we had a keen eye and dedication to content, respect for one another and our colleagues, and a dedication to figuring out if this technology could work well. Many, many hours and episodes later (70+ episodes, 5 series and 100+ hours of broadcasts), this model has mostly stood the test. We have experienced podcasting as an example that technology is still providing methodologies that can be used in deep and powerful ways for twenty-first century education.

By accessing our weekly podcast, teachers around the globe can "click into" timely, quality, and helpful professional development on the uses of technology for teaching and learning. They can do this 24/7 based on *their* own schedule. What takes this beyond the already established phenomenon of online learning and online courses though, is that this content can be listened to anywhere. Our Web-based broadcasts can be downloaded free of charge from the Teachers' Podcast Web site (www.teacherspodcast.org) or from numerous media/podcast directories (i.e. iTunes.com, podcast.yahoo.com, podcastalley.com, podcastpickle .com, etc.) and listened to on any computer or transferred to any MP3 player (i.e. iPod, Zune, SanDisk, Creative Zen, iRiver, etc.). Imagine professional development that's set free of cables, wires, in fact any restrictions of location; as mobile as music has become to the iPod generation.

As of November 2008 the Teachers' Podcast series has reached more than 4.3 million listeners.

The content of our weekly podcast offers interviews with educators, authors, and "ed techies," curriculum ideas, news resources, technology tips, and research that educators can use in the classroom. Because of the technology format, it is available 24 hours a day, 7 days a week. The podcast can be, and based on reports from our listeners, it is, easily transported to the beach, the gym, supermarket, or commute to work. Teachers who want to be "in the know" can fit professional development into their schedules rather than having to do the reverse.

TiVo for professional learning? It's actually even better than that, because you don't need to schedule the recording in advance. The online podcast databases and Web sites allow people to search for the topics they need, when they need them. It truly becomes *professional development on demand* and that puts teachers in command of their own learning!

BUILDING ON OUR EXPERIENCE

While creating podcasting can involve a high-end production process, it can also be done more simply and inexpensively. Knowing that for most educators, simple and inexpensive are essential dimensions of adoption; we were determined to establish a podcasting model in that realm. The Teachers' Podcast original series started off with a simple laptop computer, $10 external microphone, and free audio software and $5/month Internet hosting site.

Given that we tend to be a bit more technically minded than the average teacher perhaps, we explicitly concentrate on developing straightforward solutions. Therefore we offer a quick preview here of audio editing. The software aspect is not complex under usual circumstances. Basic software and the resources listed above will allow you to follow a process of: log in, click, record, click, and post. More advanced editing functions can be added later. Podcasters generally quickly want to focus on content and sound quality editing after the basics are mastered.

Aspiring educational podcasters' greatest attention, however, needs to be paid to content. Consideration and decisions need to be made in relation to use of technology, how technology changes the perception and use of information. In K-12 settings there is a great opportunity to facilitate this work with young people by having them participate in creating, developing, performing, and editing the podcasts. For professional development purposes this work more so lies in the hands of the teachers and staff developers, or teacher educators.

We have much to offer the reader in terms of our mistakes and lessons learned. We recorded the first 40 episodes under a myriad of difficult, and changing conditions and had to learn many solutions for sound editing that usual users would not encounter. In addition we learned during the beginning days of podcasting and now there is an easier road with improved equipment and software available for the everyday user. **All of this is to your advantage!** Our focus in sharing with you will be to provide solutions that will work well for you. We also want to focus on solutions that employ technology now available and likely to fit what comes next.

THEORY, RESEARCH, AND PRACTICE

Our work sounds utilitarian and technology focused perhaps, but it is fully rooted in models of educational research and practice. In particular our model is one of reflective practice (Schön, 1983) and constructivism (Harel & Papert, 1991; Jonassen, 1995). We are invested in the perspective that we need to build on pedagogical principles, and yet test our work against the measure of practice. We believe, like many before us, moving this tripartite relationship of theory, research, and practice is a strong basis for inquiry, professional growth, and the advancement of teaching and learning.

Through reflective practice we gain a keen insight into the perspective of the educator from the beginning, through the process and afterwards. Rather than looking at teaching and learning as a sterile process, the reflective practitioner gives us an "on the ground" and "within the process" perspective that can closely examine how to understand and improve both our understanding and future efforts.

The frameworks of critical thinking and constructivism provide careful examination of the present conditions and construction of new pursuits. Rather than casting about with random attempts, building skills, and practice with critical thinking provide strategic coping skills to succeed in a rapidly changing world. Constructivism is then the model by which to operate with those skills.

Together we use this platform to frame our work in professional development and podcasting in order to communicate a much larger lesson. We are communicating a worldview and skills for lifelong learning to our educators. We desire for them to become educators who can succeed on their own and extend practical application further, reaching beyond the scope of even our understanding, taking curriculum to new places. The view of revolutionizing education is about constant improvement and change from the experience of ourselves as teachers and learners.

VISION

Our vision of revolutionizing education through this new technology is based in part on our understanding of the professional development of educators as adult learning (King, 2002, 2005). Fundamental to our educational philosophy is that educators are adult learners and the focus of our professional development efforts is to support them by identifying and satisfying their learning needs. Above all, we urge integrating technology in critical ways that make it capable of radically *transforming* teaching and learning (Gura & King, 2007; Gura & Percy, 2005; King, 2002, 2005). The icing on the cake is that through Podcast for Teachers we are providing important educational technology programming far beyond our reach and usual scope at our New York campuses.

In our podcast we include educational news from across the United States and around the world; we offer not only information, but critical views and debates about these topics as we discuss them together and with our colleagues. *Beyond the* conversation and interview dimension of Teachers' Podcast "grouptalk" we go considerably further to support our colleagues. The www.podcastforteachers.org Web site is replete with resources much needed by a community of educators that's hungry for material that can help them improve their instructional programs through the application of technology to content areas. The site comprehensively lists all resources mentioned in each podcast episode, including links through which listeners can access them.

Nonetheless, Teachers' Podcast pushes the educational podcasting envelope even further through interactive elements that provide opportunities for teachers to contribute to the show. As seen in Figure 1.3 teachers may submit their own descriptions of educational technology and podcast uses via email, MP3 audio files, and phone call-ins.

How to Participate in the PD on Demand?
Complete TTPOD Contact Information:

"Click in" and listen to Teachers' Podcast
Broadcast over the Web - available 24/7
WEB SITE: www.teacherspodcast.org
Podcast FEED: www.teacherspodcast.org/feed.xml

Send us your comments and examples of podcast use:
EMAIL: www.teacherspodcast@gmail.com

Figure 1.3. How to participate in the PD on demand.

The critical element which seems to be missing in many informal podcasts is content and that may be why many universities experimenting with podcasting simply record lectures for the most part, missing the bulk of this technology's potential. Developing content requires some forethought, planning, and scheduling. It also requires insight into how this new technology subtly changes the dynamics of information exchange between speaker and listener and how this must be accounted for through the format. We have experienced, however, that the opportunity to reach educators with quality professional development at their convenience is so great that the effort to surmount these challenges pays great dividends in quality and impact.

Our vision of podcasting as revolutionizing education has been materializing and we offer you the opportunity, through this book, to learn from that experience and benefit from it. Based on the rapid growth in our listenership, the responses we receive from them and the innovations we have developed in professional development content and creations. Thankfully we do not consider that this book will hold the final chapter of podcasting in education, we do not want to offer that! Instead we have an unending vision—one of a revolution that you can be part of and carry forward with us.

CHAPTER 2

WHAT IS THE PODCASTING REVOLUTION ALL ABOUT?

PODCASTING IN EDUCATION PRESS REPORTS

Dateline: October 2008
Millersville Elementary Digital Media Voices Arise
Millersville, PA

As I approached Mr. Millers' class in Millersville Elementary School it was perfectly clear that excitement was in the air. Upon looking in the windowed-door I could see groups of students were deeply engrossed in working around laptop computers at various locations throughout the room. Their equipment included a simple desktop microphone (I have seen this in Radio Shack and CompUSA for about $10-15), the laptop computer, and software that made graphic wave patterns as they spoke into the microphone.

At first I canvassed the room and listened to the activity at each group, they were working on writing historical reenactments of explorer adventurers. One group represented Christopher Columbus, another Magellan, a third Lewis and Clark, and the fourth Marco Polo. Upon interviewing these young historical reporters my concept of school history study was radically changed. In the Lewis and Clark group, Billy told me that he was the researcher *of the group, Ruby the* producer*, Jim the* fact checker *and* script writer*, and in the readings Joey and Billy were Lewis and Clark and*

Podcasting for Teachers: Using a New Technology to Revolutionize Teaching and Learning, Revised Second Edition, pp. 17–31

Ruby, the narrator. *These students had not only dissected the tasks involved in researching and producing the work, but they had made choices about who was assigned to each task.*

The level of collaboration was beyond my expectation. For some reason I had expected them to do their work individually and then just merge it, instead I found that today they were reporting on their progress, discussing it together, and making recommendations to each other for further development. I thought about how collaborative team work was incorporated into their learning at such early ages, and how they would not have the same hurdles of adjustment that we faced when we entered the workplace and had to shift from our traditional form of individualistic academic work styles. Imagine the additional years of experience in this mode of work, development, and interdependence they would have when they approached the workforce at age 18 or 22 compared to our generation. They stood to make great advances beyond that which we have been capable.

The excitement heightened and then abruptly stopped as a recording was begun, Ruby was introducing the second episode of their "L&C Adventures into the Wilderness," hand signals lead individuals from one part to the next, each member of the team read their script with expression and careful articulation of the words. When the recording ended they hooted with excitement and immediately played it back on the computer. They were also taking notes as to what parts to alter or rerecord. It was clear that these fourth-grade students had clearly mastered a process of writing research, design, and dramatic reading, collaborative learning, and audio recording, and editing.

FLASHBACK
Dateline: SEPTEMBER 2004

Birth of Audioblogging AKA Podcasting—Plugged for Sound! Somewhere, USA and Rest of World

A small group of technophiles have plugged in together via the Internet to listen to Adam Curry broadcast his first in a series of "podcasts." These web-based broadcasts are not commercial based and not affiliated with any broadcasting agency. The content of the shows are music and talk, but it is the technology and "Freedom From Control" that has people buzzing.

Podcasts, which is commonly understood to be a combination of the words iPod and broadcast, are audio files which are posted on the Internet, and then able to be accessed via a free "podcatcher" software program and downloaded to your computer. The broadcast is in MP3 audio format which is played through many computer music programs like, Music Match, iTunes and Windows Media Player; but what is even more radical is that the files can also be transferred to a MP3 device such as an iPod and the user can then take the music with them and listen to it whenever and wherever they desire to. It was Dave Winer and Adam Curry who had explored how to make this happen (Lafferty & Walch, 2006).

As of September 2004, there are very few podcasts available. Will this technology catch on? Will people take the time to create podcasts? Will the technology be simple enough to create them and to listen to them? Time will tell.

FAST FORWARD
Dateline: JULY 2006

Dateline: July 2006
Adoption of Podcasting—9 million—Phenomenon Rising
USA

The latest reports from Neilsen research reveal that as of July 2006, over 9 million people have downloaded and listened to a podcast (Neilsen, 2006). In and of itself this may not seem like a remarkable number given the vast number of Internet users today. However this is truly a remarkable trend because just 22 months ago podcasting, then called "audioblogging" began with the work of Adam Curry and "What was just a handful of 'audiobloggers' on Labor Day of 2004 turned into a group of a few hundred 'podcasters' by New Year's Eve 2004" (Lafferty & Walch, 2006, p. 8).

This growth in podcasting listeners is a difficult number to arrive at and only represents USA numbers. However it reveals a 900,000% increase in listeners over a 22-month period of time. Many factors contributed to this widespread adoption, including greater ease of use of software, popular technology distribution, and the integration of podcast directories into iTunes, Yahoo and other mainstream Internet directories and portals.

At the same time, how many people are producing podcasts? The adoption of medium as a consumer is different than as a producer. Recent statistics demonstrate that the number of podcasts that are available have risen to at least 100,000 in September 2006. This represents the number of podcasts identified in Feedburner.com (2006) 66,879.

Furthermore, podcasting has moved from geeks'-only phenomenon to a social phenomenon. The range of topics are not just music and technology topics (geek talk). Perusing the recent listing women's talk, sports, language learning, games tricks, Gay-Lesbian-Bisexual-Transgender (GLBT) inter-

ests, university courses, natural animal healthcare, dramatic readings, family updates, and everything in between and beyond can be found on the podcast directory listings. Indeed the places to find podcast listings are increasing daily. One of the master lists of such directories provides a broad array of sources to find podcasts that may not be found in mainstream sites, but can be great gems of interest and quality: Podcast 411.com's Directory of Directories *(http://www.podcast411.com/page2.html)*

FAST FORWARD
Dateline: MARCH 2009

Dateline: January 2007
Mobility of Podcasting—On the Move
Next Door and Anywhere, World.

This infiltration of MP3 players is everywhere but it is more than the music iPod craze; this is handheld, personalized, mobile digital audio and video created by people in all walks of life and listened to … Well let's see! Talking to people on the street, in the gym, and on the beach we have gathered the latest reports on this trend.

"I can take my favorite podcast to the gym with me. It is like fitting time with my favorite professors, Mark and Kathy, into my schedule (Podcast for Teachers). On the treadmill is my favorite time, I get into my zone, and can really tune into the conversation."

"Oh my goodness sometimes the wait in line at the supermarket can go on forever, the long wait at the doctor's office, or picking someone up at the airport? But I have found the greatest way to splice my life! I pick out my best podcast choices, put them on my MP3 player and then click through them when I have time. It is amazing how much in between time can be turned into useful life time! I get so much more accomplished when I am not aggravated by necessary waiting."

"Taking my laptop to the beach was a nightmare. I do not recommend it. Sand found it's way into more crevices. Pretty foolish to even try it. BUT! I can do this with my MP3 player, I have one of those tiny iPod Shuffles, the little inexpensive flash players. I see lots of people on the beach with MP3 players. You don't just listen to music. I listen to books on them, and my favorite podcasts, some are about educational technology, others are like old time radio shows, or talk shows. There is so much to choose from. I usually stick with my favorites and am able to catch up with the series while I am laying on the beach or jogging. What is more, most of the podcasts have Web sites where they post information; they call them show notes, so you can go

back and get details and links about the show. Therefore you don't have to try to scribble notes on your lunch or in the sand ;-)"

Certainly podcast listeners have a sense of humor, but I am also seeing a great deal of creativity in exploring how they can use this technology to fit their lifestyles. A greatly mobile community is thriving on a mobile opportunity for learning.

OVERVIEW

From MP3 players on the beach, to students reenacting explorers of the high seas, podcasting has stirred a revolution since coming on the scene in 2004. What is this podcasting revolution all about? The greater realm of podcasting gained its roots in a movement originally dubbed "The Voice of the People," "Democratization of the Media," and "Radio on Demand," when it emerged on the public technology scene in 2004. In 2001, Dave Winer and Adam Curry discussed using the Web, XML, and RSS formats to deliver audio and video. Winer created the technology, but as we said above it was Curry who popularized the format in 2004 with the release of the software iPodder and the launch of his podcast *The Daily Source Code* (Lafferty & Walch, 2006).

In this chapter we will explore the major trends of meaning of this media revolution. As seen in our opening *dateline news stories* a major trend is *mobilization*: people take these broadcasts wherever they go. Additionally we saw evidence of students, experts, and average everyday people hitting the broadcasting stage through this dramatic breakthrough of the restraints of media conglomerates: These are some examples of how *Democratization of the Media* is brought to life in education.

In addition there is a dramatic experience of *Discovering Your Voice* that has brought results from young people and adults as they take to the microphone and leave their usual public speaking hesitations behind. Certainly this is a *Medium of Discovery* that we have seen used in many ways in people's lives as they employ it. By learning to podcast they gain not only audio and video technical skills, but media literacy, and basic literacy skills are also authentically and critically embedded. This is not a technology which stands in isolation apart form society and learning, it is a technology embedded in the life and flow of our world, it is creating a revolution of its own. Join us as we explore it.

THE MOBILE TECHNOLOGY DIFFERENCE

The impact that e-learning has had on education over the last 20 years is significant, especially in higher education (King & Griggs, 2006). The creation of distance learning programs within colleges and universities, and indeed whole colleges developed *solely as distance learning* institutions, has changed the way we think about pursuing education after high school. And yet, the impact of distance education on K-12 education has not been as widely pronounced.

Audio and video podcasting as mobile learning stand to provide a very different dimension of distance learning. And this is especially on the basis of two accounts: one, podcasts are seen as smaller segments of learning, it is not necessary for people to expect to always learn whole classes through the medium at this time, and we may remain open for a good period of time to paradigms that accept smaller segments of learning and development. Two, instead of being restrained and constrained to a desktop or videoconference room, podcasting learning truly can be "anytime, anywhere."

As illustrated above, people of all ages are already, moment by moment, discovering the many places they can personalize their use of podcast listening. From the classroom, to the gym, shopping mall, and to airplane, learners of all ages are exploring how to use mobile technology to improve their personal learning.

What makes a *podcast* mobile technology? The most complete answer is that a podcast is a series of audio files stored and available on the Internet and published via an RSS feed which enables each episode of the series to be "pushed" to subscribers. However sometimes a picture can be a great communicator, therefore as a reminder, Figure 2.1 again provides a graphic representation of the definition of podcast.

Or as Geoghegan and Klass (2005) describe,

> a podcast is audio content available on the Internet that can be automatically delivered to your computer or MP3 player. Strip away all the upcoming potential confusion of feeds, aggregators, subscriptions, and so on, and what's left? Audio on the web.
>
> So what's the big deal? We've had "Internet radio" on the web for over a decade.... Why is podcasting *different?* To summarize quickly, podcasting is ***automatic,*** it's ***easy to control by the listener,*** it's ***portable*** and it's ***always available.***" (pp. 5-6, emphasis added).

((audio)) + www + XML = PODCAST

AUDIO file + The Web(Internet host) + XML = Podcast

Figure 2.1. Essential elements of a podcast.

Dissecting this definition reveals that the audio series is a music and/or spoken word MP3 file that is from the same source (organization, podcaster, or "broadcaster") and linked together via a scripted language file which is posted on the Internet. These files are digitally recorded to be compatible for most current Internet browsers, MP3 programs (such as iTunes, Windows Media Player, Music Match, etc.), and MP3 players such as iPod, SanDisk MP3 players, Microsoft Zune, Creative Labs Zen, or any other brand.

The simple life of the podcast listener:
Select your podcasts, download them, and take your MP3 player with you.
Plug it in again, update it ... on the road again!

A simple diagram in Figure 2.2, Comparison of Audio Delivery in a Digital Age, will help explain the difference among podcasts, MP3 music, and Internet radio. You might say that podcasting provides a combination of features that are "value-added." That is the podcast is in a compatible, portable MP3 format, but widely available via the Internet and usually access is free for them. Therein lies the mobility factor!

What makes the updating of podcasts work? A critical element in this mobilization magic is that podcast listeners have what we call "the simple life." Today general, nontechie, technology users expect "plug and play" ease of use. Podcast technology is able to provide this through the power of XML and RSS formats that run in the background with every podcast.

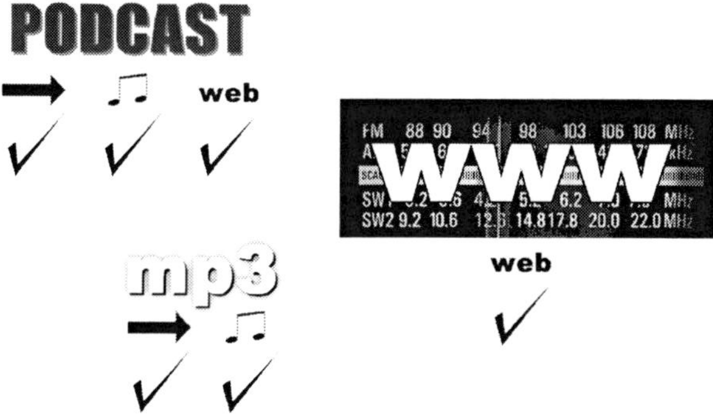

Figure 2.2. Comparison of audio delivery among podcasts, MP3s on the Web and Internet radio. Which elements do they have? Portability, audio, Web-based.

The Most Common Podcast Question Answered!

Do you need an iPod to listen to a podcast?
The answer…. No! Look at the figure above, you can listen to the podcasts on your computer, but you won't be mobile.

And for mobility, you can use an iPod or another brand of MP3 player or mobile audio device.

Figure 2.3. The most common podcast question answered!

As we mentioned earlier Dave Winer and Adam Curry had been working on the technology to deliver audio and video that would become podcasts via the Web. They had expected to use XML and RSS formats since 2001. And it was Winer who in fact created the key technology (the enclosure tag RSS 2.0 specification) (Lafferty & Walch, 2006).

Every podcast not only has the MP3 file posted on the Web, but it has to have a specific RSS feed created for it. This file is usually named feed.xml and is written in XML scripting language. The feed can be written in XML code or by feed creating software, or podcasters can use all-in-one Web sites which automate the recording and publishing process.

The RSS feed is similar to a specialized table of contents which has identifying information about the podcast and then details for each episode, or item. All the critical details of the "item" are included: the creator's name, an e-mail address, podcast title, episode title and number, date, description, and any other comments that may have been included, along with the essential "enclosure" information. The enclosure information is the file's name, size, location, media type, and publication date and time.

The absolute "magic" of this RSS feed is that it puts the "power" in the audio file series. Without this XML file one would just have an **audio-post** (an audio file posted on a specific Web site, accessible only by visiting that particular site and downloading or playing the file from there). But with the RSS feed the podcaster has an audio file for which people can subscribe and which is "delivered" to their computer's "RSS readers" whenever it updates or they open the program. This dynamic format is called "push" technology that sets RSS feeds and podcasts apart significantly from files which are solely posted on a Web site.

Consider Figure 2.4 as an illustration of the difference between an audio file solely posted on a Web site and an audio file which is also distributed as part of a podcast. One is only accessed when people visit the

Figure 2.4. Audio posted only on Web site versus podcast with RSS feed.

Web site. The podcast is accessed whenever a listener's podcatching program automatically opens and checks the podcast for updates.

Podcast listeners then use those podcast programs called, "podcatchers" to troll the directory and check the feeds for the latest information. In this way the most up-to-date information about each podcast feed is presented right to your desktop and the latest episode is downloaded for you.

What does the user see? You open your podcatcher program (iTunes, Juice, jPodder, FireAnt, HappyFish, podNova, Happyfish.com, Mediafly.com, Castroller.com, or Odeo) and go on with your other work. Later you check back to see what has updated and can plug in your MP3 player and the program updates the player for you. It is very different from having to go to each Web page and check for an update, or keep checking e-mail, blogs, or Web-based bulletin boards for updates! This podcast with RSS feed is a very different kind of delivery model. The portable player takes the ease of delivery even further making it totally portable!

Select your podcasts, download them and take your MP3 player with you.
Plug it in again, update it. On the road again!

Timeshifting

One more spin on the whole mobile advantage is that listeners can also time shift their podcasts. Not only does a podcast listener receive updates as soon as possible through their podcatching software, but their files can be "time shifted!" That is, users decide when they want to listen to them—the listeners can shift the schedule. In many ways, users can "cut the electronic cord" and take their podcasts away from the computer and make them mobile using a portable media player. Therefore, users decide *when* and *where* to listen to podcasts.

As we think about the radical changes that are experienced through making our listening to popular radio talk, music, and educational podcasts mobile, what about the roots of this movement and what it means to bypass the usual distribution control channels? The next section of our chapter explores a fundamental theme of the podcasting revolution: *Democratization of the Media*.

DEMOCRATIZATION OF THE MEDIA

How could more than 100,000 new "radio shows" have been added to the airwaves in less than 2 years? Even only addressing nonpolitical restraints such as limited bandwidth space and FCC regulations, they couldn't! "Democratization of the Media" refers to the fact that podcasting is not limited by physical bandwidth/air waves, FCC control, corporate control, nor financial backing. "Big corporations" do not own the podcasting "air waves." In podcasting, inexpensive hardware, software, and Internet space can make anybody a broadcaster.

There are in fact few limits to podcast development because disk storage space and bandwidth are very inexpensive if carefully chosen and there is no FCC (Federal Communications Commission) control of podcasting content or language (at least as of this writing in 2008). In addition, because the services of a broadcast station or financial sponsors are not needed, podcasters are not required to demonstrate a minimum audience size.

Today, a tour of some of the major podcast directories of current content reveals the breadth and variability of both topics and broadcasting expertise. In June 2008 these directories include iTunes (www.itunes.com), Podcast Alley (www.podcastalley.com), Podcastpickle.com (http://www.podcastpickle.com/), and about 100 others. From politics to tech talk, dating to music, science fiction stories to psychics, and history to business management, you can find the full spectrum of interests in all varieties of views, expertise, and sophistication, in the world of podcasting.

What does this mean for personal and formal learning in the world of education? Two major areas are evident: (1) a technology to create and deliver is accessible, easy, and inexpensive, and (2) there is a wide base of users: creators and listeners.

Some other technologies have held the opportunity to being the voice of the people to the public, but fell short. Consider teleconferencing and the expense of the equipment that was needed in the 1980s and 1990s. But podcasting has grown out of the blogging movement, which in June 2008 was estimated at 112.8 million blogs increasing at a rate of 175,000 new blogs per day (Technorati, 2008). Podcasting is part of this same digital media approach and mindset of chronicling thoughts and sharing perspectives; digital natives, people born after 1980 expect to use technology for these purposes. Within this context we have a rich environment in which to teach important lesson to our students:

- multicultural understanding and appreciation;
- international relationships;
- issues of foreign trade and its impact;
- globalization;
- media literacy;
- digital literacy;
- foreign languages;
- geography and changing international borders; and
- many more.

In addition, the wide base of users means that classrooms and students can find partners from across the city and the world to communicate with on a one time or ongoing basis. They can partner with other classrooms on collaborative projects. They can see how others view the same topic and compare their work for the type of work, level of work, and perspectives. The dialogue, collaboration, and skills that they can experience will be able to lay a foundation for a worldview that will morph as rapidly as the international boundaries they will live among during their lifetimes.

Our students are growing up in a world of change more rapid than even that which we have been experiencing. They understand that change, they look at it, and process it in different ways than we do. Through engaging in global experiences and generative projects such as podcasting not only are we affording them the opportunities to grow and learn, to expand beyond the four walls of the classroom, but also to reach beyond the scale of our knowledge and to provide us with a glimpse of the worlds they are creating.

Somehow this medium has the power to create experiences of learning, dynamic creations, and generative experiences that break down communication among nations, classes, and even ages. These are the possibilities of *Democratization of the Media* through podcasting and other digital media for teachers and learners.

In the next chapter, we will be further developing not only this understanding, but also the impact for education and it may be that it is also a democratization of the *classroom*—when we look at teachers and learners as true colearners in projects such as these. Chapter 12 provides a broad survey of Who's Using Podcasting in Education and we will take you on a tour of some examples of how classrooms are accomplishing some of these feats. These examples of classroom use include the breakdown of barriers, and the new developments and new perspectives. Join with us as we see how new technologies can bring new dimensions to teaching and leaning.

FLASHBACK AND FORECAST—DISCOVERING VOICE THROUGH PODCASTING

During some of my graduate studies I took a voice music class, and no the results were not that dramatic! And the experience was daunting to say the least. Each week we had to practice a song with a cassette tape (yes, this was quite a few years ago) and memorize it to prepare for our in-class solo. What made it worse was that I was only a graduate student and had very little natural talent in this area!

However, the turning point is seared in my memory as I distinctly remember my robustly voiced professor proclaiming across the fully attended classroom to me one day, "Kathleen, you are a soprano, not a tenor! Go find your voice!"

Thus began a series of highly embarrassing treks to the practice room with the cassette, breathing exercises, trills, scales and many assorted screeches. Low and behold one day this high voice popped through what seemed to be the top of my head. I nearly jumped out of the room, thinking someone else had come in.

However with much maneuvering and sweat, and then practice over the course of that semester I was able to somewhat consistently reproduce an octave within that range. Somehow, that former opera star turned dedicated educator had been able to encourage this mediocre talent to discover her mezzo-soprano singing voice.

Well, I can safely say that if you tune into our podcasts you will never hear me sing. However you may still hear me talk about "finding your voice," because what I and others have found is that podcasting can enable a different *kind* of voice to be discovered. Regardless of whether your pitch is bass, tenor, soprano, alto, or anything else, we have seen that podcasting provides distinct opportunities for teachers, students, and podcasters of all walks of life to experience new confidence, new efficacy, and sometimes new personas.

For instance you have the students assembled to do simulated newscasts of the nightly news. At first when they take on the project they may hand off the reading part to the last person in line. But within a few episodes, they are vying for the anchor seat and polishing up their delivery styles. When you listen in to any number of podcasts performed by young teens it is totally contradictory to the popular depiction of adolescence reticence to speak in public, to mutter, and slur their words.

When I was 18 years old I began to lead small educational circles for my social group. At these times I would be steaming hot under the collar, sweating profusely, and in full-fledged anxiety for 15 minutes prior. Listening to these students, they appear to have few of these anxieties as they create frequent broadcasts, develop scripts, enjoy repartee, ad lib with one another, and sometimes include kind-hearted jokes about and dedications to their teachers.

When you think about the common understanding of "discovering your voice" usually you think of sound quality such as in singing or speech coaching, but our colleagues in podcasting and in education know exactly what we mean regarding this experience. Listen in as I share some examples from some colleagues describing the connection between podcasting and a similar impact on discovering their voice. The first from the host of the science fiction magazine, Escape Pod podcast.

> I just came back from Dragon Con [a popular gaming conference] and one of the things I noticed is how podcasters are more comfortable talking in a group than other people are.... And it made me wonder about myself.... I have gained confidence in public speaking since doing the podcasts....
>
> I can remember being a lot more shy than I am now ... put me in a crowded room and I would fade into the background ... I think a lot of it is the podcast I do each week....
>
> It takes a certain threshold of confidence to turn on a mike and start talking into it week after week even if you have written content. But it also builds confidence. And that confidence extends to other social settings....
>
> I think the key to confidence is simply knowing what you say is important to say ... if you are shy and not comfortable with it ... then getting a mike and starting a podcast might be the way to do it ... and you will have some nervousness ... it will take awhile ... but the fact that you are putting your voice out there will make you feel like you have something to say. (Stephen Eley, Escape Pod, www.escapepod.org)

In addition, in this example from a student podcast project, we see that they list one of the goals of podcasting explicitly as the development of voice:

> Empower students to develop a real voice through podcasting, an emerging and exciting technology that is breaking barriers in the world of communications. (SMASHcast student podcast goal #1, www.smashcast.org, Level Playingfield Institute, 2006)

My own experience, Kathy's, was much like Steve Ely's even though I had been teaching for more than 20 years, when you put a microphone in front of me I would really get nervous. But beyond the nervousness, I could not settle into who I really was with the podcast until my cohost and I discussed more how we interviewed people as a comfortable "conversation." There was a definite change from false starts and nervousness to confidence when I gained my voice with podcasting. In addition, the confidence I have gained through podcasting has definitely carried into my speaking with a microphone in public, being videotaped and recorded, and interviewed. For me, I describe it as there being a sense of "I know how to wrap my mind about this experience. My public voice comes from a consistent place of who I am as an educator, professional and person."

With so many needs ahead of students in their lives to have to speak in class, in their future workplace, publicly, and advocate for themselves and others in a variety of situations, the opportunity to integrate this development of their voice into a fun experience can be a priceless one. As we explore the podcast in classrooms in future chapters, you will see many examples of young people standing up for their opinions, learning the quality of production they need to learn, and gaining confidence in who they are. What a great opportunity for us as teachers to help build that self-sufficiency.

A MEDIUM OF DISCOVERY

Based on the developments in our work of podcasting I believe a common theme emerges and that is that podcasting is *a medium of discovery.* It is a generative medium. From the development of mobile learning opportunities when we did not have them prior to the democratization of the media and creating opportunities for thousands of broadcasters who would have not reached the "airwaves" otherwise, to providing rich proving grounds for young and old to discover their voice, podcasting is one of discovery and creation.

Some technologies are confined to just a few dimensions, but although much of the easier podcasting right now is in audio format, it would stand to reason it could be rather "flat." However this just does not seem to be the case. Instead, podcasting is a very rich medium. We have the depth of media literacy, we have the audio, the nuances of meaning, the persuasion that may be hidden or blatant, and the related Web sites in which the message is delivered. Then there are the host of literary styles that can be explored in a medium that seemed to have been skipped over when the radio age was eclipsed by television. Podcasts seem to be renewing interest and depth of understanding in dramatic performances, narratives, soundscapes, and more. Furthermore, the role that book reading in podcast form can take and the many ways they can be used by those who are disabled and people who are not can open many additional opportunities. And then there are the multitude of technologies that can be learned in the process of development, support, and enhancement of podcasting from Web page development, to video production, to blogging, bulletin boards, e-book production, audio book production, serialization, and emerging technologies that are but the opening of the door of possibilities.

The general podcasting movement has also been a community of discovery for these first 2 years. It has been very much a generative group of people, sharing information and supporting one another, helping one another to learn, and giving back to the community. We hope to support this perspective especially in the K-12 educational podcasting community as perhaps this movement develops further. There have not been too many linkages among K-12 podcasting efforts although there could be many opportunities developed.

CHAPTER 3

FROM POP CULTURE TO KILLER APPLICATION FOR EDUCATION

"IS THIS MY GRANDMOTHER'S ENGLISH CLASS?"

Cecelia Dabrowski confronted the same battle each day of class, how to get the ear buds out of the students' ears and their focus on their literature readers. The literature for fifth grade included some introductory pieces to fine writers around the world. This was the time in her life when her world had opened up; the boundaries of her small farming town had fallen behind her and her imagination had been unleashed.

However she had not been able to connect with her students in the same way. She had believed that just as the words, characters, and storylines had leapt off the pages for her some 15 years ago, they would do the same for this generation of students. But their approach and their expectations of literature, narrative, and storytelling seemed so connected to their world of entertainment, that she could not seem to breakthrough with her planned, traditional literature education approaches.

Cecelia found almost a disdain in the students' faces as they looked at the readers, they could not "see" how they could be relevant. She needed to find a way to figuratively "plug in" to their world. She talked with them about how they were using their media devices; they were all listening to music on them.

Podcasting for Teachers: Using a New Technology to Revolutionize Teaching and Learning, Revised Second Edition, pp. 33–46

From the door of the bus, through the halls, secretively during class time, in hallways, during lunch, throughout the school day, and as far as she could observe students outside of school hours, when they had they had the opportunity, they were continually connected to their digital media devices. And when they were not listening to them they were on computers, chatting, instant messaging (IMing), with one another or doing both listening and IMing at the same time.

What were they listening to? What were they looking for? What did they expect? How did they make choices? It wasn't too obvious to her at this point, but these would be great questions to use as a springboard to talk about music lyrics as language, analysis, and interpretation. Maybe given some opportunities in this realm, she could find new ways to open conversations, open dialogue, and it could lead to more applications to the course content?

Considering the MP3 players with which so many of the students were engrossed, she wanted to find a way to capture these devices and the students' attention for teaching and learning. She thought about audio books and about the many different genres of literature she loved and had studied. Cecelia mused whether there was a way to port over, or even transform, literature that she wanted them to study and analyze into the media with which they were already absorbed. Were there ways to use these MP3 devices in order to communicate, retell, interpret, perform literature, or student work? Was there a way to create a media empowered Trojan horse so to speak?

BEDLAM IN BELLEFIELD OR DIS-INTEREST/DIS-SCIENCE CLASS

Steve Fielding unlocks the door of the classroom and braces himself for another battle in Bellefield. Oh yes, this is science class, not war, how could he forget? The past few months had been less than spectacular; they had been downright harrowing. He had been teaching for 10 years, but lately the students were slipping further and further away from him. He was losing control of them and based on supervisor reports it was not just a matter of discipline, but also lack of interest.

The students were not seeing the relevance of the science classes. They were not interested in the content. How could he make it more interesting to them? He had been trying several approaches, but they did not fit his teaching style and they were not working with the students either. Today he had something different to attempt. He had some short audio broadcasts from the Web that other students had created. They were created like the nightly news, but they were about famous scientific discoveries. He was hoping the students might find the ones he had picked out interesting and that they would prompt some focus to the day's lesson. Maybe it would be the right kind of "hook" to get them interested in the introduction to atoms.

As the class assembled he booted up the laptop and the LCD projector. Some of the students were watching what he was doing when he plugged in his portable speakers. And there was murmuring. Then he opened the podcast directory he had been using and asked if any of them listened to music or podcasts on the Web. He had some takers and what is more, he had some attention from his students!

Within a few minutes the class had listened to a students' news broadcast about atomic science discovery. In fact, they had actually listened closely, and had several questions about who the students were, how they had gotten on the Web and how they had created their newscast. Then he focused them with some questions about the content. Wow! They had caught the content! After a few minutes of further discussion, he went into the lesson of the day and they mostly stayed with him.

The next day he went a little further but included a computer activity into the lesson that circled back to the new episode from the student news and podcast site he had used that day. There were some more murmuring noises and furtive glances his way. This was odd reticent behavior on their part! He asked what they were talking about. They asked if they could help find some more science podcasts for the next few classes. Something good might be starting in what had mostly been bedlam.

OVERVIEW

Even though they were having difficult experiences, Cecelia and Steve had some critical characteristics that set them up for successful possibilities in their classrooms. They were seeking to understand their students and connect to their culture and understanding. In addition, they were building on their own pedagogical expertise. These are characteristics of teachers who are both confident and humble in themselves as people and professionals. It is also evident that these teachers were very dedicated to their students' best interests. They were persistent in discovering ways to connect their students with their assigned content areas. Cecelia and Steve were colearners with their students. And their approaches are surely pedagogical models for us, but also, more importantly, we would consider that they are lifelong learning models for their students.

Without promising the "silver bullet" solution for education, in this chapter we will explore how podcasting builds on today's pop culture and is becoming a powerful, potentially "killer application" for education. Our approach is to connect the students' great interest and understanding of digital media with your expertise as educators. To build on what we know excels in educational environments and great powerful learning opportunities that will extend teaching and learning. Beyond the simple application of technology to education, we look at this connection to the current and evolving forms of digital media as transforming it. In this chapter we will be providing some quotes from teachers, and examples of student podcasts that demonstrate this potential. Where are we headed? We are creating new dimensions of teaching, and learning that bring teacher expertise and student creativity together in unlimited possibilities. In the twenty-first century and beyond a killer application should not be narrowly defined, it should be capable of constant regeneration. Podcasting offers this possibility to education.

POP CULTURE CONNECTIONS

The culture of digital media today is built on a plethora of experiences that may not be very familiar to some generations of teachers. Students' lives are embedded in their common experiences of digital media culture, perspective, and products.

Young people expect to be constantly connected by technology. Technology is transparent to them. Today's students are constantly involved in computer gaming, DVDs, DVRs, MP3 players, IMing, texting, blogging, cell phones, and Internet surfing for many of their social and information needs.

As was mentioned in a previous chapter, in this world of constant digital connection and communication, a group of techies in the fall of 2004, pioneered podcasting—then dubbed audioblogging. Later in September 2004, further advancing podcasting by making downloading podcasts easier, Adam Curry and Dave Winer released the first key podcatching software, iPodder (now called Juice), which automated the downloading of podcasts. Tying popular movements with technological advances, Adam Curry himself had been identified with pop culture and MTV through his "vee-jay" days there.

However despite the multitude of hours invested by podcasters prior to June 2005, it was Apple's move at that time that created a great impact on podcasting in pop culture. By including a podcast feature into the home page of its iTunes software, Apple pushed podcasting into the mainstream (Lafferty & Walch, 2006). Maybe more importantly, Apple understood the urgent desire for young and old users for "Plug and Play" simplicity: the iTunes interface enabled Apple's iPods to be updated with new podcast episodes just by plugging them into a computer with iTunes installed (see Figure 3.1).

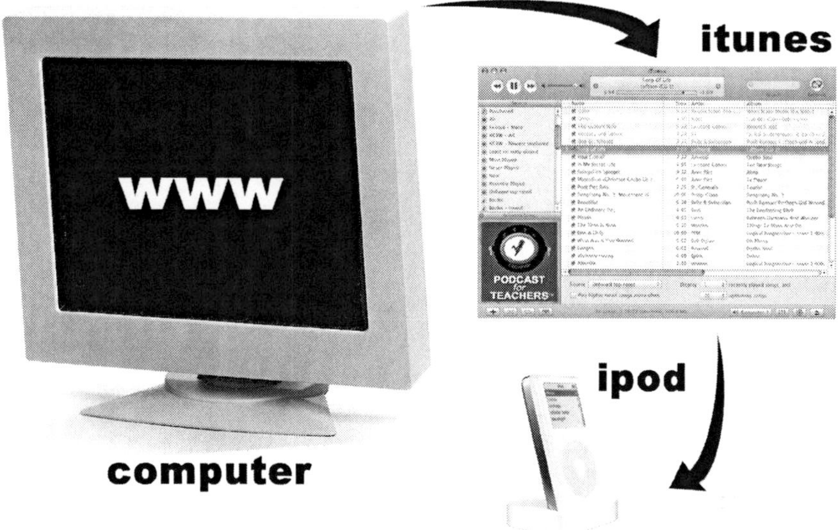

Figure 3.1. Diagram of computer—iTunes—iPod.

This relatively transparent incorporation of the iPod media device with podcasting built on the success and ease of use iPod users had already been experiencing through iTunes with their music. Therefore there was a built-in user base there. But now there was an entirely new body of information and media format available in podcasting. That which had been inhabited primarily by the more technically minded (okay, we were geeks), was now being widely made and easily available to the general public.

And the public downloaded those podcasts with great vigor. From the first introduction in June 2005 when people were saying "pod-whating?" to June 2008 when the trend reached 49% of people participating in a worldwide survey indicating they listen to podcasts (Universal McCann Survey quoted by Lewin, 2008, May 5). This illustration may become the *definition* of the adoption of a technology into the mainstream culture!

By June 2006 the trend reached millions and millions of podcasts being downloaded each day just in iTunes (Friess, 2006).

We podcasters had been working for months to try to educate people about podcasts: what they were, how to get to them, how to download them, and so forth. Yet the integration with iTunes in June 2005 had an amazing impact on the development of the podcasting community.

Now in 2008 we have many options to not only find podcasts using podcast directories, but also "catch" or aggregate them using podcatchers. Examples of programs that can be downloaded today (February 2007) and used to index, search, and collect podcasts, AKA podcatchers, include, but are not limited to:

- iTunes (http://www.itunes.com),
- Juice (http://juicereceiver.sourceforge.net),
- FireAnt (http://www.getfireant.com),
- Mediafly.com (http://www.mediafly.com), and
- Mypodder (http://www.podcastready.com).

Also try Podcatchermatrix (http://www.podcatchermatrix.org) to compare podcatchers.

By providing the means to easily find, access, and subscribe to audio and video podcasts from around the globe, listeners now have a huge repertoire of content available to them (see also Felix & Stolarz, 2006).

You could almost imagine young people watching as adults who were more used to traditional broadcast radio or television as their main source of entertainment, began to hear the voices and music of everyday people from around the globe, not just on Web sites, but in Web-based, portable "broadcast formats." And here perhaps is the greatest connection we as educators need to make with students—it is to realize that the globe is communicating with us and that **our students expect to have a global voice.**

Podcasting brings with it not only *exposure* to other views, but the opportunity to easily and inexpensively **air** your views. Democratization of the media doesn't need to be a theoretical conversation; the floodgates of point of view, dialogue, and articulation are thrown open in the classroom when the podcasting mike is turned on. A tremendous reciprocal process occurs with the floodgates of understanding others' perspectives through podcasting, because as students research and produce their own work, they listen to that of others. These are prime opportunities for listeners to *engage* in listening, understanding, reflection, and critical thinking. See Figure 3.2 for a schematic diagram of this process.

Students expect to have a global voice

When students have worked hard to carve out their own understanding and to carefully collaborate and hone their words for a script; when they have read their words aloud, or coached one another and then edited the recordings for hours to get it "just right;" they have pride in their work. They are "pumped up" and ready to see what impact they are having on

Figure 3.2. Tremendous reciprocal process that can happen through podcasting.

the world. When their broadcast/podcast goes out on the Web on that automated feed it is rather like pressing the electronic send button and wondering who is on the receiving end and considering what their reaction will be.

Young people are deeply vested in thought, reaction, and consideration. By creating their original writings and readings and making them public, solo, or collaboratively, we provide a great opportunity for them to enter into a worldwide discourse. Such is a venture into the twenty-first century digital media and a first-hand introduction by immersion into the skills, critical thinking, collaboration, team work, and problem-based learning that are all rolled into an authentic problem-based learning experienced.

Rather than learning isolated skills by rote or for a unit assignment, these students have the opportunity to learn digital media skills in real life application. They are contributing to the conversation of "the real world" and under the guidance of their teacher facilitator they stand to gain a tremendous amount about how to participate in each step of the process better.

Furthermore, the students are primed for consideration of other people's work. As podcasters they are authors, broadcasters, and creators of digital content. Now that they are participants in the media, they can not stand aside and be idly disinterested nonparticipants. They are involved and they must have opinions. By virtue of the fact of their participation they can now assess the work of others. They can see the effort that goes into audio and video productions in a new way. They can consider the flaws and greatness of people who write, produce, and speak in media. They can consider that there are real people behind those newscasts and articles they see moment by moment on the Web, and in news, and print articles.

These are prime opportunities for listeners to *engage* in listening, understanding, reflection, and critical thinking. With the experienced guidance of their teacher-facilitator they can ask deeper questions from these perspectives. They can learn additional critical thinking skills. They can learn new questions to ask, and new research skills to help ferret out background information to test the truth of what they read, see, and hear.

When we connect the excitement of pop culture's voice in podcasting with digital literacy and critical thinking in the classroom, we have teachers and students as colearners. We have the colearners' potential of reaching beyond our current experiences of teaching and learning—a generative, cocreative experience of transformation.

"KILLER APP" REVEALED

Podcasting has the generative possibilities of a killer application (killer app) for education: creating, extending, and transforming learning. Establishing new dimensions of creativity, extending teaching and learning in new directions, and transforming educational experiences, these are what podcasting is making possible today. Imagine our future!

Teachers and students around the globe have already been doing tremendous work in creating our futures in podcasting and digital media. More than traditional teaching and learning, these pioneers are characterized by teachers who tend to work with these students in facilitative roles and have a vision of new developments and creativity.

Listen in to our eighth podcast of Podcast for Teachers (PFT), based on our experience in educational technology; we could see the trend already:

PFT Episode 8: 10/8/2005
Mark Gura: We need to transform—not just integrate or adopt [education]

Kathleen P. King: Yes. I found an article in the *Chronicle for Higher Education*. It was from their September 9, 2005 issue (Read, 2005). It is talking about how Purdue University is abandoning cassette tapes, okay. It is going to be using podcast lectures for almost 50 courses. What they are talking about in this article is that instead of distributing lectures on cassettes, they are only going to be distributing lectures on podcasts. It will no longer be available in the other format.

> They are moving to a podcast phase there at Purdue. In addition, Purdue they say is not the only university, Drexel University is handing out free iPods this fall to freshmen and have created what is called a "PodPage" where students download the orientation materials or sign up to receive recordings from the Education School's Division of Distinguished Lecture Series. This is interesting because ... it is a little underwhelming in the sense that it is lectures delivered by podcasts. It is the same sort of teaching methodology, only it is being delivered over a podcast.
>
> **Mark Gura:** You know we see this time and time again. I remember when the Web came out and people were thinking about how this might influence texts for students or even without the Web, just CD-carried software. Lo and behold, there were Web sites and there were CDs that had really nothing more than the same text exactly. What you would find in a hardbound book is now in digital version on the Web or the CD. This is always the way it is when a new technology comes out. People adapted to kind of promote the old way of doing things. It takes a while for them to make the connections that, "Gee, the whole equation has been shifted somewhat." Let us really think about how we can do different and better things with the technology. It is not surprising that we are seeing people simply recording lectures and then uploading them as a podcast. In a sense, there is some value right there. I think we are under whelmed by it because we sensed that there is so much more really could be done. (King & Gura, 2005a)

And yet while we knew that this was the limitation, we were trying to point out that there were some possibilities that were embedded in this model and had the potential for something more advanced. That is to say, even with course casting, (the approach described above) schools might transform teaching and learning experiences.

> **Also PFT Episode 8**
> **Mark Gura:** To give them some credit, it sounds like they also have ancillary materials. They are using this as an opportunity to distribute enhancements. Truth be told, producing cassettes is really unwieldy, not just that it is an inelegant technology, but each cassette you produce has a cost and the mailing of it and [or] distributing of it—and here if you upload, it is virtually, not precisely, but virtually limitless as many people can do as many downloads as they can. They are all advantages. (King & Gura, 2005, October 17)

By PFT Episode 24, February 6, 2006, we were discussing articles that were being published in the *New York Post* (Andreatta, 2006) and the *Chicago Tribune* (Silverstein, 2006) about students sleeping through lectures knowing they could download podcasts later. The responses from professors varied. The responses from students about deciding to go to class or not was telling (King & Gura, 2005, October 31).

Basically students seemed to be deftly identifying the creative and extending possibilities of podcasting. If there was not added value to go to class, why should they attend? However, it would stand to reason that it would not be such an issue if there were reasons for students to attend and *participate* in class. That is, if there was content, meaning, interaction, and material they could not be gained only through recordings. One professor we interviewed in the summer of 2006 aptly and descriptively described such course casting as fossilizing lectures (Umbach in PFT Episode 54; King & Gura, 2006, September 11; CUNY Matters, 2006). Fossils preserve the status quo, but they don't make your presence urgent.

How possible is it to create dynamic podcasting? Examples may be the most powerful way to communicate the potential of dynamic podcasting in education.

Creating new dimensions of creativity. At first listen/look, one might think this teacher is all over the map, but what he is about is choice: Jeff Bradley (http://www.slausonpodshow.com/) is giving his students plenty of choice when it comes to listening to podcasts and *creating* podcasts with him. When we interviewed Jeff on our Podcast for Teachers podcast (PFT Episode 53) it was resoundingly evident that he had great passion for teaching and learning, and tremendous creativity for facilitating independent learning with a lot of hands off, but definite guidance, from their friend and teacher "Mr. Slauson." To quickly get clued into student culture, take a look at the student's topics, show notes, and graphics choices at Slauson Podshow http://www.slausonpodshow.com/. And to see how a teacher can loosely, but effectively corral that energy and independence, that next level up of organization gives some of the same flavor: http://slausonpodshow.com/.

One example of creativity and extension that really captured us when talking to Jeff was the "Gertie Tacoma Bridge" narrative assignment. When talking about this work with the students, this seems to be history content, but in fact Jeff effectively extends and involves his students in creative exploration of the scientific principles behind an historical event. Not stopping there Jeff had his students extend their learning by creating first person accounts of the event. He posed questions to them such as,

- What did the bridge feel like?
- What would it have experienced?

These activities created critical learning experiences for the students to delve into and to comprehend scientific principles, historical events, and critical thinking through collaborative experiences. Rather than reading an account or observing a video, they were active learners and creative thinkers. That is, these students created a meaningful product which will be richly instructive for other students and also serve as a guide for teachers (PFT Episode 53, King & Gura, 2006, September 4).

Extending teaching and learning in new directions. Another example of creativity and extension may be found in the work of Radio OWL at Mansfield Elementary School, Mansfield, CT (http://www.mansfieldct.org/schools/vinton/vnradio/index.htm) where students create special research topic reports for their podcasts. While this may not seem too stretching, think about the grade level of the students. These are students in Grades 4-5 creating reports and broadcasts about Native American religions and cultures (Radio OWL, Episode 3, 2006). In addition, a sister school of theirs hosts Radio Southeast (http://mansfieldct.org/schools/southeast/radiose/). Their third graders created and recorded their first episode The Wonders of Winter, which is a blend between a student report and a newscast (Radio Southeast, Episode 1, 2006).

In addition to the research they also scripted and performed their podcasts fully cognizant that they were speaking to a global audience. Far from the realm of a classroom presentation or a Friday morning auditorium performance, these students have taken on the world as their audience. To create new forms of authentic outcomes and to extend these learning experiences to include *finding* and *expressing* the *voices* of these young people—all accomplished through simple audio recordings and skillful teacher facilitation.

Transforming educational experiences. Transforming teaching and learning might be seen in several examples of educational podcasting already. However one that particularly stands out in our minds is that created from a group of students in California called the SMASHcast (http://www.smashcast.org) (Level Playing Field Institute, 2006). These students are wildly excited about math and science learning and overly anxious (is that possible?) to share that excitement with other students.

Their podcasts stretch the boundaries of usual classroom presentations and encourage students and educators to think about what is possible. Their tagline is "SMASHcast is a group of students from the San Francisco Bay Area who like to tell it like it is" (SMASHcast, 2006).

With topics ranging from how Coca Cola exposes seem to be overstating physical trauma, to religion science and death penalty debates to an episode about flat feet, it is interesting and totally random! (SMASHcast, 2006, Aug. 12). These students are able to greatly express themselves through this podcast. You can see a great deal of youth culture through this podcast, but don't be tricked the teacher and students seem to be very astute. Just when you think the podcasts are "over the top" and that you are just watching teens having fun with a microphone, they produce technology help episodes like SKYPE mobile "how-to's" (SMASHcast, 2006, June 3) and environmental science and ecological responsibility (SMASHcast, 2006, April 29).

SMASHcast is another example that when teachers work with students, guide them, let them run with learning in creative ways, and extend their experiences, what results we all can experience! These students are going to be something else to deal with when they become the future legislators of the world!

Another venue for creating podcasting and video podcasting is rapidly gaining ground. Watching the media demonstrates the current rampant interest in viral videos (Arnold, 2006). But several schools have already been avidly walking that delicate balance between full fledged video production and more "shoot from the hip" vlogging.

When used as a medium to explore and express student learning, vlogging can be a tremendous medium. The difficulty at this point has been the time intensiveness of video editing. So that the projects in video formats take so much longer to produce than audio. However with each month we are seeing more resources and more streamlined software that make the process easier (Feeley, 2006; Wired, 2006). Eventually we should be able to reach the level of ease with video podcasting that we have today with audio podcasting. The fact that podcasting is so powerful in just audio format, magnifies the case that creative medias have such inherent power. And a good portion of that power is found in the discovery, liberation and development of voice.

Ultimately whatever media we use to create, extend and transform dimensions of teaching and learning will open new visions of possibilities for teachers and learners. The unusual occurrence and dynamic potential with podcasting is that these generative and transforming dimensions are encapsulated in a relatively simple format. Podcasting is a format that is identified with a mainstream digital device, and digital trend (music). Building upon that we are already seeing how we can capture it and transform those fundamentals into powerful experiences for teaching and learning.

SITES YET UNSEEN

With the connection of pop culture to transformation learning opportunities, podcasting in education truly is a "killer application." We believe building a framework to use podcasting in education will set a precedent for similar digital media technology use now and into the future. In this chapter we have sought to provide a solid understanding of both of these perspectives and possibilities. In the next two sections of the book we aim to equip educators in models and procedures for podcasting in education as well as a conceptual framework for their growth—personally, professionally, and curricularly.

Over the years we have seen that theory and research are powerful. However without the lifeblood of application they can be stale (King & Wang, 2007). Our work with podcasting is bringing together several models of formative development, best practice, and innovation. It is an approach that seeks to work from a stance of action research and reflective practice and continually asks such questions as:

Regarding Pop Culture and Learning

- Why has podcasting caught the interest of pop culture?
- How can we make the best educational use of that deep interest?

Regarding Pedagogy and Podcasting

- How do we as educators best serve as facilitators of students' creativity, extension, and transformation of their learning?
- How do we best engage students as co-learners with us in this discovery experience?
- What lifelong learning skills are they gaining that tie pop culture back to the world in which they will have to successfully thrive in order to later succeed?

Developing Models of Practice and Inquiry

- How can we systematically explain the podcast development process?
- How can we effectively analyze the benefits and costs of podcasting and other educational technology pursuits against the expense of varied resources?
- What approach can we take that will allow for a dynamic, interactive process of podcasting and student learning?
- How can we understand the path of learning educators experience in learning podcasting in education?

Our work with podcasting since August 2005 and years of professional experience and training as educators has enabled us to develop these working models and provide guidance for educators to build on. Those we present have been developed, tested, and honed for months; some of the models and approaches have emerged from prior research and work we have conducted individually.

What we are so very pleased to be able to offer is not just these working models, but also a vision that we hope you will work with us to continue to create; the future of podcasting in education. We are headed for "sites yet unseen." The creativity and generativity of this medium does not stop with the broadcast and uploading of the podcast. The synergistic creative, productive, power of this work is found in the process and learning experience itself. Teachers and students bring it to life and it is all of us together who will chart the course yet unseen—continuing to discover:

- New interpretations of literature, history, science, math, and so forth;
- New collective voices of those who have never joined together before;
- New cross-cultural and global perspectives of society, politics, economics, and related issues;
- New creative forms of digital media;
- New formats of delivering content through podcasting (beyond interviews, reports or lectures); and
- New extensions of learning into content and fields of which their teachers and their teachers' generation have never known.

How tremendous these discoveries are. Join us; it is happening now. You are right on time to create the next generation of learning experiences with your students.

PART II

PODCASTING "HOW TO" BASICS

CHAPTER 4

THE PFT MODEL OF PODCASTING

***Cherryvale, MN**—Ms. Marion Barber's literature class is studying American genres this year. The middle school students are not especially excited to be reading the classics in fiction, nor poetry. Marion has been talking with Ravi about his summer activities and found out that he and his mother have been listening to some sort of Web-based broadcasts of detective stories it seems via their home computer and his MP3 player. This gives her [PAUSE], so to speak!*

The above is a situation that we have seen several times since the summer of 2005. Building on the age-old need of teachers to make their content area interesting and relevant for their students, teachers are plumbing the interests and experiences of their students. During this time we have seen teachers finding that students use computers and the Internet, of course, for their entertainment, as well as their MP3 players and gaming devices. Questions continue to arise, however, how do teachers capture the attention, abilities, and investment of students in these media and turn them to educational benefit?

What Ms. Barber had stumbled across with her student Ravi was indeed the use of podcasting. He and his mother had been evidently searching about the Web and finding podcasts that were detective stories and then he was downloading them for listening to his MP3 player. Many teachers

Podcasting for Teachers: Using a New Technology to Revolutionize Teaching and Learning,
Revised Second Edition, pp. 49–62

will retrace the steps that Ravi, and other students like him in similar classrooms around the world, will describe to their teachers and so they may in turn find other podcasts. And they will see the potential to use the *audible book* style podcast which easily enough translates to their classrooms.

After all, one can imagine the students listening to a poem or two via podcast, or an occasional chapter in this manner in order to introduce a book, series, or genre. Benefits can include capturing students' attention, helping those who are auditory learners, or providing additional, auditory experience to the written word.

> *What about going further? Marion enjoyed involving her students fully in the literature; when she could find the means to do so!*
>
> *She began wondering about how involved it was to create these podcasts, because she noticed some schools and teachers created their own podcasts. But there were not many easy to read instructions on this topic and she really liked personal instruction—at least to start.*

Having had so many teachers contact us from around the United States with the same situation as "Ms. Marion Barber," we at Podcast for Teachers, Techpod started to offer the live virtual workshops, Podcasting Education in June 2006. Through these experiences we have been able to discuss what podcasting is, how it is used in education, and how to develop podcasts. And through the live format we have been able to provide rich dialogue in the process.

As we discuss the "how to" aspects of podcasting we find that breaking it down into a few significant steps is most helpful. Our Teachers' Podcast (TTPod) Model of Podcasting not only helps people to efficiently carry out the process, but also helps them conceptualize, or as Kathy likes to say "wrap your head around" the concept from the start.

PFT MODEL OF PODCASTING

The TTPod Model of Podcasting has two phases of five stages each: **The Set-Up Phase** involves the stages: (1) **Create:** plan, create, and record content; (2) **Edit:** edit and export MP3 files; (3) **Web site:** create Web site, post MP3 file to Web; (4) **XML:** create the XML File; (5) **Publish**. And the **Continuing Phase** has five similar stages except that in stages 3 and 4 the files are edited rather than created. Figures 4.1 and 4.2 illustrate the model and will be used to guide the discussion in this chapter.

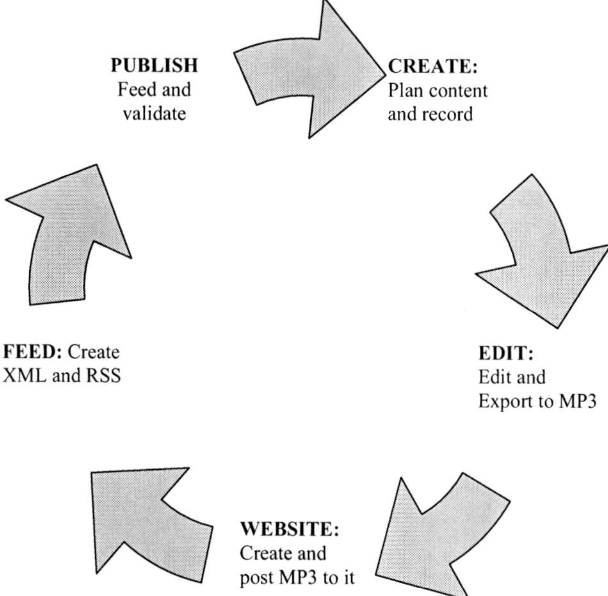

Figure 4.1. The TTPod model of podcasting set-up phase.

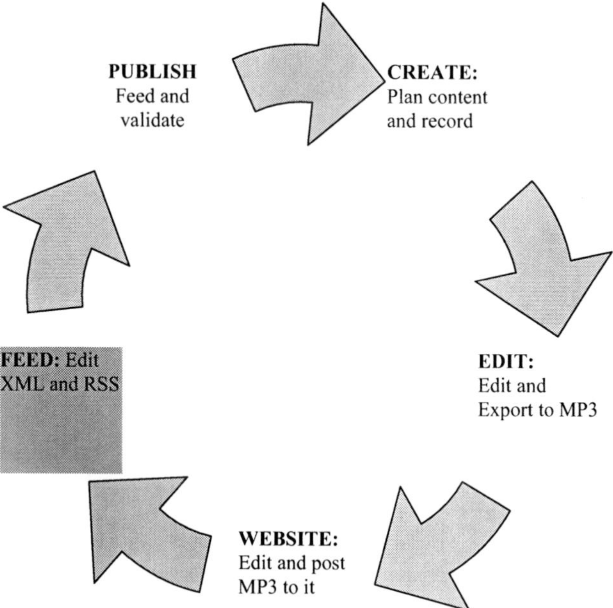

Figure 4.2. The TTPod model of podcasting continuing phase.

THE SET-UP PHASE

Having two phases in the TTPod Model of Podcasting reveals the fact that podcasters have to follow a different process the first time they create a podcast than they do each time they create additional episodes afterwards.

When one creates a podcast it has to have an XML and RSS file created so that it can be announced to the world in formal and informal ways. Because of the power of these programming formats, later on when one posts subsequent episodes it is only a matter of updating the master files. In this first of the five stages of the Set-Up Phase is Create, which includes Plan and Record the Content of the podcast.

Create: Plan, Create, and Record Content. Much, much easier said than done, this stage of development can take educators and students anywhere from 2 hours to 2 years. However, like many of our approaches, we would suggest that a modest favoring of the shorter end of the scale be pursued. That is, perhaps 2-3 weeks should be spent in researching the topics, interests, and approaches that the teachers, students, and team (class as a group) would like to, or need to, invest their efforts.

While we greatly enjoy the technical aspects of our pursuits, this stage and focus should continually be dominant throughout the podcasting development, editing, and continuation process. Teachers and students alike should keep a careful, critical, and constant eye for improvement on the balance of content in their educational podcasting pursuits. Podcasting is a great opportunity for a problem-based learning endeavor that provides real-life lessons about cost-benefit, quality control, learning on demand, and lifelong learning! Focusing on content is one of those primary opportunities.

Content planning and development takes form in terms of identifying a topic, conducting research, developing series outlines and episode outlines, assigning responsibilities for each episode, and deciding on how the content will be documented for the listeners. One can see how each of the next stages is dependent on content: sound editing, Web site updating, creating the feed descriptions, and ultimately publication.

Thus at this point you have the framework of the podcast series and perhaps several episodes envisioned. Regarding the project timeline, it may have been underway for a month or two, or more! (And yet there may be some settings where older students, high school to college, could easily be creating podcasts and be ready to record within a week two; therefore the timing is difficult to generalize here.)

Recording the podcast includes identifying a software program to run on the computer and then a simple microphone with which to record. Care is taken to have clarity of voice, make the speakers comfortable in their environment, and give them the opportunity for several retakes. All of this is done with full knowledge that the next steps provide the wonderful platform to make them sound like a professional. Sound editing has become very easy and the uhhhms and ahhhhs—the stumbles and pauses—can all be deleted easily. Just knowing this and/or seeing a demonstration **can give them great confidence.**

Edit: Edit and Export MP3 Files. Moving along in our bird's-eye view of this podcasting model we see the sound editing process. Through much experience we realized that the way to describe this process is that sound editing is done in several "pass throughs." The first few times that one listens to a recording the focus really can be on large errors and the content with the more final editing being a focus on the fine sound quality. This separation of the assignments really assists in what could be otherwise overwhelming. Much like editing written content, at first one needs to learn to grade papers by focusing on content and then going back to look at mechanical errors, or vice versa. But it is very difficult for the novice to correct both concurrently.

Once the sound file has been content and sound edited to the quality that is accepted by the podcast developers, then a process is conducted which is called "mixing down." At this point, if separate sound files have been recorded, the recording software patches them together into one seamless file. Whichever format they were started in they should now be exported into the more universal portable format of MP3 with parameters that will make the podcast small enough to download quickly. In chapter 6, "Demystifying the Podcast Techtalk," we succinctly explain sound recording and editing and will provide details on the process and settings, but at this point we will continue our overview so that we can get a global view of the podcasting development process for the first time.

Web site: Create Web Site and Post MP3 File to Web. As the podcast audio file is now ready for distribution, the teacher and students can now begin to look at other dimensions of their podcast production. Podcast distribution is much more than posting an audio file as a link on a Web page or sending it out by e-mail. One needs to consider the purpose, audience and focus the contribution of the podcast is going to make to the larger "community" that you intend to reach. This focus especially comes into concern with the Web site for the podcast. Certainly when starting out a teacher, or teacher and students, might consider only a homepage that lists the contents for each podcast, or "show notes."

However, at this level of the endeavor for most teacher and student projects the home page will likely be posted on the school Web site, and your school technology people should be contacted to see if any special Acceptable Use Policies (AUPs) need to be addressed. Then the teacher and students can plan out how they want the site to be developed, including ease of user navigation and later updates. Such planning should keep in mind that the Web site should coordinate with the ongoing distribution of the episodes of the podcasts. Web pages need to be linked together for show notes and also eventually, as the episodes build in number, an archive where users can easily find a list of previous episodes by date and episode number. A blog format for posting show notes is another popular option.

Another podcast setup scenario involves teachers creating podcasts on their own. In that case they may want to use an independent podcast host provider for their Web site, MP3 file storage, and even include a blog with it. This arrangement is a viable option:

- to provide materials for other teachers outside of your school to use;
- for topics you want to explore that might not relate to your specific content area; or
- even if your school does not have Web site (FTP) space available for teachers at the current time.

Chapter 6 provides options in this respect, but be assured you can set up the whole arrangement for $10-20 per month with significant bandwidth for audio podcasting, and still have control over your Web site name, and your audio file formats. Please note that if you intend to also video podcast on a significant level, your storage and bandwidth needs and costs will increase. Remember "free" is not always the correct answer as *reliability* of your file availability and *control* of your podcasting features are of great importance. Hold tight and read on in the next two chapters so you learn more details before you plunge into this venture; it will really benefit you not to take shortcuts in this process.

The final issue with the Web site is that the MP3 files will need to be posted, but if a podcast becomes heavily used, very popular with other students, or the general public, this can become a problem for your school's Web site or Internet provider. Therefore it is wise that an outside podcast host be used for the MP3 files, at least so that the traffic that is retrieving those files does not overburden the school's network. In technical terms, this is called bandwidth usage and it is a real issue for podcasters who do not plan ahead. There are several quality providers who provide services for as little as $5-20 per month with unlimited or close to unlimited bandwidth that will give your school technical administrator peace of mind and keep your podcast in service 24/7. (Check our resource list at the end of this chapter for information about podcast hosting.)

XML: Create the XML File. As you can see from Figure 4.1 the fourth stage in this Set-Up Phase has us working with the "mysterious" XML files and RSS feeds. And really these are not so mysterious at all. These formats enable podcasts to be distributed in a sequence, so that your listeners know that the next episode is ready for their listening enjoyment!

XML is simply a different scripting language, a simplified programming language used for very specific purposes. Similar to the Web page language of HTML it uses tags and brackets to identify functions with the file sequence. Most beginner podcasts can use a great RSS feed creating program like Feedforall (a trial version is available and you can make your first fully functional podcast with it) for this. Some podcast host sites like Libsyn (http://www.libsyn.com) or Switchpod (http://www.switchpod.com) enable you to have the RSS feed created for you automatically when you fill in a few identification markers and upload your MP3 at the site (see Figure 4.3). In either case, these inexpensive solutions provide a robust way to create sea-worthy RSS feeds that are written in accurate XML code. What has to happen is that the XML file will then best be named feed.xml and also be posted in your podcast directory. This file will have the information the podcast directories then send to your listeners.

So What Lies Beneath That Mysterious Code?

This section is optional and offered to demystify the world of XML. Ninety percent of the people creating podcasts do not get into the code

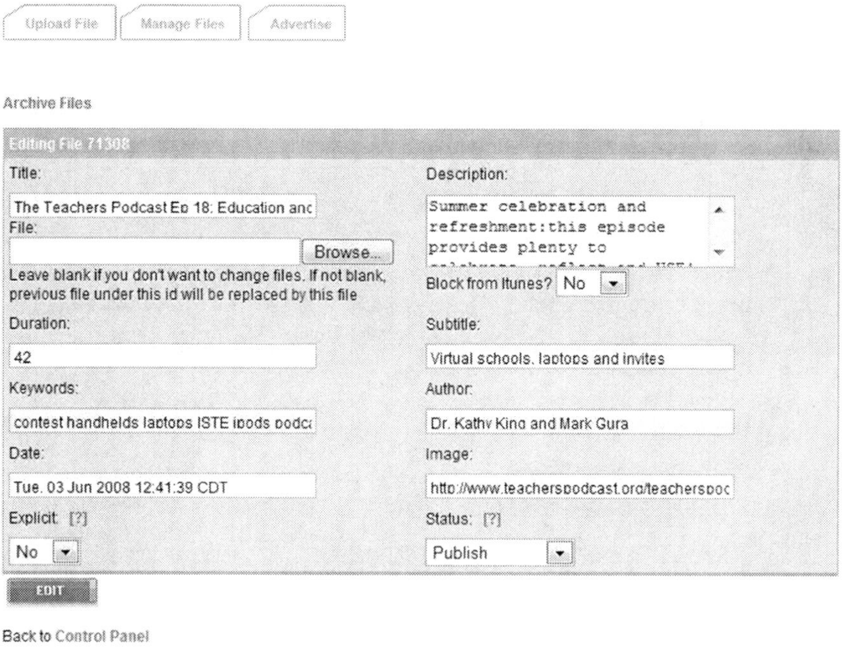

Figure 4.3. Switchpod.com podcasting episode publishing and editing interface through http://switchpod.com © Switchpod 2006.

level of XML, they use automated features. But I promise you theses few pages can demystify what is a very orderly system, and knowledge is power!

The content of an XML file is assembled exactly like the right hand column of Table 4.1 The left hand column provides an explanation of each set of instructions in the XML file. As you examine the code line by line you will see that first of all the code identifies the version of RSS and XML it is using so that the programs reading it will know how to read it. Then the first group of instructions is about the Podcast series in general. What is the name of the series, description of it, Web address, copyright holder, managing person responsible for it, Web master, etc.? This part of the Feed.xml file is gathering information about the "channel" and includes among the information the date it originated, was last updated and whether it has a logo for the feed and where it is on the Web, its assigned name, its file size, etc. You can think of XML files as saying, "Just the facts, ma'am! I am trying to figure out how to process your information accurately, just the facts!"

The ITEM section is the one that is provided for each episode. So with episode 1, I fill in the information requested for that episode much like above for the podcast series, except it also wants detailed information about where to find the MP3 file, how big the file is (length) and the "type" of file audio, video, mpeg, other. This critical information is held in the all important ENCLOSURE tag and is usually obtained once you upload your MP3 file to your podcast host.

One of the magical occurrences for me as I entered into this world of XML scripting was how this system worked when you added episode 2, 3, 4, 5! What I discovered was that each newer one is placed closer to the top of the list, but just **below** the channel information. It is in this manner that the podcast readers know which episode to serve up next to listeners!

Publish, Feed, and Validate. You have come a long way through your first round of creating that new podcast! Now we move onto the final steps. Once that feed has been created we need to publish it on the podcast host site, and then check that the feed validates. This step can be done at several Web sites including Feed Validator (http://www.Feedvalidator.org) and Atom Feed (http://www.atomfeed.org), validating a feed checks the XML code.

Once at the validation sites you type in the full address of your newly posted feed address and let it check it for you. If it says "Congratulations you are validated!" then you feel very good about yourself and know that the feed is working. If not, join most first timers, second, third, and veteran podcasters when sometimes there is a glitch in the code. Not to worry, these feed validators are really quite helpful and will have the problem areas underlined and usually short notes to try to clue you into the

Table 4.1. XML Code Explained

	Explanation	*XML Code*
1.	XML version	<?xml version listed here>
2.	RSS version	<rss ver listed here>
3.	Channel marker just says we are starting the section that identifies the name and source of this podcast series	<channel>
4.	Title of your podcast series	<title> Podcast for Teachers, Techpod </title>
5.	Description include title, purpose, who, where	<description> Live from the Bronx it's Fordham University's Podcast for Teachers, Techpod with Mark Gura and Dr. Kathy King </description>
6.	Your Web site for the podcast	<link>http://www.podcastforteachers.org</link>
7.	Topic category	<category domain="K-12">Education</category>
8.	Copyright holder	<copyright>(C) Fordham RETC, King & Gura </copyright>
9.	Instructions for RSS coding (standard line all feeds)	<docs>http://blogs.law.harvard.edu/tech/rss </docs>
10.	Language of the podcast	<language>en-us</language>
11.	Last edited	<lastBuildDate>Mon, 20 Feb 2006 00:57:59 -0500</lastBuildDate>
12.	Who manages it	<managingEditor>Podcastforteachers@gmail.com</managingEditor>
13.	When was it posted	<pubDate>Mon, 20 Feb 2006 00:47:56 -0500</pubDate>
14.	What is the rating	<rating>G</rating>
15.	Web master for the podcast	<webMaster>Podcastforteachers@gmail.com</webMaster>
16.	Information about a podcast logo is coming next	<image>
17.	Web address of the podcast logo itself	<url>http://www.podcastforteachers.org/PFT_LOGO.jpg</url>
18.	Title of the logo	<title>Podcast for Teachers - TECH POD-Live From The Bronx- Ed Tech You Can Use!</title>
19.	Link that you want people to go to when the CLICK the logo	<link>http://www.podcastforteachers.org</link>
20.	Description of the logo	<description>www.Podcast for Teachers.org Logo</description>
21.	Width of logo image	<width>144</width>
22.	height	<height>144</height>

(Table continues on next page)

Table 4.1. (Continued)

	Explanation	*XML Code*
23.	End of image information	</image>
24.	Beginning of First Episode!	<item>
25.	Comment information (can be the same as description- shows up in some additional places in some directions) <!--- starts this section	<!--Podcasting Grows, Tips, Tricks, Interview, Podcast via Internet Radio and Resources for Schools and Teachers. One Laptop per Child for Thailands (USA Today); Tech humor; KPK interview; Tech humor registration for podcasting on cellphone (VoiceIndigo) reveals humorous questions! Podcast for Teachers book in process- updated research being shared;
26.	---> ends this section	PFT's name and content is developed, produced and copyrighted (p) by Fordham Univ., King and Gura, 2006."More Ed Tech You Can Use Today and Tomorrow from Podcast for Teachers(sm)!"All rights reserved.-->
27.	Title of this episode	<title>Podcast for Teachers, Techpod, 51st Episode 8/21/2006: Podcasting Grows, and Grows, Tips, Tricks, Interview, Podcast via Internet Radio, and Resources</title>
28.	Description of the episode Begins with <description>	<description>Podcasting Grows, Tips, Tricks, Interview, Podcast via Internet Radio and Resources for Schools and Teachers. One Laptop per Child for Thailands (USA Today); Tech humor; KPK interview; Introduction to Kathy's interview on Podcast 411 with Dave Walch; ASCD SmartBrief- models of pd.
29.	Description ends with </description>	PFT's name and content is developed, produced and copyrighted (p) by Fordham Univ., King and Gura, 2006."More Ed Tech You Can Use Today and Tomorrow from Podcast for Teachers(sm)!"All rights reserved.</description>
30.	ENCLSOURE tag very critical After posting your MP3 file on your podcast host server You need the accurate and full 1. URL name 2. number of bytes in the file (length) 3. identify type of file (it could be audio or video for instance	<enclosure url="http://media.libsyn.com/media/retc/PFT_51_8_21_06.mp3" length="9422171" type="audio/mpeg"/>
31.	When the file was posted to the server for distribution	<pubDate>Sun, 13 Aug 2006 12:02:16 -0500</pubDate>

(Table continues on next page)

Table 4.1. (Continued)

	Explanation	*XML Code*
32.	A GUID is a genuine unique identifier being used to help databases. One way is to use your complete file name for that MP3 file	<guid>http://media.libsyn.com/media/retc/PFT_51_8_21_06.mp3</guid>
33.	End of information for this item (episode)	</item>
34.	Beginning of information list for the next episode!	<item>
35.	And more episodes!	
36.	And more episodes!	
37.	End of this podcast series	</channel>

problems. For example the error messages might be an incorrect file name, file not found, date is in the future, inaccurate time, and so forth.

Once everything is corrected and saved, reupload it to your server, validate it again, and eventually we are sure you will get it right. Now the power of "Push Technology" commences! Your file is out there and everyone can tell their podcasting software to "open" your URL address and their program retrieves all the information about your podcast and its episodes. What is more, every time you upload a new episode, edit the feed and immediately everyone who has subscribed to your podcast has the new episode in their podcatcher or aggregator! How does it happen? You create a new MP3 file, put it up on your podcast host, edit your feed.xml, and post it on the Web ... Wow! People immediately have it available as soon as they open their podcasting program the next time! The power of Push Technology, and the voice of every person as we get excited about implications for education! So let's continue with the stages.

THE CONTINUING PHASE

Create: Plan, and Record Content. So, we thought we were done when we created our podcast; we just do it again and again and again. Well, not quite. A few things are different as you move through the Continuing Phase of your new podcasting assignments, hobby, career, or work. The first thing is that in the **Create Stage** you really want to focus on content to keep a thriving and interesting podcast going. You want the educational content to dominate. Therefore you could have students find and use good resources, develop their best writing, share the work in well facilitated collaborative teams and use the opportunity to practice their speaking skills.

In addition, further Web site design can be developed in this stage to support the content development and to connect with other school projects, Web sites and podcasts. How can you cross-promote your program? How do you get feedback? And how do you get people and opinions involved to keep you and your students fresh with a project that will be in the public eye? This **Continuing Stage** is the one in which to think about these aspects and not just walk through the steps trance like!

For instance, consider how students and teachers alike have great opportunities to continue to learn and grow in the area of recording. They can learn how to use the current equipment best, determine when additional equipment would best meet the needs, and learn how to best use that equipment. Learning new media production includes just developing different podcast formats but also exploring different, interviewing styles, and making choices of stage presence, voice and speaking practice, enunciation, characterization, dramatization, or skills to be selected among and including background music, and sound effects. These dimensions can gradually be introduced over weeks and months to keep the experience interesting and fresh for all the learners involved. Podcasting, as a part of digital media is a constantly changing and improving field offering many expansive learning opportunities to refine and gain different perspectives.

Edit: Edit and Export to MP3. This edit stage will be an area of continued growth. Probably the first two stages in the continuing development of the podcast will be the areas of most continued growth. In addition to researching and developing new content, developing new skills in content editing and sound engineering will have a long road of challenges, but in a positive way it has great range of opportunity.

Web Site: Edit Web Site; Post MP3 file to Web. The Web site stage will be different now in **Continuation** than the first time around. At this point in the process the educator already has a Web site location and has it created. Now it is a matter of updating the information on the Web site for each episode with show notes that provide content for participants of the show, link to the show, and then start an archive for people to find previous episodes. Other features may be added as educational podcasters proceed and can be special projects for different groups of students as long as they are coordinated with the larger team and are also consistent with the overall educational goals and objectives.

Posting the new MP3 files to the podcast host server is done the same way as before EXCEPT you need to use a different name for each MP3 file. Therefore it is good to have a file naming convention that might indicate the episode and date of each MP3 file so it can easily be identified and referenced. Let's march on! We we are ready to head into that XML file again.

Feed: Edit XML File and RSS Feed. As we address editing of the XML file we move to the first <item> statement and create an entirely new entry for the new episode, and save the file with the same name. If you are using a text editor to edit your feed.xml, the copy and paste functions can aid very well when used with care. But you can also use the automated system that some podcast hosts provide (like Libsyn, Switchpod, Odeo, and Podomatic) or a feed creator program such as we mentioned previously. The key difference in this continuation step has been instead of creating a NEW file, we are only adding one small section to the same file with each new episode that is posted.

Publish Feed and Validate. Now the old feed.xml file should be saved with a new name and this file should be uploaded to the new server and validated immediately. Upload and validation proceeds like it did in the first phase of the model. Once it is in complete order then you are all set with this step. You are successfully on your way to many happy hours of podcasting.

FOCUS ON CONTENT

It is our sincere commitment that in the midst of the technical needs and descriptions that educators will not lose sight of the primary focus on *content in podcasting* efforts. There is so very much more to be developed, created and transformed through this medium. The technical aspects do not have to be overwhelming. In fact we like to keep the technical aspects simple but complete order to focus on content.

I certainly explore new equipment, new techniques, and new software, but I try to focus on what our listeners need, and how we can contribute most fully to the larger educational community. We encourage you to focus on your audience, focus on the student content, and also on your role as a facilitator. We firmly believe that with the aid of this book and its resources we will clue you into the technical aspects that will be enough to sustain you.

What is so very different with this model is that we as educators have the opportunity to bring something really different to podcasting: passion for teaching, learning and students.

CHAPTER RELATED RESOURCES

Atom Feed: Podcast, XML and RSSfeed validator, specifically of ATOM type code: http://www.atomfeed.org

Feed Validator: Podcast, XML, and RSS feed validator: http://www.Feedvalidator.org

Feedforall: XML feed generator for podcasts: http://www.feedforall.org

Libsyn (Liberated Syndication): Podcast host, one of the first ones, major directory of podcasts: http://www.libsyn.com

Odeo: Podcast directory where your podcast can be created and hosted: http://www.odeo.com

PODBEAN: Podcast host, major directory of podcasts, http://www.podbean.com

Podomatic: Podcast directory where your podcast can be created and hosted: http://www.podomatic.com

Switchpod: Podcast host, major directory of podcasts: http://www.switchpod.com

The Teachers' Podcast: Popular educational technology and professional development podcast with cohosts Kathleen King and Mark Gura: (The "new generation" of Podcast for Teachers, Techpod) http://www.teacherspodcast .org

The Teachers' Podcast, Virtual Workshops, Services and Conference Events: Events related to the popular podcast series: http://www.teacherspodcast.org

Transformation Education LLC: Educational support and consulting, professional development services, Web-based productions and more from a team of experienced educators, led by Kathleen King and Mark Gura: http://www.transformationed.com

CHAPTER 5

PODCASTING COST/BENEFIT DECISIONS

REFLECTIONS ON OUR EVOLUTION

When we considered launching into podcasting initially Kathy could see there would be a time and value in human resource investment as well as costs. However, the exact details of all possible costs for all the different aspects of podcasting we would test, pursue, and further refine were necessarily unknown. Nonetheless, almost 4 years down the road in this field of podcasting and over 40 years in education teaching, curriculum, and research development, provides a strong basis from which to provide some observations about this experience which we believe will be helpful for educators seeking to pursue podcasting.

Our approach to our educational work has always been to plan and design instruction and research in a dynamic feedback process. This enables us to gather information throughout our projects and to develop improvements based on that information on an ongoing basis, rather than only at the end of a project.

In fact this approach to research is consistent with key themes of learning many of our readers will find familiar: **project-based learning, action research, and reflective practice.** For example when we consider our research we seek to be consistent with our project-based learning approach to student learning and classroom teaching. In addition the

Podcasting for Teachers: Using a New Technology to Revolutionize Teaching and Learning,
Revised Second Edition, pp. 63–75

same patterns are also seen on a broader scale in our action-based research approach to teaching and curriculum in these observations.

However, even with such a strong conceptual groundwork, we continue to address the practical everyday instructional needs of teachers and learners and want to bring those "to the table" for discussion in our work. Indeed it is because of the groundwork we have laid that we believe the practical and highly relevant materials we provide are recognized in those ways.

Because of this unique experience in building a successful podcasting series for educational purposes, we have had to keep keen attention on needs and limits of resources and learners alike while staying focused on the powerful potential of content. This background of experience and the model of balancing costs and benefits is what we share in this chapter.

For us the unknown potential of podcasting was one of the major incentives, but this was coupled with extensive experience that Kathy had both technical details and distance education development for over 15 years. We were able to use her expertise and our technical advisors to evaluate the resources in content, time, equipment, and network needs for establishing and piloting a podcast project very rapidly because the cost for an initial pilot could be minimal with potential significant benefits.

OVERVIEW

Foundational to this approach is the model that Dr. King has developed over the years to use with educators for professional development in many settings (King, 2002, 2003, 2005; Lawler & King, 2000). This model of "Formative Curricular Development" encourages a perspective of teacher created instruction and action research. The model we applied to podcasting is often closely applied with problem-based learning.

This Formative Curricular Development model is a valuable approach to educational podcasting because it approaches **podcasting as a curricular project** that professional educators seek to make decisions about for the benefit of learners. Therefore in this model we seek answers to key questions educators ask when they develop curricular projects:

1. What are the specific curriculum needs we are addressing?
2. What are the student interests and needs that can be connected to with this curriculum and related projects?
3. What resources and technologies fit best with the curriculum and needs?
4. Which of these resources or technologies are realistically available?

5. How can we evaluate and assess what students learn and the curriculum project we design and deliver in order to improve the entire curriculum with each rendition?

The questions help frame the presentation of the model, however we also flesh out how the model helps us understand the **process** of educational podcasting.

Finally, the chapter brings us back to a key emphasis that should guide educational podcasting that will be truly relevant and long lasting. We develop the theme that our focus of podcasting embraces **constant change** on many levels. As adults we know our world changes constantly and as educators we see the evidence of change every year in new curricular trends, pedagogical favorites, and sociopolitical repercussions. A curriculum development approach to podcasting as expecting constant change can help us better cope with many aspects of our professional lives while guiding our efforts in this specific application.

MODEL OF FORMATIVE CURRICULUM WITH COST-BENEFIT-EVALUATION

Overview Description

When we as educators consider new topics of study for content areas, we evaluate many aspects of student needs, content standards, objectives, resources, instructional methods, and assessment to name some of the major aspects. In much the same way, when we look at the best ways to incorporate technology into our curriculum we examine the standards that students need to reach in content areas, within the broader technology learning standards (International Society for Technology in Education, 2006, 2007) and evaluate how to use technology to make learning more authentic, relevant, critical, and essential to student development.

With the Model of Formative Curriculum Development we build on the essential practices of **project-based learning, action research, and reflective practice.** By looking at podcasting as an extended curricular project educators can include learner-centered instruction, collaborative learning and a rich environment for students as not only a learning experience, but also project-based learning and vital student research. On another level, podcasting curriculum design also enables students to be part of action-based research. Therefore, one sees that it becomes much more than another flash of digital media. Podcasting in education can be a dynamic and powerful means of teacher and student colearning.

Model Stages via Questions

One of the ways to explore the stages of the Model of Formative Curriculum Development, seen in Figure 5.1, is as questions that can guide the process of evaluating the costs and benefits that face one approaching podcasting projects. In fact we have incorporated five key questions into the model design. These questions are represented by "questions waves" as they are **free flowing** because educators will be thinking about them and the related issues several times throughout the process of the curricular project.

The questions are represented by the phrases:

- Addressing curriculum needs;
- Student needs;
- Resources and technology which fit;
- Resources Availability; and
- Plan for assessment which improves

Educators looking at these projects have to consider curricular and technical issues all at the same time, even when they don't know the technical aspects yet. So where do we start? Let's look at the model briefly first with these questions and stages in mind, and then we will walk through it with podcasting specifically in view.

Addressing Curricular Needs: Q1: What are the specific curriculum needs we are addressing? When thinking about a new curricular project an educator needs to begin evaluation of the curricular needs that will be addressed. Asking what curricular needs are to be addressed with the project helps educators to immediately focus on the end goals and by seeking to articulate these from the beginning they can be better understood.

Another important point is that one does not need to be tied down completely to this first choice. Instead stating the curricular need can rather be like charting a course that is being shaped. Especially during a time of standards and evaluations, we know what we need to aim for; an extensive project-based learning curriculum opportunity provides the chance not only to meet such immediate needs, but also reach cross-disciplinary goals and needs and to develop additional directions as they emerge.

Student Needs: Q2: What are the student interests and needs that can be addressed to with this curriculum and related projects? A second critical question is to focus on the student needs and interests which could be vibrantly connected to the curriculum and project. We have all seen the terrible results of curriculum that fails to connect to or motivate students.

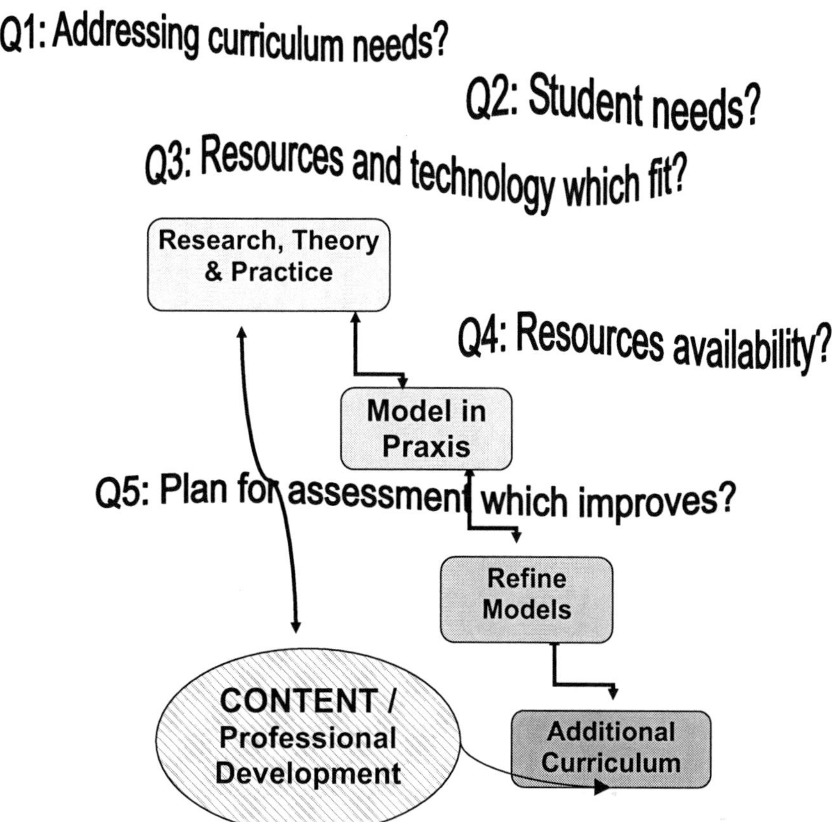

Figure 5.1. Model of Formative Curriculum Development. © 2007 King. All rights reserved.

At the same time it is not difficult to watch students, talk with them, and explore their interests. Upon doing so we can prepare to create lesson plans and activities which are meaningful and relevant.

Resources and Technology Which Fit: Q3: What resources and technologies fit best with the curriculum and needs? Within this dynamic, flexible model of curricular design the next question helps determine resources and technologies which fit best with the curriculum and student needs. Rather than forcing a favorite new technology that students are excited about into the curriculum, this question guides teachers to think about how to make choices about educational benefits.

This third question directly brings together the issues of costs and benefits succinctly. Rather than being blinded by the tempting glitz factor of new technology's lure, which education seems to have been susceptible to, educators need to look at technology, evaluate how it can be used for the good purpose of motivating students, addressing their interests and skills in digital media and twenty-first century skills, and escalate higher order thinking. But at the same time we need to ask the hard question as to whether sometimes new technology is only a matter of flash and not substance (e.g. educational benefits vs. empty promises). If we as educators do not ask the questions, no one will. By integrating such questions into the model we will be including critical questioning in our instructional design.

Resources Availability: Q4: Which of these resources or technologies are realistically available? It may seem unusual, but we have seen it happen, people oftentimes skip over the obvious question as to the realistic attainment of the technology or other resources they are considering using in their curricular project. Therefore this model builds in an explicit question to have educators consider the availability of resources. Why is it phrased in that manner? Because sometimes technology or a resource might not be immediately at hand, but it may be attained without too great a difficulty or expense. Therefore, again, it is a matter of investigation, questions and consideration in this process as one considers the project and the needs, merits and costs.

Plan for Assessment Which Improves: Q5: How can we evaluate and assess what students learn and the curriculum project we design and deliver in order to improve the entire curriculum with each rendition? The final question is one that educators often leave to others within the educational system (such as administrators or curricular oversight). In this model educators are expected to consider, plan and take responsibility for assessment of student learning and the curricular project. This tenet is a vital component because it not only determines the effectiveness of the curricular project, but it also lays the foundation for a dynamic, information gathering and always improving approach to teaching and learning.

A continuous improvement approach to instruction might sound unusual but action research is not. What is so very different is that this model aligns the individual instructor as the individual designer and operative of that research and instructional design. This model validates the curricular insight and planning that most instructors do day by day and takes it to a more formal level that also blends research, assessment, and project-based learning into it.

Stages: Reviewed

Research, Theory, and Practice. Considering the model now one can see that it articulates research and theory and practice. Because not only being based on the theoretical bases and the essential principles, this model also ties so fundamentally to practice. The entire model is one that takes the expertise of the field, weighs the costs and benefits and creates a model to test which is to put it *into* practice.

Model in Praxis. This stage means that practice is the experience of action and learning in action which is a critical element of the continuous improvement and information gathering elements of the model. Rather than just posing a model and testing the philosophical elements of it, this approach has not only a framework, but a requirement to test the model in action and then improve on that *field of practice.*

Refine Models. In this model the result of praxis is to refine the model that has been tested. In fact with each cycle, or round, the model can be revised and created in a new version or application for different contexts or revised as a holistic approach depending on the content. Models are created, tested in praxis and results are used to refine them further.

Additional Curriculum. In an even larger "circle" of development and application the model can result in the outcome of additional curricula. That is, while the model may be refined and further developed, entirely new content and models, even new curricula may be developed out of the work that is conducted. Such is an ever cyclic, continuing, yet nonlinear process and model that can frame curricular planning and teaching and learning.

Podcasting in Education Application of the Model of Formative Curriculum Development

Now as we think about applying this model to a specific curricular activity, let's work though how we would consider the costs and benefits of podcasting for educational settings. Let's say that in this situation we are considering using podcasting for a sixth grade language arts and literature class.

Addressing Curricular Needs. In addressing the curricular needs we would probably want to start on a small scale, perhaps by identifying a unit of study in Literature. This might be important in this class because the students may show minimal interest in the required American short stories and plays and have not yet developed good research skills. Already the possibility emerges here for them to research short stories in small groups and then do dramatic readings which they podcast for distribution. This will be detailed in further questions to come.

Student Needs. Q2: What are the student interests and needs that can be connected to with this curriculum and related projects? The student interests at this age and with this group are usually focused on themselves and people like themselves. So how can they determine similarities and differences among the characters in the literatures? Research arises as a tool to sell them on! Additionally students really like to communicate with students like themselves and meet new people, especially online. We can use that interest in a safe online environment and incorporate some skills and safety knowledge into learning podcasting and online learning and research. Making literature relevant and come alive, inspiring students to do research and giving them more tools to do it, and then improving communication skills and tools: sounds like our digital native students would be motivated by elements in that repertoire.

Resources and Technology Which Fit. Q3: What resources and technologies fit best with the curriculum and needs? These elements are already determined above as computer and online access for a basic podcasting setup; this has been an easy fit scenario.

In chapter 6 we detail podcasting setup requirements. However very briefly, the basic configuration may include free software and equipment you and your school already have. If you have computer and online access available sometime for your students, the cost to get started would be $0–$30. Therefore in the list we provide here we expect that if any, only a few items may need to be purchased. The specifics of the basic podcasting configuration are:

- free editing software (Audacity works for all operating systems);
- access to a computer for Web page or blog entries, recording and editing sound files;
- access to the Internet when you are researching material and posting items online;
- inexpensive microphone ($10-30 each);
- headphones or ear buds for private editing ($5-10), and speakers for group use ($15); and
- server space to upload—if not your own space then this can be about $5/month

Resources Availability. Q4: Which of these resources or technologies are realistically available? The major ticket items in hardware above is the computer and really for beginning to moderate podcasting the computer does not have to be dedicated to this project, it could be in a lab, or in the back of the classroom. The other resources are much smaller financial concerns and one setup for $30 could equip a classroom so that 20 students could cycle through in groups of four or five. This arrangement works out well because students could be assigned to different tasks: some will be writers, researchers, technical operations, and so forth. Working in teams and rotating responsibilities will also teach a great deal about using those resources responsibly and effectively.

Plan for Assessment which Improves. Q5 How can we evaluate and assess what students learn and the curriculum project we design and deliver in order to improve the entire curriculum with each rendition? Planning to Assess from the beginning always gives us a great start on our projects because we know we will not miss those great moments such as if we had been unprepared. In the podcasting situation one wants to have the students keep portfolios of all their draft work, labeled by date and draft number. Attendance in groups and what their daily group role/ assignment and tasks will also be important information for the students to later use to reflect on the collaborative process with the teacher and one another.

We highly endorse working with students to develop a rubric of evaluation. You might pose one and then have them help fill it out in greater detail as they learn the content area.

So in this case we might start working in literature and listening to some literature podcasts we had found and perhaps some of the students had found. Then we would have a class discussion about what else could be included in the literature podcasting rubric or the dramatic reading podcasting rubric. This would provide a solid basis for them to now start the research for their podcast as they know how they will be evaluated with authentic assessment of their work as well.

Stages Considered

Throughout the process of working with the students the curriculum idea will have developed into a posed model of how this interest and need for working in literature and podcasting can be a model for directing an instructional unit and managing class activities and even evaluating student work. As work continues the model is put through its paces as it were in praxis and it is stretched and twisted with the innumerable questions never imagined and irreconcilable inventions that young minds discover. Thus the model is deftly able to bend, mold, and adjust to the needs of individualistic traits of content, context and philosophy. Through this approach we can develop many models of specific practice to guide our work so that we can pursue curriculum development and student learning more vigorously and creatively,

Costs and Benefits

On the largest level this example of podcasting and curriculum brings us back to some essential ultimate questions in education where daily we make choices that mirror the large issues of cost and benefit, or as it is seen in many ways—cost and value. It is helpful to think about how exactly we can articulate the different dimensions and variations of value associated with the decisions as well as the costs. Consider this preliminary list as related to the podcasting example; they can be used as a good source for reflection and discussion

Value and Benefits: Fiscal

- Creating custom digital media;
- Preparing students with digital media skills;
- Preparing students with twenty-first century skills;
- Increasing student information and digital media literacy;
- Increasing student public speaking skills; and
- Increasing student writing, oral and research skills.

Value and Benefits: Intellectual, Social, Emotional, and Professional

- Creating custom digital media;
- Creating customized lessons based on local and state students for specific classroom contexts;
- Empowering professional educators to use their expertise more fully; and
- Encouraging leading educators in their ground breaking work as students learn critical thinking in real life application students (e.g., students learn to follow simple legal guidelines for digital media use [Creative Commons, 2006; EFF, 2006]).

Costs: Fiscal and Human Resource

- Teacher time spent way from basic education and spent on involvement in teaching technology skills;
- Teacher time spent assisting in editing student written work;
- Teacher time spent on facilitation and supervision of collaborative research groups;
- Minimal computer and recording equipment for podcasting; and
- Legal risks schools already face—students need to be protected from illegal Internet activity. Schools need comply with the Children's Internet Protection Act of 2001 (Federal Communications Commission, 2006).

What we really want to think about as we look at educational technology choices is whether in the big picture of our work we are fossilizing old patterns of education or we are creating, extending and transforming education in meaningful ways. We would think those new meanings would be critically important for the field of education itself and also for students and teachers.

In many ways, you can not place a price tag on inspiring the minds of the future when they enter our schools. Nor should we be minimizing the needs of our schools and educators. Costs and benefits—such difficult choices. Our urging to you is that at whatever level you work make the best choices on cost and benefit and to choose value for learning. As classroom educators we have those choices all day long and this model is one that provides strategies to look at your work in the eyes of educational value and pedagogical questioning.

Podcasting Focus, Like Learning—Change is Constant!

Figure 5.2 illustrates how some constant behaviors are needed in this model. There needs to be a constant focus on content needs. Needs for learning may start at some point, but as learning progresses, new pathways open up, new learning deficiencies may be revealed, and new inter-

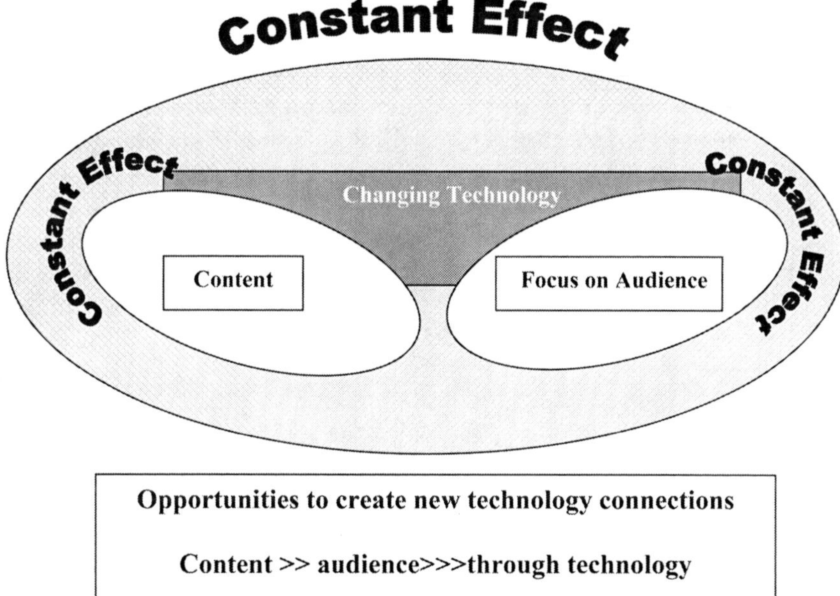

Opportunities to create new technology connections

Content >> audience>>>through technology

Figure 5.2. New opportunities for learning—to create new technology connections.

ests may emerge. In each of these few examples educators must consider when and how to address these potential content needs. It may be best to address the learning needs immediately or later. However, the indications, otherwise formerly known as "findings," that are revealed need to be recognized, discussed, and recorded so they may be returned to later.

In another dimension in podcasting there is the constant need to focus on the podcast audience, and in the case of educational podcasting, the learners. While this attention needs to be constant and unwavering, and podcasting educators must stay true to the mission of serving those needs, the podcaster must also realize that the audience can change. That is, unlike the traditional semester long or year long classroom composition, the very composition of *who* is listening can change day by day. In addition, our listener's needs, the reasons they are seeking out the podcast, the historical and political context in which they live, might change day to day, month to month as they may not be connected to a podcast for a specific traditional educational outcome such as credits, diploma, or degree. So here again arises the constant attention to a baseline that will shift and change frequently and constantly needs tracking.

Finally, on a very elementary level the third major factor to consider is the constant change that is happening in technology development, availability and user adoption. What is happening on the user level with technology? This landscape of events can change frequently with the release of new software programs, upgrades, media player devices, and company takeovers. If you do not keep up with the changes, your podcast could end up being in a form that is obsolete or unobtainable for a large number of potential users. As educational podcasters you need to be technologically savvy and address tech needs—specifically as they translate into and apply to the technology using needs of your listeners. Constant attention is also needed to this changing landscape.

Working through this interrelationship of constant attention to changes, educational needs, learning, and podcasting, one realizes there is a risk. As educational podcasters we could become entangled, even *strangled* in the technology and miss the message entirely, or we could never step on the technology highway and enter the conversation at all.

If you have reached this point in our book we know you are eager to be part of the conversation; therefore we provide an insight to steer through this potential entanglement. Instead of being tangled in the constant onrush of technology reinventions or missing the needs of the learners, we offer Figure 5.2 as a way to create New Opportunities for Learning. We focus on CONTENT in the midst of the constantly changing landscape of technology, tech user, and learner needs. We aim to steer with an eye on each, keep appraised of the status, steer a course that adapts and includes the changes, stay in the conversation, include your learners/listeners, and focus on how to communicate the content they need in the way/s they need it.

In this model technology and educational innovations may not mean a brand new curricular design; it may not mean a roaring new success of technological innovation immersed in curricular application. Instead these educational innovations are happening in the classrooms, on the Internet, in the MP3 players and on the Web daily and moment by moment by educators who are using and applying technology in new ways because they have an eye for what technology does, they understand what learners need, and they understand the *content*. The usual high-end information technology specialist does not have this content expertise at hand; however, educators do. If we as educators keep our eyes on these landscapes, if we watch the trends and developments, if we understand what the learners need and use, we can bring the content and the learning to intersect. These intersections create educational innovations that are powerful because they meet the needs of those learners today and tomorrow.

CONCLUSION

In this chapter we have explored how a model of curriculum development can guide us through considerations of costs and benefits as we consider podcasting in education. By using a dynamic model which builds on teacher expertise and critical questioning, one has the potential to create new curriculum activities, units of study, and branch into the development of new content for students and even teachers.

At the same time this model has embraced and practices problem-based learning, action research and reflective practice. Rather than just engaging in the use of technology for the sake of keeping up with current trends, educators can demonstrate to their students and one another how to critically evaluate choices, gather information, research, analyze, and continually improve their perspectives and work. In such a way we build podcasting in education is a living example of teachers and learners as co-learners in a lifelong process.

CHAPTER 6

DEMYSTIFYING THE PODCAST TECHTALK

Html ... XML ... pods ... blah ... blah ... ISP ... host ... feed ... feedster ... Feed me please!

RSS ... URL ... FTP ... http ... BLOG ... bandwidth ... bands ... garage door ... audacious ... blah ... blah ...

MP3 ... wav ... oggs ... eggs ... export ... mash-up ... mix-down ... mash potato ... the hustle ... import ... tariffs ... podsafe ... safepods ... escape pods?

Wait a minute? What are they talking about?

—*Thoughts of the beginning podcaster*

OVERVIEW

In this chapter we aim to help you decode and demystify the technical jargon and "tech-talk" which swirls around the podcasting world. Probably more than in any other area of innovative technology, in quite a while, podcasting seems to overrun those who seek to break into the new technology with techno-speak. With terms ranging from XML to blogs, feeds, MP3, WAV, RSS, export, import, to mix-down, educators seeking to bring the power of podcasting into their teaching and learning may be tempted to run from the room. Thankfully the days of overwhelming volumes of

Podcasting for Teachers: Using a New Technology to Revolutionize Teaching and Learning,
Revised Second Edition, pp. 77–103

requisite techno-speak seem to be fading and podcast production and hosting interfaces are becoming more user-friendly.

Nonetheless, as educators, most of us would value the statement that "Knowledge is power." And it is from that perspective that we provide this chapter to help you decode and master the language *and* power of podcasting for education.

This chapter will begin with an overview of podcasting setups and descriptions, the technical language, and details of hardware considerations, connectivity, software considerations, and sound recording, editing and production. You might use this chapter in several ways; first as an introduction to the terms and concepts and then later as a reference guide to assist you in decision making and troubleshooting. Podcasting in education is all about how we can create teaching and learning opportunities; therefore, we want to provide enough details that are relevant to make that happen and yet not muddy the waters.

PODCASTING SETUPS

An overview of podcasting setups and their descriptions does not have to be complicated. As stated, this section is meant to be an overview and guide. As always you will want to check online to determine what hardware configurations, software programs, and versions are the most recent and well-equipped, as no printed publication can keep up with the industry day to day. As a rule of thumb, when considering what you will need to create and fully produce a podcast, educators can approach the issue by thinking about at least three different degrees of complexity and expense: basic, moderate, and advanced.

As a framing paradigm educators want to consider the reasons why they are pursuing their podcasting project.

- Is it a first time venture, or is it a school—or organization-wide rollout of prior successes?
- Will the podcasts be used for student use, teacher use, individual classes, schoolwide, general public, and/or potentially global distribution?

Answers to these questions will guide educators in determining how much to invest in their first podcasting setup. Our approach, with our Podcast for Teachers, Techpod series, was to invest a minimal amount until we saw whether podcasting was a medium and format that met our needs and fit our resources. Once we evaluated those conditions, we invested further. Such an approach is usually one that helps fledging podcasters get started in educational settings where resources are not abundant and they can demonstrate the worthiness of their projects to administrators.

Basic Configuration

As illustrated in Figure 6.1, in the **Basic** configuration, a podcaster would have *access* to a computer, Internet, microphone, sound recording, and editing software, and Web and podcast hosting service. If you have Internet and computer access, Table 6.1 demonstrates that podcasting production and hosting can be accomplished on the inexpensive side for a one-time expense of $10-30 for a microphone and $5-10 per month for worry-free hosting. If your school or organization has a server available that will allow you to post your podcast Web site, audio files, and feed on their server, then you will not have the monthly fee.

Among microphone options one way to simply distinguish among inexpensive microphones and their uses and benefits is a desktop, clip-on, or headset model. The clip-on and headset microphones are good for

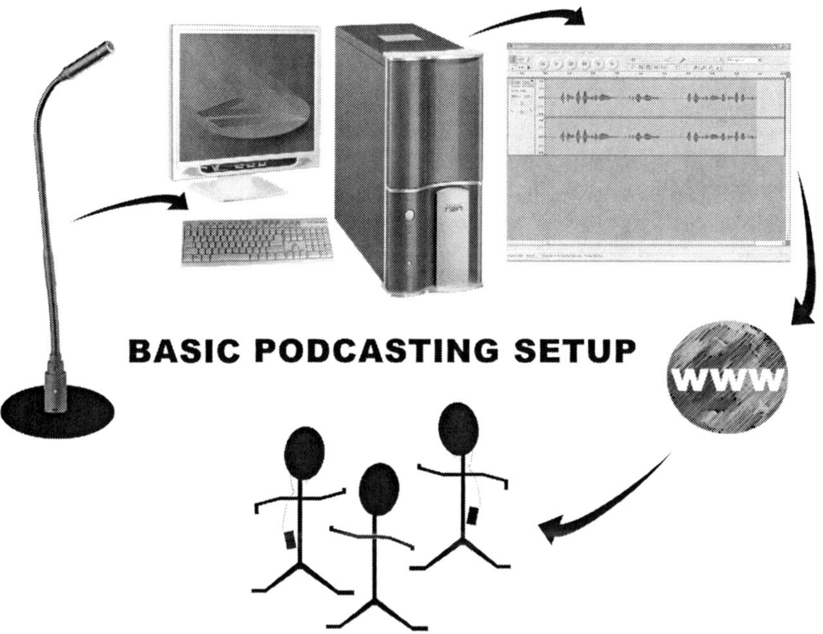

Figure 6.1. Basic podcasting setup: microphone, computer (software), access to computer, Web, and podcast host on the Internet.

individual podcasters as they follow the individual when they turn his or her head. The desktop model will be better for one to three people assembled **very** close together.

If for some reason you do not have a computer available for occasional access or any Internet access, then your total cost for podcasting has to include these resources. This unusual situation would of course increase the total cost of the educational efforts. The approximate additional total cost of $500 initial computer plus $10 monthly Internet access would be needed. Again it would be unusual that a school or teacher would not have a computer available for at least occasional use through a computer lab for instance. A dedicated computer is not needed at all.

Therefore in most childhood and adolescent schooling educational settings the setup costs for a basic configuration would be $10-30 and there may be a $5-10 monthly fee for a reliable hosting services in order for a classroom and school to be launched into the digital media dimensions of podcasting in education.

Moderate Configuration

Returning to Table 6.1 a **Moderate** configuration includes the same basic elements of the Basic configuration—*access* to a computer, Internet, microphone, sound recording and editing software, and Web and podcast hosting service. The differences include upgrading selections in the microphone, sound editing software, and a sound mixer (see Figure 6.2), and the fact that it would be easiest to have access to the same computers for recording and production sessions. The one-time setup cost or upgrade cost is $180-300 and of course can be done in stages. None of these are recurring monthly costs.

In addition, at this Moderate configuration level you might be expecting to use more than an entry-level **computer** which might be valued at $800-1,200. Again, as regards the computer access, we expect that most educators will have access to one on an occasional basis. We want to repeat that it is not necessary to have a computer solely dedicated to this project. At this Moderate configuration level, however, it would be best to be able to use the same computer each time, but it could certainly be used for other purposes.

Let us now return to the matter of the upgrade of the equipment we mentioned—the microphone and mixer. Among **microphone** variations, not only are there "desktop," clip-on, and headset models, but also plug, or attachment variations. In terms of the models, the clip-on is still an option but there are wireless options in this price range. With headsets, we have not only the 1/8" headphone/audio jack that you see on comput-

Table 6.1. Podcasting Set-Up Costs

	Microphone	*Mixer*	*Sound Editing Software*	*Headphones*	*Total Setup Costs*	*Podcast Host*	*Total Recurring*	*Access*	*Internet Connection Monthly Fee*	*Computer*
Basic	$10-30 Model: desktop, clip-on, headset Plug: 1/8", USB	0 Not necessary	0	Helpful	$10-30	$0/mo	$0/mo	Access to Internet and computer needed—not purchase—nor does it need to be solely designated to this project	$10/mo	$500
Moderate	$50-100 Model: desktop, clip-on, headset Plug: 1/8", USB, XLR	$80-150 Model: USB	$50	$20 (recommended)	$200-320	$5-20/mo	$5-20		$10/mo	$800
Advanced	$50-800 Model: desktop, clip-on, headset Plug: 1/8", XLR	$80-400 Model: USB Firewire	$50-200	$50-100 (recommended)	$230-1,000+	$5-40/mo	$5-40	At this level it would be good to have an area set aside for podcasting—but computer still could be used for other applications	$10/mo	$1,000

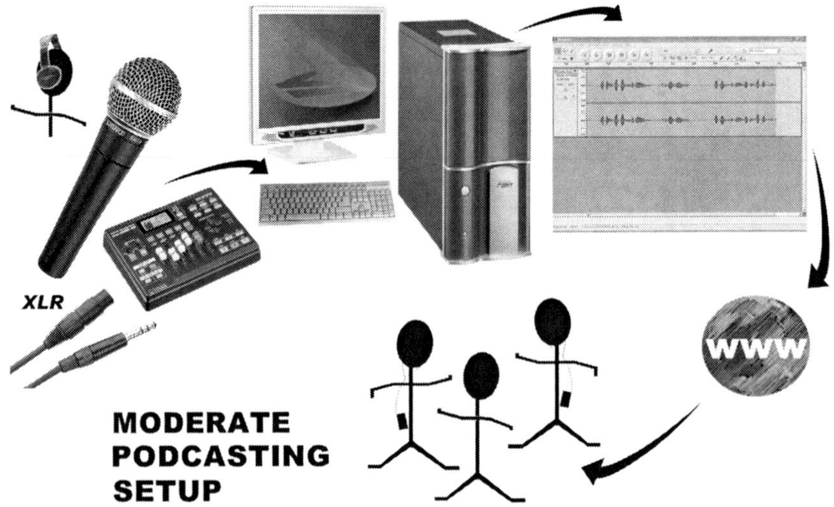

Figure 6.2. Moderate podcasting setup: microphone with XLR plug, mixer computer (software), access to computer, Web, and podcast host on the Internet. Headphones are recommended.

ers and other audio players, but also USB versions which give superior technology integration. The most familiar microphone which enters this price range is the larger type "professional" microphone which has the XLR plug/jack on the end. Such microphones are classified as condenser or dynamic microphones and require an additional power source, which is called "phantom power."

See Figure 6.3 for diagrams of the microphones and Figure 6.4 for illustrations of the XLR plug and related cables. The microphones can then be positioned by attaching them to a small desk stand, floor stand, or boom (long arm) that can be rotated to many angles. None of these setups are expensive, large music stores and online warehouses can provide these stands for $10-15.

In Figure 6.4, I have included the images of the XLR plug and cable for people not previously involved in recording, and after all most of us are not music educators, so this might be a bit puzzling. The XLR plug is the large adapter on the end of the professional microphone and you need the heavy microphone cable to connect to your computer or mixer. The first cable connects from XLR plug to XLR plug, the second cable illustration in Figure 6.3 is an adapter so you can use the professional microphone with the XLR plug and connect it to a 1/8" plug in a computer or mixer and you need to provide the "phantom power" through

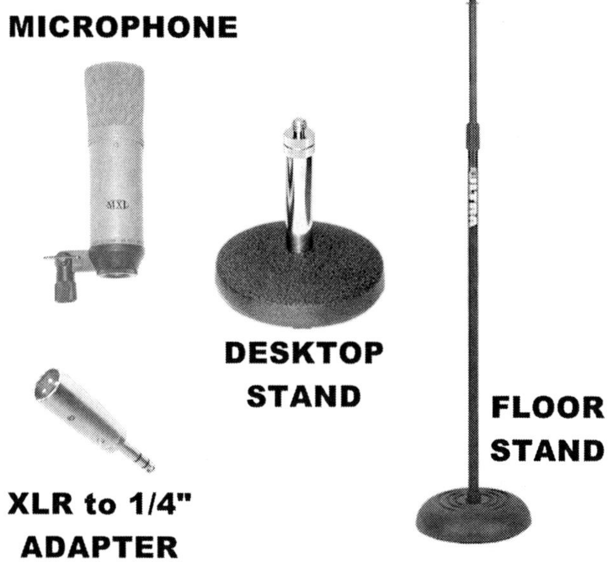

Figure 6.3. Microphone, adapter, desktop stand, and floor stand (microphone photo is a Marshall Electronics MXL V57M Studio Condenser Microphone, photo licensed for use by zZounds.com. Used by permission.

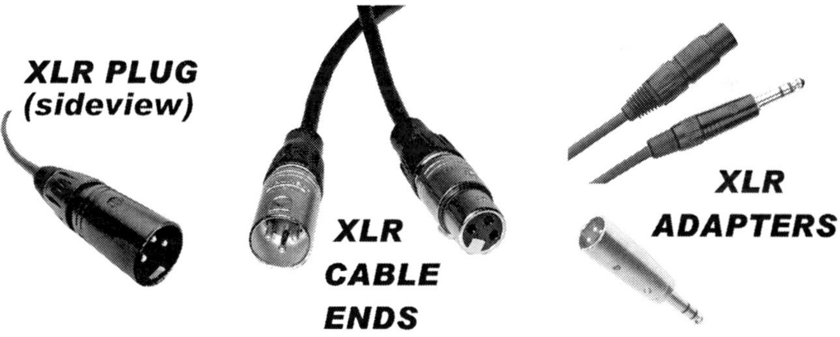

Figure 6.4. XLR plug (sideview), XLR cable end views, and XLR cable with adapter to ¼" stereo plug (diagrams and photos licensed for use by zZounds.com. Used by permission.

the plug, the microphone or the mixer. The diagrams should help to clarify this relationship.

Next we consider **mixers**; in Figure 6.2 you can see the sound mixing board which connects the microphone to the computer in this configuration. A sound mixing board and amplifier not only can allow multiple inputs, but also volume control, amplification, and digital effects to be accomplished at the time of recording. One of the major advancements in technology since 2005 is that these mixing boards can be connected to personal computers with a USB or FireWire connection. Previous to this, in order to assemble a setup with comparable capabilities of mixing boards, amplifiers, compressors, and so forth, one would need thousands of dollars in highly specialized computers, to record—to tape or disc—and then transfer to high-end computers.

Alesis was one of the first companies to market a reliable, high quality, but inexpensive USB mixing board product in this area (http://www.alesis.com/). We have used an Alesis model since mid 2005. Now there are other companies including Yamaha (http://www.yamaha.com) and Behringer (http://www.behringer.com) who also make quality inexpensive mixing boards with a full range of features for personal computer use. For example, in 2006 FireWire connection (instead of USB) mixing boards came into the market that were more expensive but still not in thousands of dollars and allowed the added capability for the channels/microphones to also be split separately.

In terms of **sound editing software** when one moves up from free software there is an extremely large improvement in production quality. In this respect my number one choice has been Adobe Audition and the educator discount makes this a reasonable choice. Equally important is the fact that regardless of how advanced you and your students want to get in podcasting and sound editing production in the future, you will not need another program. Unfortunately very few educators seem to make the choice to step beyond free podcasting software and they never gain the benefits and power they can have for $100 of cost. When one considers that these sound editing programs' retail and street values exceed $300, **and** the benefits to be gained from their use, educators, and administrators should be making this their first choice of upgrade for any group committed to podcasting.

Sound editing software that is more powerful has the capability of including more recording tracks, scores of filters which can eliminate sound problems and improve sound quality, and a basic programming engine which "mixes down" the recorded tracks to a higher quality product. Simply stated the benefits of a smaller investment in sound editing software are: greater quality and options throughout the sound editing process—from recording, editing, to output.

For the beginner configuration it is possible to use a free software program or to tryout an online recording solution once or twice, but if one is going to pursue an educational effort, please invest the money in sound editing software. Adobe Audition (http://www.adobe.com) is top notch;

iLife (http://www.apple.com/ilife/) has a lot of positive aspects, but falls short in some regards. See Table 6.2 for more details and my own ratings based on my experience and testing. You will also find most companies provide free 30-day trials of their progress for you to test drive; therefore you can do a few test recordings, and evaluate the ease of use of the program and help files in addition to the sound quality of the results.

An additional product to support the project is a **small digital camera** ($15-50) that can be used to document the learning process in developing a group or individual portfolio. This documentation can be a matter of pride of work or also be used in the learning process as another form of assessment. The pictures, without student names, and with parental permission, can also be used on the podcast Web site. Having a camera nearby throughout these projects is indispensable. Students will remember these experiences for a long time. Even if it is just for them to have a positive keepsake of their meaningful work, this is a way to build pride in intellectual growth, collaboration and school work. These results are all the type of excellent outcome we yearn for as educators.

Again, your approach to podcasting configurations is that you can start with a modest setup and see if you will be staying with the project and gradually build on to it. If the project and educational effort is really advancing, that is it is becoming a significant curricular focus and you are having multiple participants, the **Moderate** configuration is really the best place to go to next. The step up in software, microphones, and mixer will have substantial benefits for recording, production, and overall educational benefits because the experience in production and results will be so much better. The next level of **Advanced** configuration will take the educational podcasting project to the top tier of capabilities.

Advanced Configuration

What distinguishes the **Advanced** podcasting configuration is that the educational podcasting project has evolved so that it meets greater needs and expectations. Some reasons may likely include, but not be limited to one or more of the following:

- multiple participants,
- perhaps an additional source of sound input (such as a prerecorded or live music source),
- the need to separate multiple recording tracks,
- advanced sound editing with digital effects and/or filters,

Table 6.2. Comparison of Sound Editing Software That May Be Used for Podcasting

Title/ Program	*Quality Rating (1-5*) Price (1-5 $)*	*Comments*	*URL*
Adobe Audition 2.0	***** $$	Great product, powerful editing, and mastering. Incompatible with Vista.	http://www.adobe.com/products
Adobe Audition 3.0	***** $$	Powerful audio editing, added features, even better. Vista OK.	http://www.adobe.com/products
Adobe Soundbooth	**** $	Basic audio editing features, ease of use, Adobe quality.	http://www.adobe.com/products
Audacity	*** free	Free, but limited. Very popular. Many online tutorials available.	http://audacity.sourceforge.net
Clickcaster	* $	Record online—limited quality. All-in-one production options	http://www.clickcaster.com
Hipcast	* $	Record online—limited quality.	http://www.hipcast.com
iLife '08 Garageband	*** $$	Mac only. Integrated podcast record and post features. Audio and video.	http://www.apple.com/ilife/ garageband/
Profcast	**** $$	Mac based only. Podcast your PowerPoint.	http://www.profcast.com
Podomatic	** Free to $	Record online. All-in-one production options	http://www.podomatic.com
Propaganda 2.0	** $$	Podcasting recording and posting software. Used to be free—but now more reliable.	http://www.makepropaganda.com/
Snapcast	****** $	PC based. One stop podcast creator, feed and upload! Also able to podcast your PowerPoint.	http://www.snapkast.com
Sony Sound Forge Audio Studio 9	*** $$	Basic features, 24 bit, beginner, easier than full packages	http://www.sonycreativesoftware.com/
Sony Sound Forge 9	***** $$$$	Professional production power, full features, 24, 32, 64-bit	http://www.sonycreativesoftware.com/

Note: This table was developed based on my own testing and experience with these programs as of 6/15/2008. Of course you are encouraged to test the free trials available for most of the programs to see which will be meet your specific needs and uses. *Always ask for educational discounts!* (K. P. King)

- creating a variety of output formats—podcasts, CDs, DVDs, archives, and so forth, or
- additional processing power for mixing larger and/or multiple files.

The **Advanced** configuration will include the same Basic configuration components, but in order to be able to pursue this it is expected you would have a dedicated computer, purchased one or more microphones, sound recording and editing software, and have access to the Internet, and Web and podcast hosting services (see Figure 6.5.).

Regarding the **microphone** upgrades for this category, microphones provide a variety of models from dynamic and condenser and several patterns in which they record sound. An additional microphone distinction should be noted. If you will solely be working with a mixing board you can conveniently use a microphone that requires *phantom* power because you will be plugging into a device that can provide it. This set-up means you will not have to worry about replacing microphone batteries.

For educational podcasting the major benefit of the Advanced level investment may be in several microphones, or that a higher-end model will be within reach. Microphone performance can be very specific to the voice of the podcaster. I have found that some large music stores have

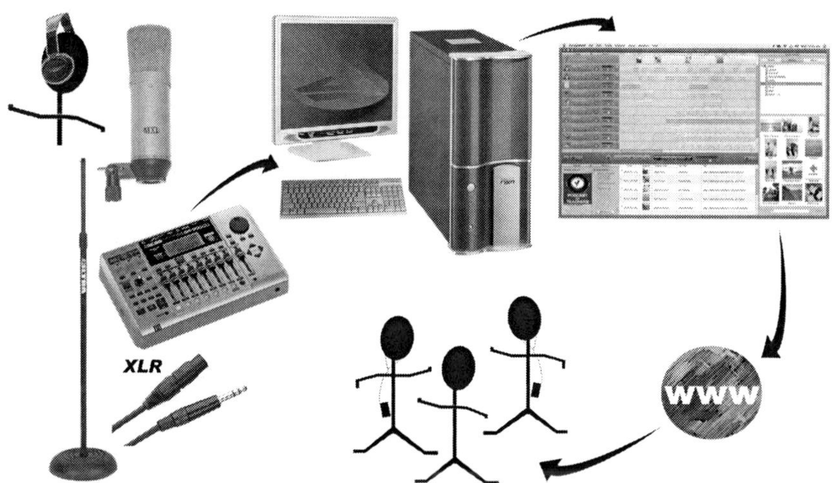

Figure 6.5. Advanced Podcasting setup: Multiple microphones with XLR plug, advanced mixer, advanced sound editing software, designated computer, advanced headphones and higher costs for server space.

bays of microphones wired so that you can test them and monitor yourself on headphones. This prepurchase testing ground is ideal before launching into a high-end microphone purchase. Many podcasters favor MXL and Precision microphones in particular. In addition, the condenser microphone designs have the capability of recording the multiple levels of the human voice very well. One detail to note in microphone terminology, podcasters are intending to use them for speech and not "vocals," which refers to singing.

In the area of **mixers**, an addition to the educational podcasting studio that would provide increased production capabilities includes USB and FireWire mixers. What also enters at this Advanced configuration level are many additional inputs, outputs, digital effects, and monitoring capabilities, to name a few of the features. Alesis, Behringer, Yamaha, and Phonic are a few of the names that have continued to lead the industry at this level.

A very good Behringer EuroRack is the UB 1832 FX Pro at about $329; the advanced one I use and favor a great deal is the Phonic Helix Board 16 ($400). You can easily spend more than a $1,000 for a mixer. Again you are looking for features you will use and not just copious additional switches and effects that will never be used. Otherwise you will be in a financial sinkhole! Personally, when I go looking at these devices I always go on exploring missions with no credit card or cash; I gather information for a few months before I decide on a model and then I compare prices locally and online.

For **portable recording** there are several options and it depends what exactly you are expecting to do. If you are taking a laptop on the road and want to plug in a tiny USB device, the Fast Track USB model is manufactured by and is available from M-Audio (http://www.m-audio.com), but of course it is limited in its capabilities. Another approach is to use a digital voice recorder that will record and save in high-quality MP3 format. In fact in 2008, this is our favored setup for The Teachers' Podcast. Another solution is to attach a digital recorder to an iPod (such as a Belkin Tunetalk) or use an inexpensive ($40) digital voice recorder/MP3 player combination device. The top of the line solution is a recorder, such as the MicroTrack2496 (http://www.m-audio.com) or the immensely popular Edirol R-09 (http://www.edirol.net/products/en/R-09/).

For microphones in portable settings your choices vary **greatly.** You might use your laptop, iRiver or MP3 player and plug a condenser microphone (with a battery in it) into any of those and use a cable that converts the XLR plug to the ¼" plug or carry a portable pre-amp like the Behringer Eurora cvkub ($50). Conversely you could also use that same line-in plug in the recording device and plug in a very small lapel type or table top microphone with a 1/8" jack. Major issues in these "on the road" settings include background noise, echo, and people being too far from the microphones. The best advice is to do a test run in the environment with several types of microphones and have plenty of backups and batteries, plenty of water, and good humor.

Sound editing software provides another opportunity for upgrading the possibilities of recording and production. Moving up from the Basic configuration packages to the Advanced provides new features, many more input options and greater processing power. Back in Table 6.1 the appropriate pricing is listed for the relevant programs and you can be assured that the additional price provides much greater features. The untold difference is the ease of use for you personally and the particular needs and goals you and your learners have for the sound editing programs.

Therefore you need to look at some technical reviews and comparison charts to ascertain the most recent comparisons. Kathy always turns to places like the following sources for reliable and complete reviews and user-friendly comparisons of software and hardware and this certainly includes sound editing and video editing software. See Table 6.3 for a convenient list of magazines and their Web sites that provide such comparisons.

Figure 6.6 is a sample review from one of these sites; in this case it is for a less expensive sound editing program but a very popular one, iLife. This sample review shows that in addition to the description of software features via numeric ratings and text, some sites also leave the opportunity for users to rate the products as well. This information can be very helpful as you spot people who have configurations or goals like your own and who either have success or difficulty with the product you were considering purchasing. The point of looking at software and hardware reviews is that we no longer have to go into investments uninformed, there is an abundance of information available that can help us be self sufficient in these decisions.

Computer processing is a critical element in podcasting production that may go unnoticed until you reach this level. Based on our experiences producing podcasts, we can tell you that with *multiple* inputs, tracks and larger files, an entry level computer and many laptops will begin to fail the grade. In 2008, for an Advanced configuration I would expect one would be looking at dual processors, 2 GB RAM and at least 120 GB hard drives. In addition, external hard drives are simple to add and are a very good choice for backup and portability which is needed in many education-related projects.

Much of what we do in education is not computing power intensive. However graphics, video and sound editing at this advanced level will be

Table 6.3. Short List of Major Information Sources of Hardware and Software Ratings

Source	*URL*	*Focus*	*Hardware*	*Software*
Videomaker Magazine	http://www.videomaker.com/	Amateurs, students, professional videographers	Computers, cameras, video sound equipment, recording equipment	Sound editing, video editing, anything photo related
PC Magazine	http://www.pcmag.com	Technical magazine with extensive online format and features. Also provides comparison studies of equipment and software	PC hardware	PC software
CNET	http://www.cnet.com	Provides reviews on products and also technical articles	All	All
MAC User	http://www.macuser.com	News, information and reviews about everything Mac	MAC hardware	MAC compatible software
MAC World	http://www.macworld.com	Technical magazine with online' format and features- provides reviews, specifications and information.	MAC hardware	MAC hardware
Podcasting News	http://www.podcastingnews.com	Announcements and ads of the newest equipment specific to the field of podcasting	MAC and PC	MAC and PC

demanding so there will be justification to get a better computer than standard issue in the organization. At the same time a high end $3000 "gaming madness machine" is probably not going to be rationalized very easily in a school budget unless it is directly related to the students' curriculum. Our chapter 5 discussion of cost-benefit arises again, doesn't it?

Also in our experience a high quality set of **headphones** can make the work of sound editing much easier. While not absolutely required the

An Excerpt and Abridged Review of iLife '06 from CNET
iLife '06 http://reviews.cnet.com/4505-8033_7-31661463.html
At a glance

- **Release date:** January 10, 2006
- **Editors' rating:** 7.3 Very good
- **Editor's take:** If you don't already have iLife and you deal with digital media, you should get iLife '06. If you have an older version, think carefully about whether the new features are worth the price.
- **The good:** iLife '06 improves performance and integration between applications. GarageBand 3 has podcast studio capabilities, and iWeb lets you create Web pages easily.
- **The bad:** Some applications, especially GarageBand, are RAM hungry or require a .Mac membership to realize their full potential. iWeb is not yet mature. Also, service and support for iLife has waned since last year's version.
- **The bottom line:** If you don't already have iLife and you deal with digital media, you should get iLife '06. If you have an older version, think carefully about whether the new features are worth the price.

CNET editor's review

Reviewed by ; Daniel Drew Turner
Edited by ; Felisa Yang
Reviewed April 19, 2006

With iLife '06, Apple offers an evolutionary revision to most of its consumer digital media applications, casting an eye toward the social networking of your content. iPhoto 6 gets a performance boost and new "photocasting" abilities, while GarageBand 3 becomes a full-featured podcast-creation studio. The new iWeb offers an elegant and simple way to create media-rich Web pages, though it still needs to mature. The other applications in the suite--iMovie HD 6 and iDVD 6--integrate better and work with your iWeb pages, enabling you not just to create digital content but to share it, too. If you're already happily using iLife '05 and don't need iWeb, you may want to stick with what you have. On the other hand, if you don't own iLife or if you want the new features, $79 is quite a bargain, considering the tools you get.

Setup and Interface (Excerpt)
Installing iLife '06 isn't a mere one-step process, but it's not onerous either. An installer program walks you through the steps, which include agreeing to the terms of use and deciding whether to install optional extras. If you're tight on hard drive space and don't plan to use GarageBand 3 as a music-making machine, you can save a lot of room by not installing that application's many extras........

Features Described (Excerpt)
The iLife '06 suite is composed of iPhoto 6, iMovie HD 6, iDVD 6, GarageBand 3, and the new iWeb. None of the older programs gets a radical revision in iLife '06, but they all get new and welcome features.

(Figure continues on next page.)

Figure 6.6. Sample comparison of software features. (Excerpt from CNET.com © 2006 CNET.com. Used by permission.)

We've already reviewed GarageBand 3 **in depth as a powerful music-creation tool**. In short, with this third version, Apple has added interesting podcast-creation tools. GarageBand 3 includes automatic ducking, great filters for voice recording, and integration with iChat. The last is particularly interesting in that it enables you to record interviews using iChat's voice feature, with the interviewee's voice on a separate track. **There's a downside to using GarageBand 3 as a podcast studio, though: it's a resource-intensive application with heavy RAM requirements and gigabytes of sound files that will fill up your hard drive. [emphasis added]**

Performance
Service and support (Excerpt)
As with Apple's iWork '06 consumer productivity suite, the price of iLife '06 does not include any dedicated tech support per se—a step back from the support offered for iLife '05. ....

User comments---[*people write these in via the web---take them for what they are worth!*]
Average user rating Very good 7.6 out of 10
Average user rating: from 9 users

User rating Spectacular 9 out of 10
Essential upgrade or must buy if you don't have it
by MacsRG - January 15, 2006
Pros: can publish iWeb pages to non-.Mac site. Easy podcast creation and iWeb.
Cons: Lose some features when uploading to non-Mac site.
2 out of **3** users found this user opinion helpful.

User rating Average 5 out of 10
Limited functionality without .Mac subscription
by l22 - November 20, 2006
Pros: Excellent, intuitive software
Cons: Some essential features only work with a .Mac subscription

User rating Excellent 8 out of 10
Good, but being anti-mpg is Apple's HUGE MISTAKE
by cl- July 30, 2006
Pros: easy to use, beautiful interface, complete, no need of [sic] pro software
Cons: Iphoto, quicktime and Imovie don't like mpg files!

Basic specs for iLife '06 Compatibility-- **Mac** Distribution media-- **DVD-ROM** License qty-- **1 user** License type-- **Complete package** Min processor type-- **733 MHz**	Buying choices for the iLife '06 Buy direct from Apple Computer, Inc. $79.00 AtomicPark. com $73.00 | In stock: Yes Buy.com $73.01 | In stock: Yes See prices from all 15 stores

---

http://reviews.cnet.com/4505-8033_7-31661463.html

Figure 6.6. Continued. (Excerpt from CNET.com © 2006 CNET.com. Used by permission.)

amount of time and effort saved can be remarkable especially when your group may be producing more than one or two podcasts per month. Even a high quality set of headphones only needs to be about $50-100 at the most. We have found Sennheiser, AKG, and Sony to be among the best quality and they can be found very reasonably in music stores and online sources. An example of one model is the Sennheiser HD280PRO, which has a street price of $99.

A **video camera,** to start taking video, exploring and developing a video podcasting project with the students is another branching curriculum project. The added dimensions of video bring in disciplines of moving art visual composition, and increases the dimensions of research, writing, and production through another strand so that not just storyline and sound has to be prepared, but also the visual. A good video camera can also be used to document the podcasting work of the students for an authentic assessment and portfolio of their learning process.

With the totality of what we have described in this Advanced configuration section the podcasting educator should be very well prepared to ramp up and pursue podcasting projects on more of a professional recording and production level.

OF MP3 AND XML FILES

As we can continue our discussion of podcasting technical aspects, identifying the terms MP3 (MPEG Audio Layer 3) and XML (eXtensible Markup Language) will help clarify matters greatly. MP3 files are the format that the audio podcasts are exported into and then uploaded onto the Internet for users to access (see Table 6.4). MP3 is a compression technology used for audio and now video files. How much can it compress a file? While the standard comparison is that a 40 MB CD quality music track would be about 4 MB in a MP3 file (Farlex, 2007a).

Why MP3 format? A few basic reasons include that in this format audio files maintain a good quality of sound, and yet are compressed to much smaller sizes. MP3 format has become a de facto file format that is widely recognized and exchanged among music media players. It has become a major "currency" of audio files in the digital age.

Now to get to the master term of mystery as it were, XML. XML files are specific RSS feeds. That is, they are programming scripts written in a specific programming language named XML. XML stands for Extensible Markup Language and is widely used to format information in a uniform method so that it can be passed along and processed. In many ways it is more a format than a formal programming code. It also can be used so that the [tags] can be very readable phrases so that people who are non

Table 6.4. Audio File Formats

Audio File Formats and Abbreviation	*Comments*
MP3	Preferred format for podcasts **MPEG-1 Audio Layer 3**, uses a compression format that greatly reduces size of file but is widely compatible **MPEG** stands for the Moving Picture Experts Group
WAV	Very common file format, large files however Waveform audio format, is a Microsoft and IBM audio file format standard for storing audio on PCs. Compatible on PCs and Macs.
WMA	Windows Media Audio files proprietary format created by Microsoft
Mpeg4, mp4	Video standard used primarily to compress audio and visual (AV) digital data. Introduced in 1998.
M4u	Audio portion of the mpeg4 files
Ogg	Open source audio format Ogg Vorbis. Being used in more and more mobile media players because it is open source.
Aiff	Audio Interchange File Format uncompressed audio file format used mostly on Apple computers
AAC	Advanced Audio Coding proprietary audio format used by Apple in iTunes and Sony's Playstation
Mkv	Alternate audio format developed in Europe, but found to be highly susceptible to viruses being embedded in it

programmers can follow the logic of the script (Farlex, 2007b). This means it is helpful for podcasting because it is a formatting script that enables podcasters to easily tag their information to send it to the podcast directories and it is universally recognized.

Again, the power in this development was envisioned and leveraged by Dave Winer and Adam Curry as they saw how to bring MP3 files together with XML coding. When you marry the two technologies, you end up with a script that enables your audio files, episode after episode to be "pushed" to people who are interested in them. Chapters 6 and 7 of this book go into great detail on the development of RSS feeds for podcasting.

INTERNET CONNECTIONS

In considering the connectivity issues related to podcasting, we have already addressed most of them, but a section that summarized them provides a ready reference and cohesive explanation. Podcasting involves three major aspects of technology connections that the podcast developer needs to account for, they include:

- Internet access,
- podcast file storage space (MP3 host), and
- podcast Web site and feed host.

I identify these items separately because they entail issues that can develop into unexpected costs if not planned for appropriately.

Now returning to the issues of connectivity, we repeatedly refer to **Internet access** because in order to develop and produce a podcast one does not need to have constant 24/7 Internet connection for all phases of the work. Teachers and students need access when uploading files and doing web-based research, but access is the key phrase. Broadband connection is preferred, but most educational podcasts are not over 30 minutes in length and do not have to be high fidelity files, therefore, it is possible that files could be uploaded over modem connections. This detail is provided because we do not want to exclude the possibility that schools and educators may be in settings across the globe that do not have broadband connections ubiquitously, or at all, available.

An educational podcast will not only have MP3 files that are uploaded to an Internet server (**MP3 host**), but also an XML file that is uploaded to a server (feed host) and a Web site. In reality the greatest demand on the Internet servers for files will be for the MP3 files. This demand for the MP3 files is called traffic, or bandwidth, and the larger the files, the more information has to be transmitted. In addition the more people access the files, the more demand and traffic there is. Therefore you have a multiplying effect in play, as more people listen to the podcast your bandwidth increases, and larger files will also increase it. What kind of impact could it have? A large demand could pull a typical organizational network to its knees. Therefore, it is well worth planning to host MP3 files on an outside server so that the demand on resources is not overtaxing your organization.

In comparison the podcast Web site and XML file do not cause a large demand on network bandwidth and your organization will most likely want to have your educational podcast closely identified with it. With these concerns it becomes very beneficial to host the Web site and XML file on the organization's server if possible; therefore, your podcast will have that identity in public.

SOFTWARE AND SOUND PRODUCTION

Now that we have demystified some the terminology of equipment and Internet connections and file formats, the focus for podcast developments needs to turn to a discussion of introductory terms and principles of sound production software and processes.

For those of us who have never been involved in sound production before this is a new world. However the terrific news is that digital recording, editing, and production have become simplified with the recent advances in technology. In fact for Kathy this was one of the major reasons she launched into podcasting in 2005. In addition to content potential for education, the technical interfaces had become much easier. We can honestly say "Get ready to have a lot of fun and to see your students get very excited!"

SOUND PRODUCTION SOFTWARE

Earlier in this chapter we described software packages that might fit in different levels of podcasting configurations and price categories. Table 6.2 can be returned to as it has much detail about comparisons of this software. Some significant considerations and details when examining sound production software production include the following and are self explanatory:

- More is not always better—you might want to start with basic or free software and ramp up once you determine your level of interest and commitment to podcasting.
- Once you become committed to podcasting, seriously consider upgrading to a more advanced software program.
- At this time, all-in-one online recording systems and phone recording (aka phone casting) do not provide the quality of a stand alone podcasting station like those we have described has.

You want to be sure to check that your sound production software has suitable capabilities and flexibility for recording, exporting, and mixing down (final production) of audio files for your podcasting work. Thinking in terms of the different levels of podcasting (Basic, Moderate, and Advanced) helps users realize they don't need to be advanced technology users at the beginning of learning this new field and technology. Instead, focus on the content and educational benefits while you learn what you need to produce basic products.

Our approach with all of our podcast series and this book is not to let the technology get in the way. Instead, let technology be a catalyst for what you want to accomplish for teaching and learning.

Sound Recording

A basic principle to keep in mind as you work through the production process is to balance the best quality sound you can record with the most reasonable cost. This choice is a constant tradeoff, but once you make your recording and save it you will be editing it and the quality will degrade continually. Therefore it makes sense on many levels to start with the best recording product at the start. This quality depends on your recording equipment, software, and *environment.*

The latter is easiest to control in certain respects. Plan your recording session so that you have a time or place that will be the quietest and least echo producing environment possible. In addition, assemble the people optimal distances from the microphones and instruct them not to touch the microphones or cables while recording (or you will have a lot of "noise" in the recording).

How do you know when you have the correct configuration for your recording environment? Unfortunately there is no simple answer to this question. The best approach includes a few points along with those above:

- Choose a quiet environment
- Decrease echo in the recording environment (use a smaller room, with objects, or curtains on the walls and furniture in it)
- Use a quality microphone and recording software
- Position participants optimal distances from microphones
- Adjust volume of microphones so that all voices are near equal volume (using a mixer, microphone volume buttons or adjusting distance of the microphone)
- Do a brief test recording with all the participants and listen to it on headphones to check the sound
- Record and save the recording at the highest quality bit rate

In recording audio files you will be using an interface with buttons that look much like those of most recording devices. As seen in Figure 6.7, the recording interface has icons which represent and work like buttons for the basic functions of rewind, play, record, stop, forward, and pause that can be pressed with the mouse.

Recording. A brief discussion of recording must start with the reminder that the quality of the recording product is based on the equipment, conditions, and content. All three of these have criteria and dimensions for podcasting educators to control. Conditions are discussed in the section above; content is discussed throughout the book and equipment is

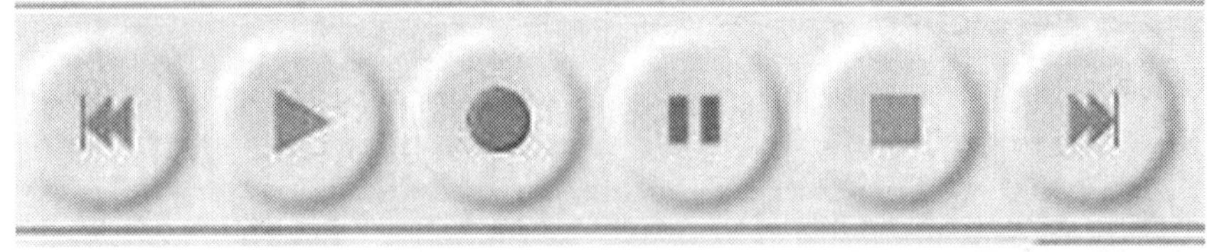

Figure 6.7. Recording icons representing recording buttons. [Image from Audacity recording and editing software. Audacity can be downloaded for free at http://audacity.sourceforge.net. Audacity is a registered trademark of Dominic Mazzoni and the software is available under the terms of the GNU, General Public License. Images used by permission.] For tutorials for learning Audacity visit http://teacherspodcast.org/podcasting-help/

discussed in our section on different types of microphones, plugs, cables, mixing boards, portable recording devices, and so forth.

Our focus here is to round out those issues by introducing some terms that may be new to readers. These terms include two major groups The first is 8 bit versus 16 bit versus 32 bit. Recordings are made at a certain bit rate which is a major factor in determining the quality of the recording and the size of the final file. As might be guessed 8 bit files have the lowest quality sound, and create the smallest files. In general the choice to record should be to record in the **highest** possible bit rate so you have the best product to start from in your editing work. However especially if you are recording with a portable device your storage space might be a real hindrance and might instead force you to limit recordings to 8 or 16 bit.

Mono and stereo settings are much like what we are used to in other audio settings. Again if your recording equipment allows you the space to record in stereo go ahead and capture the recording the fullest format you can. However when you mix-down your file you may want to change the settings to mono for educational podcasting because it is usually spoken word and you can save a lot of file space in the final product. A smaller file size for the final product makes it less taxing on your podcasting host limit and your listener.

Editing. The ease of editing audio files was one of the greatest surprises to us in early 2005. Basically, consider it this way: sound editing is using the same highlight and delete, or highlight and copy then paste procedures we have become so familiar with in word processing only we are doing it with a sound file, not words on the page.

When you speak into a microphone that is hooked up to a computer and sound recording software you see a wave form on the screen that represents your voice pattern. Remember school grade science class where

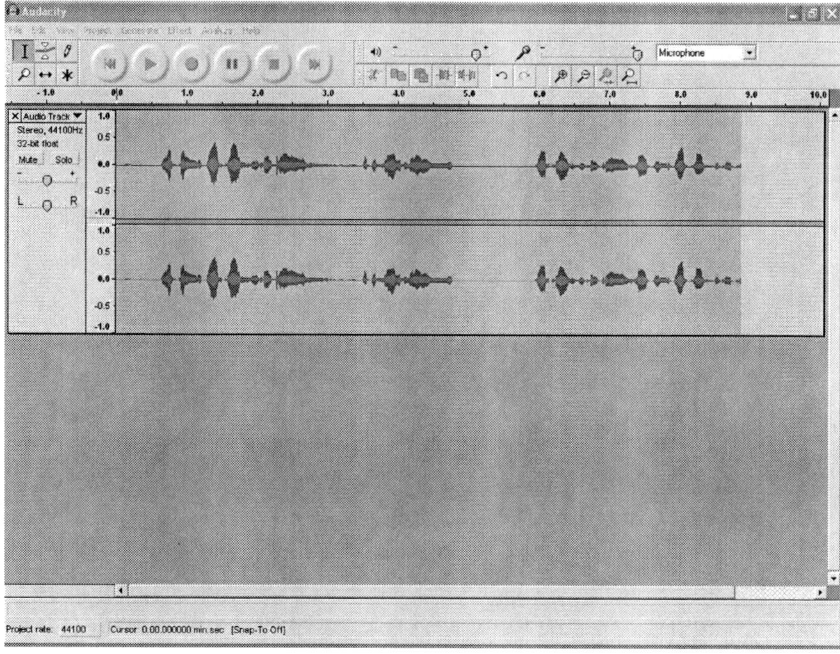

Figure 6.8. Sample sound editing file screenshot: single voice wave in stereo (Audacity software was used. For information on Audacity visit http://audacity.sourceforge.net. Audacity is a registered trademark of Dominic Mazzoni. Image used by permission.)

you learned sound is really made up of waves? Here it is! Figure 6.8 shows just what it looks like in the program Audacity.

In the process of recording, of course I make mistakes, but I have gotten into the habit of repeating my phrase if I have an error because I know I can easily go in and "clip out" the fumbled phrase with the sound editing software. How do I do this?

- I listen to the file by pressing the play arrow.
- I press STOP when I find the error.
- I use the mouse to highlight the error word or phrase
- I play the highlighted word or phrase to make sure I am deleting the correct part!
- Then I press the DELETE key on the key board. Poof! Now my sentence is perfect.

Sometimes when I am sound editing I need to move a phrase or discussion to another part of the recording. In that case I follow the same above steps EXCEPT instead of pressing DELETE, I select from the pull down menu EDIT and then COPY (or control key + C), move the cursor I-bar to the new place where I want it and then select the pull down menu EDIT PASTE (or control key + V).

So here are the steps for copy and paste of a soundclip:

- I listen to the file by pressing the play arrow.
- I press STOP when I reach the area I want to move.
- I use the mouse to highlight the word or phrase
- I play the highlighted word or phrase to make sure I am moving the correct part!
- Then I press pull down menu EDIT and then COPY (or control key + C),
- Then I move the cursor I-bar to the new place where I want it
- Then I press pull down menu EDIT PASTE (or control key + V).

Of Tracks and Mix Downs. One of the main differences in this form of digital recording on a computer is that you can record more than one "**track**" at a time. Tracks may be considered to be entirely separate recordings that are all held inside one meta-recording. Figure 6.9 provides a screen shot from Audacity software where you can see two recording tracks within one audio file.

An appropriate scenario is to think of two people each sitting at a different microphone and their voices are each recorded on a separate track. Another configuration is having a voice track and then a music track that you will blend in at the beginning and the end.

When you then bring the tracks together you are in effect "splicing" together files as it were. In fact the sound production software works very intensely at this point to "**mix down**" these files into one seamless track.

Less expensive software usually handles fewer tracks; therefore you would be restricted in how many different layers of music, sound effects, voices, and other files you could incorporate into one file mix down. In addition, less expensive software and less expensive computers (those with slower computer processors and less RAM memory) will mix down files less favorably. We have seen definite differences in performance in this regard so that your better sound production software and better computers will produce finer sound files once you start creating complex projects.

Mixing Down. As explained above this is among the last steps of the sound production process as the many different recording parts are digitally assembled. Just think about that for a moment. Perhaps in this single podcast you and your students are using

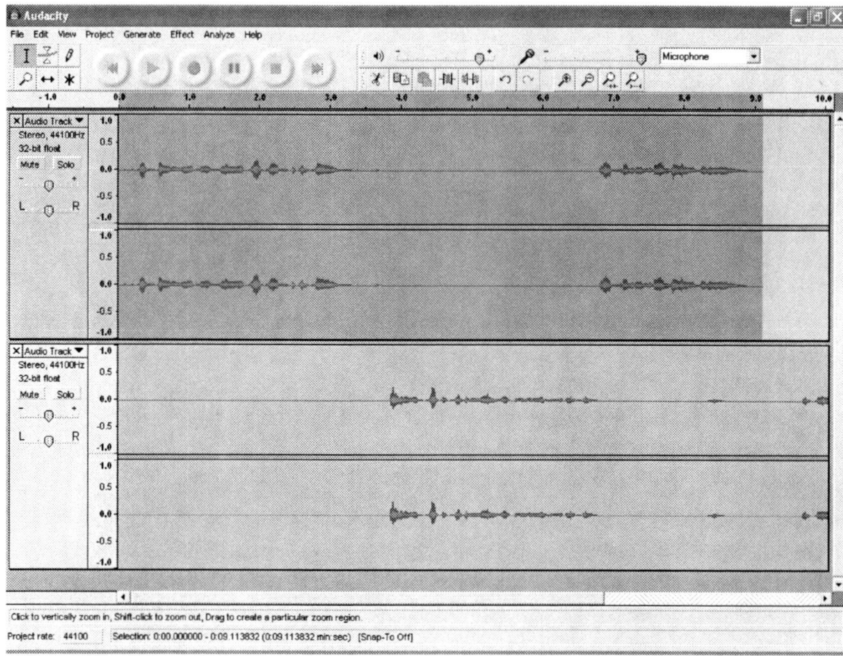

Figure 6.9. Sample sound editing file screenshot: two stereo tracks, two voices in one conversation (Audacity software was used. For information on Audacity visit http://audacity.sourceforge.net. Audacity is a registered trademark of Dominic Mazzoni. Images are used by permission.)

1. podsafe music on a theme fitting the podcast topic of choice (Podsafe music is that which independent musicians have made freely available for use on podcasts);
2. a student group narrative recording;
3. a student report from the most recent school event;
4. teacher greetings to students, parents and community; and
5. various copyright free special effects to help illustrate points in the student work.

When you mix down the file, all these tracks are "spliced" seamlessly together to create a single continuous audio file. Along the way you will select several settings including

- Bitrate (8, 16, 32, 64, 128, etc.)
- Mono/stereo

- Sampling Rate: Mhz (11000, 22000, 24000, 48000, 92000, etc.)

The goal continues to be to produce good sound quality but achieve a portable size so people don't have long downloads. As a guideline we try to keep our 30-minute audio podcasts down to under 10 MB based on feedback from our listeners.

FLASHBACK—

Are you more in the know with the tech talk now? Test your increasing technical comfort level with this hyped up podcasting scenario.

The podcastforteachers.org/index.html Web site has a new podcast episode available. It also announced today that they have a new ISP partner, BX Internet and that it is using Feedforall to create its RSS and XML feeds for its podcasts.

Any podcaster can FTP their files with their universal URL and have them designated with an http address. However be sure to take bandwidth considerations into account when you pick your podcasting host and consider what other services you may want such as blogging, bulletin boards, email, etc.

iLife, Audacity, and Adobe Audition are popular choices for sound editing programs so your can edit your wav file and export it into a MP3. Of course we would only ever include podsafe music to supplement our shows but more on that in our next chapter. Recording sometimes includes multiple tracks which need to be mixed down. But there are always those issues of technical specifications such as bit rates that help determine file quality and size. We get to be master of the educational audio universe! You get the gist of empowerment through understanding more techtalk!

CONCLUSION

We have tried to create a fun chapter about what can often be a confusing or daunting topic. We know most of our readers are educators who are not specialists in recording and media production and therefore are using this chapter as an introduction to the terms and processes involved in these aspects of podcasting for educational purposes.

We have sought to decode and demystify the technical jargon and "tech-talk" which pervades the podcasting world. For several reasons this area of innovative technology is shrouded with techno-speak: from XML to blogs, feeds, MP3, WAV, RSS, export, import, to mix-down. We hope this chapter will reduce some of the fear and peel back several layers of mystery so that more educators and their students can enter the world of podcasting and begin to contribute their voices and perspectives to this global conversation.

By providing a framework to consider different podcasting setup configurations, schools, and teachers can better assess where they want to start with their initial work in this area. And with the descriptions of upgrades and technical specifications these choices are not made blindly, but with future steps in mind.

We have also worked to provide a macro and micro view of podcasting, that is from connectivity to mixing down. In this way educators can step back and say on the larger scale what is *needed,* and on the planning level, what will I need to *do*?

We expect people will use the chapter in several ways; as an introduction to the terms and concepts and later on as a reference guide that they return to for assistance in decision making and troubleshooting. Podcasting in education is all about how we can create teaching and learning opportunities; therefore, we want to provide enough details that help clearly guide us toward that goal, and yet not muddy the waters. Future chapters will help us continue on this common journey.

RESOURCES

Alesis. Manufacturer of a full line of professional audio and musical instrument products. http://www.alesis.com

Audio editing software titles and URLs: See Table 6.2.

Behringer. A designer, manufacturer and distributor of professional audio equipment, musical instruments. http://www.behringer.com/

Edirol R09. Portable recorder. http://www.edirol.net/products/en/R-09/

Hardware and software reviews (many sources): See Table 6.3.

M-Audio. Digital recorders and mixers.http://www.m-audio.com

Yamaha. Designs, and manufactures a full line of professional audio and musical instrument products; has music education programs. http://www.yamaha.com/

zZounds.com. Online source for recording equipment. http://www.zzounds.com

CHAPTER 7

TALKING TO THE WORLD

Podcast Format

So we have our content area of focus and are creating a general podcast idea. With an overview of the podcasting process behind us and some introduction to technical terminology (chapter 6), we now aim to address the critical questions of:

- How do we go about talking to the world through our podcast?
- What are the overall elements of a podcast broadcast and production?

Later chapters, chapters 10–15, will provide details about creating podcasts as resources, setting up classrooms and classes for podcasting, podcasting uses in education, and curricular connections. This chapter will provide a working overview of the elements of a podcast and podcast production so that educators will have a foundation on which to build educational creations, applications, and extensions.

In the first section of the chapter we will discuss the elements of the podcast and then move on to possible podcast formats. This is a potentially expansive section that we will confine to some strategic selections and also provide resources for educators and students to explore through reading, listening, and research. From the onset let us be clear, the podcast format is one of the areas of podcasting which is fertile ground for development, creativity, and transformation.

Podcasting for Teachers: Using a New Technology to Revolutionize Teaching and Learning,
Revised Second Edition, pp. 105–124

PODCAST ELEMENTS

One valuable way of at looking at all of the elements of a podcast production is that it includes: the podcast episodes, podcast feed, show notes, Web site, listener email feedback, directory listings, optional blog and optional bulletin board. Many other features could be added and are sometimes used, but as a good starting point and intermediate steps, these are very good elements for which to plan.

Podcast Name. The cornerstone of podcasting are the episodes that are distributed through the podcast directories such as iTunes (www.itunes.com) and Podcast Pickle (www.podcastpickle.com), and are also available from a podcast's Web site. The podcast individual episodes are the most obvious element of the podcast and the part that people think about first. What will we talk about? What will be our focus? How frequently will we record and release the episodes? Who will be the broadcaster? What will the format be and where will we do the recording? This topic is discussed in episode 10 of Podcast for Teachers (King & Gura, 2005, October 10).

But also included in this are the broader topic and the essential element of the podcast name. The podcast name is the identifier of all the episodes that will be released under that podcast. While you might immediately focus on individual content, backtrack a bit and think about your overall goal, purpose, and audience. How will they know what you are communicating? How will they recognize your podcast? What are the identifying words, key words, that should be in your title so they will quickly recognize your podcast will be of interest to them?

Next, go to the podcast directories we list at the end of chapter 8 and conduct some searches to make sure the names you are considering are not already taken and then do a general Internet search for the same. Once settled on a name, write, and edit, edit, edit and hone your description so that you can communicate clearly and crisply the purpose and value of your podcast for potential listeners.

Podcast Episodes. Regarding the episodes, these are the sound files, the MP3 files, that you will upload each week to your specific Internet server (podcast host), and add to your feed.xml file. Your listeners will then go to their podcast reader program, also known as a podcatcher, or aggregator, and when they select your podcast they will see all your episodes, with the most recent ones usually listed first. Caveat: you can have them listed in another order if you wish by listing them differently in your feed.xml file, but most recent first is the usual convention.

When thinking about your podcast episodes, here again think about content, format, and names. Do you want to do a series on a specific topic? Will all the podcasts tie together? Will there be several *mini*series within the whole podcast series? Will the same podcasters be broadcasting on each podcast? Will you have guests? What will be the format of all your shows? Or will you perhaps use different formats for different shows? As you can see there are many choices in the format area and we will focus on this in the second section of this chapter.

However regarding the "podcast episode" the decision regarding the title of the episode and the description is likely best made after the recording and editing are done. With this information best in mind, the podcast manager/producer, can make the decisions to clearly communicate the content and provide titles that will convey that content and value to the audience. Again be aware that many people will be looking at directories, searching directories, or scanning the titles on tiny MP3 players or iPod screens, so every word counts and the first two or three words matter the most. You can gain many ideas on naming choices by looking at your favorite podcast and evaluating why those names work, and why others might not appeal to you or to your potential listeners.

Podcast Feed. The podcast feed will be that feed.xml file that provides access to the podcast for your listeners. As we described in chapter 4 each time a new episode is released, the information is added near to the beginning of the XML file script. It actually gets inserted in the feed.xml file script right after the "channel," or main podcast, information. The podcast feed file is the "power" of how podcasting is automated for the listeners. It enables each of your episodes to be "pushed" to the desktop of your current listeners, subscribers.

Table 7.1 provides examples from two of our podcasts with each of the podcast elements listed. Notice the consistency in the URL addresses among the major features of the podcast. This practice carries through to the feed naming. Be sure to upload and store that feed.xml file in either the main directory for your podcast or a RSS subfolder, subdirectory.

> ***Valuable Tip from Kathy and Mark:*** *Notice we use feed.xml as the feed for both of the podcasts. That is because it is the most widely expected address and creates the least amount of confusion on the listener's end of the process of finding or retrieving the podcast.*

Show Notes. The show notes of a podcast can take a variety of forms from a simple outline of the episode, to detailed narrative, transcription, and many other renditions. However most podcasters will find that listeners will appreciate and more listeners will be drawn to the podcast if you have a companion shows' note page which identifies the topics and Web links or other resources that are mentioned in that particular episode. You can just imagine driving along the highway and listing to a podcast on your morning commute, a very popular practice of many adult podcast

Table 7.1. Podcast Elements—Examples

Podcast name	**The Teachers' Podcast**	**Transformation Education LIVE!**
Podcast episode	**Episode 18-Education Bridges: Transparency, Learning and Disruption**	**Ep 17: Using New Media in Higher Ed Classrooms**
Website/blog	http://www.podcastforteachers.org	http://transformationed.com/podcast/
Podcast feed	http://www.teacherspodcast.org/feed.xml	http://feeds.feedburner.com/transformationeducation
Show notes	http://www.teacherspodcast.org/	http://transformationed.com/podcast/
Show notes for this episode	http://teacherspodcast.org/2008/06/02/ep-18-education-bridges-transparency-learning-and-disruption/	http://transformationed.com/podcast/2008/05/21/ep-17-using-new-media-in-higher-ed-classrooms/
Listener e-mail feedback	teacherspodcast@gmail.com	transformationed@gmail.com
Directory listings (same for both)	iTunes.com Podcastalley.com Podcastpickle.com Podcast411.com Blubrry.com Podomatic.com	Podpusher.com Odeo.com Castroller.com Pageflakes.com Singingfish.com Podscope.com
Other options	**Facebook group:** http://fordham.facebook.com/group.php?gid=9953658948 **Distribution of Feed through E-mail:** http://www.feedblitz.com/f/?Sub=5004 **Distribution via cell phone** http://mobilcast.com/ http://voiceindigo.com **iPhone and iTouch feed** http://iphone.wizzard.tv/web/external/feed/?rss_url=http://feeds.feedburner.com/teacherspodcast **iTunes link:** http://phobos.apple.com/WebObjects/MZStore.woa/wa/viewPodcast?id=264496274	**Streamed during recording** **Live call-in and chat during recording** www.blogtalkradio.com/transformationed **Companion radio station distribution:** www.blogtalkradio.com/ **Distribution of feed through e-mail:** http://www.feedburner.com/fb/a/emailverifySubmit?feedId=1432831 **Distribution via cell phone** http://mobilcast.com/ **iPhone and iTouch feed courtesy of Wizzard** http://iphone.wizzard.tv/web/external/feed/?rss_url=http://feeds.feedburner.com/transformationeducation
Satistics via	Feedburner Podpress Libsyn Switchpod Server stats	Feedburner Podpress Blogtalkradio Server stats
At this time podcast hosted at	Switchpod and Libsyn (of Wizzard Media)	Blogtalkradio.com

listeners, and trying to scribble down the URL on your coffee napkin. This is not behavior we want to encourage among our listeners!

Therefore, for the sake of continuing the longevity of all podcast listeners, *please* create those show notes as a simple reference page. It is your chance to be recognized and indexed by the search engines and guide prospective and current listeners to what they will hear on the episode and later to help them find the resources and information you shared in your show.

> ***Valuable Tip from Kathy and Mark:*** *The element of show notes is one of those highly valued and certainly expected features of podcasts. It really is a demonstration of inexperience and incomplete production if a podcaster does not provide this feature.*

Web Site. Your podcast Web site is really the hub of all these podcast elements. Figure 7.1 provides an example of a podcast home page. This sample podcast homepage is from the Radio Owl podcast, which we discussed in chapter 3.

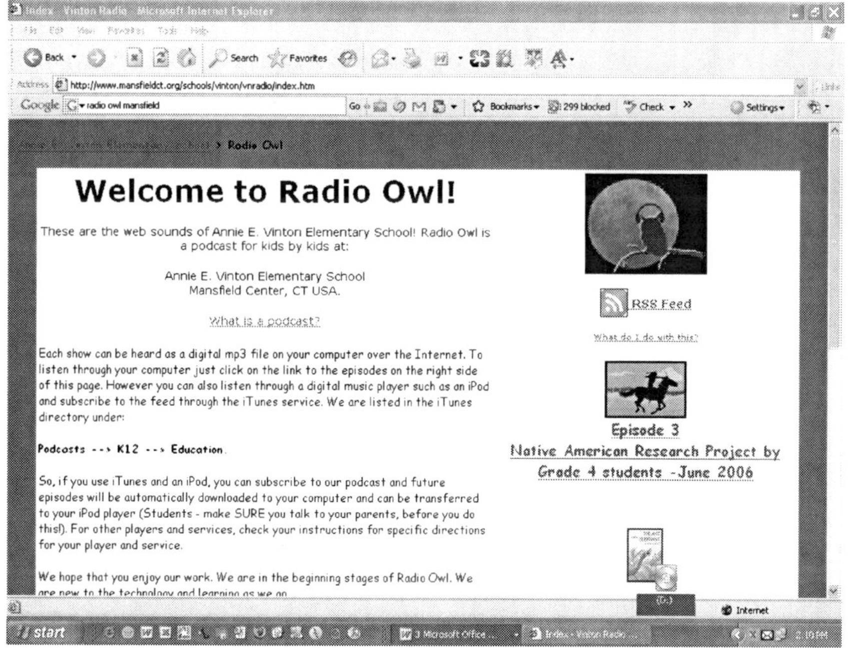

Figure 7.1. Radio Owl Podcast at Annie E. Vinton Elementary School, Mansfield Public Schools. Screenshot used by permission. http://www.mansfieldct.org/schools/vinton/vnradio/index.htm

The podcast Web site will have your home page for the podcast, the description of your podcast, information about the podcasters themselves, and then link in the show notes for each episode. It also needs to include icons, buttons; that easily enable people to find the RSS Feed information so they can subscribe to your podcast in their podcatcher program. 1-click subscription enables potential users to click one icon and then the related podcatcher, such as iTunes or Yahoo, opens and the user is subscribed to your podcast.

> ***Valuable Tip from Kathy and Mark:*** *Several Web sites will automatically create the Web site code (html) for these 1-click subscription buttons. Visit http://fireant.tv/buttonmaker for an example of the one for FireAnt podcatcher.*

Listener E-mail Feedback. All podcasts need to have a current email address. In fact you cannot register your podcast with any of the podcast directory databases without a confirming email address. In addition, you will also want to provide opportunity for listener feedback and the simplest form is email. Looking at Table 7.1 you will see how you can set-up an email account for free with some services such as Gmail and still have a great deal of storage space. Or you might have a related organization, like the iLearn Radio podcast example, that you want to use that email address. Whichever way, you need to arrange the email correspondence, be sure it is current, reliable and monitored closely because you could have a variety of inquiries about your podcast.

These email inquiries can range from listeners providing pats on the back, the podcast directory needing to confirm your sign-up information with them, or to people telling you that the podcast feed is not working. You need to be sure someone responsible will be watching for those correspondences on a regular basis and be able to knowledgeably respond to them.

Directory Listings. Thinking about the distribution of your podcast, this is an area that most people do not know about. When you create a podcast, unless you register it with the podcast directories the only way people might find it is by you sending out emails or fliers, word of mouth or Internet search engines. There really is a much more powerful way built into the podcasting process. As of July 2008 there are over 100 podcasting directories, among the most well known are iTunes, Podcast Pickle, Odeo and Podcast Alley. At this point in time there is no universal way to register your podcast in all of those directories at once.

Podcasters need to go through the long process of submitting their podcasts to each of the podcast directories that they think listeners who would be interested in their podcast might be looking for it. Again as mentioned previously among the best lists for the podcast directories is at Podcast 411 (http://www.podcast411.com/page2.html). Podcasting News (http://podcastingnews.com/topics/Podcast_Directory.html) also has a good list that is kept up to date. Usually you just have to go to each of the directories find the button to submit a new podcast, and fill in the fields they ask for.

> ***Valuable Tip from Kathy and Mark:*** *Information requested by a podcast directory may include from 1 to 10 fields of information, but all the features we have discussed above, need to be in place before you can complete this process.*

Once you register your podcast with a podcast directory they will send you a confirming e-mail and often they will review your podcast, before they allow it to be added to the directory. Why? They are guarding against spam submissions, duplicate submissions, and also against people putting "g" ratings on content that is not "g" rated. You can imagine that they want to keep their huge databases efficient and also reduce any liability they might have on their side.

Optional Blog. Beyond the basics of podcast production many podcasters also have blogs which they might, in fact, use for their show notes. In fact, podcasting was originally called audioblogging back in the olden days of September 2004! There are many similarities in how some podcasters and bloggers approach the content creation and focus of their work.

However today, not all podcasts, especially in education, have blogs because of the potential of spam and the consequent need for time intensive monitoring of blog content. However a password-protected blog may be very effective as a value-added component to your classroom podcast for your student participant. A good Web site and discussion about the educational value of blogs is Support Blogging at http://www.supportblogging.com/.

In a similar vein, a wiki might serve very well. The difference is that a wiki is more of a collaborative document that many users can edit, whereas a blog is an ongoing conversation among participants. Both elements can create additional dimensions for listener dialogue and participation in podcasting and are very worthwhile for educators to consider how they fit into the overall purpose, goals, and value of what is being produced, now and maybe later on. Some wikis that can be used for free in K-12 education and be password protected include, but are not limited to: Wikispaces (www.wikispaces.com) and PBWiki (www.pbwiki.com) (see example in Figure 7.2).

Optional Bulletin Board. Without discussing every possible additional feature for a podcast, another major one is the bulletin board. The focus

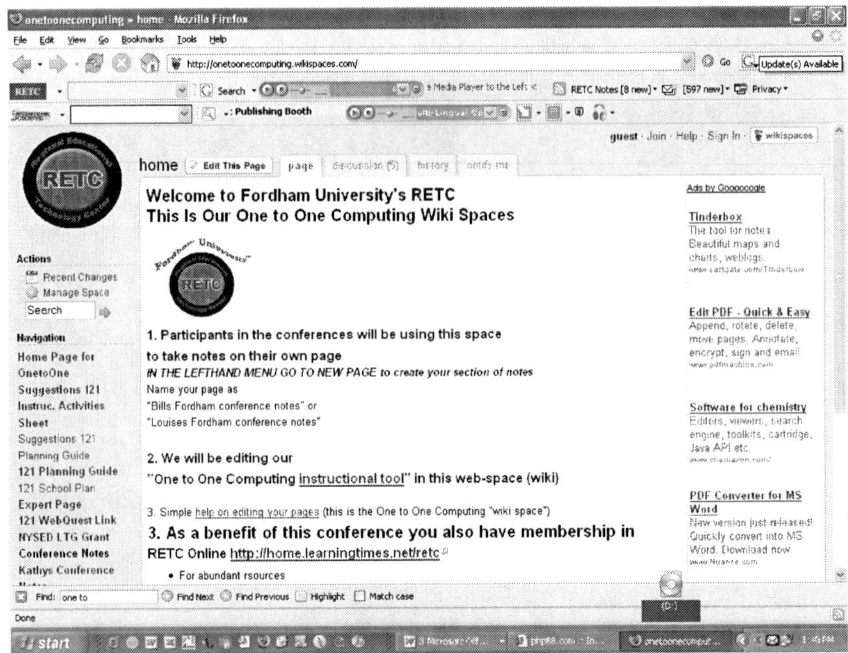

Figure 7.2. Wikispaces example from Fordham Center for Professional Development. http://www.wikispaces.com © 2007 Tangient, LLC. Used with permission.

of its use is to provide a forum where listeners can converse on different topics with one another. Some schools might have access to an online bulletin board system that they could link into. If your school is running a Linux server, the open source PHP bulletin board system can be downloaded, installed and used for free. This PHP Bulletin Board (http://www.phpBB.com/) is a favorite among podcasters and therefore is an interface that people recognize and know how to navigate very easily. Figure 7.3 shows a screen shot of what this bulletin board looks like and it closely resembles how many others are configured as well.

In order to read a topic, the user just selects the topic by clicking on it with the mouse, reads the item and then selects a reply button, types in a response and selects "post" or "submit." Podcast managers can set up a bulletin board so that users can post anonymously. However public posting is probably not advised in educational settings, or perhaps only if participants they are registered and approved by the bulletin board/podcast manager. This management provides control over the content, but can be time consuming. Once again we have a cost/benefit decision to consider!

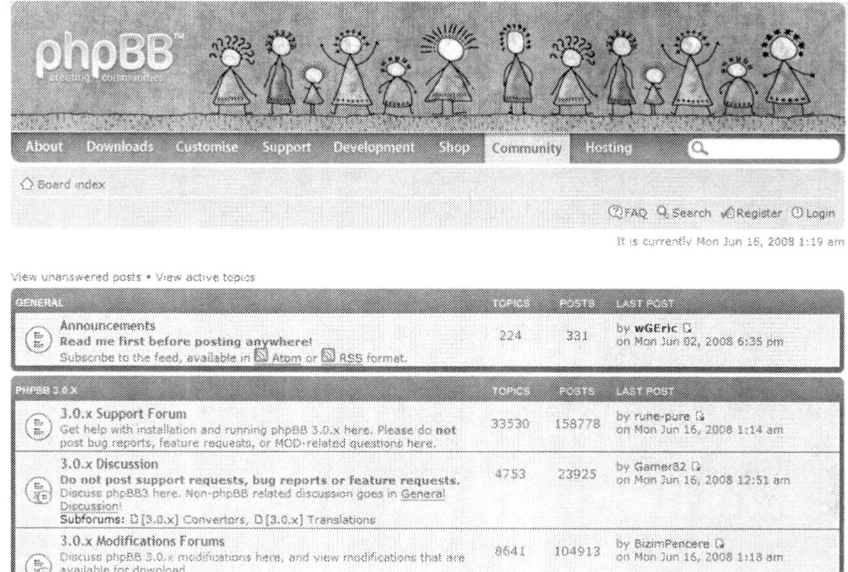

Figure 7.3. PHP Bulletin Board—community bulletin board area. http://www.phpBB.com © 2001, 2003, 2007 phpBB. Used with permission.

With our overview of podcast elements complete, we can now focus on some finer points of podcast format as they apply to podcasting in education.

PODCAST FORMAT

Having laid a foundation of the standard elements of podcasts and some of the optional features, this section of the chapter provides some examples, guidance, and resources of podcast formats as they apply to educational settings. Specifically, this section will focus on podcast format planning, format options, script-related models, and because interviews are such a prevalent podcast format, interview tips.

In this section of the chapter we will also be peppering the explanations with examples from other podcast formats so you can get a taste of the ever-expanding rich variety available through your nearest podcast directory. We know you will gain a great deal from this chapter, so in the format of one of our favorite podcasts we'll say, "Put on your thinking caps and fasten your seatbelts, it's time for Podcast Formats!" (Paraphrase of Escape Pod tag lines, 2006).

> ***Valuable Tip from Kathy and Mark:*** *Steve Ely of Escape POD (www.escapepod.org) provides different humorous, somewhat goofy tag lines just before his short story science fiction episodes begin. They have become one of his hallmarks and listeners look forward to what he will have in store for them each week. They are brief, quick witted, often silly, but the important point here is that they have become a much anticipated, predictable part of his podcast format. Steve has a repartee with his listeners through this simple literary device; something to think about for your own development.*

Podcast Format Planning. As educators we are well accustomed to planning our work ahead of time. We think through our educational audience, consider our objectives, content, text, instructional materials, tools, and select instructional methods and assessments. Much in the same way we can take that planning orientation to educational work with podcasting and it will have great benefits. When we first started off we really had not made that connection, but early on we realized how much our podcast preparation was like our educational planning process, because we had educational, professional development, purposes in mind for the Podcast for Teachers series. Therefore we offer the following suggestions as outcomes from our many, many hours of preparation and podcasting so that you may gain from our experience. However we have full expectations that you will combine these suggestions with your own teaching and class preparation style.

Preplanning. Given that you have already gone through the earlier stages of researching the need, topic, and areas of your podcast and are up and running (see chapters 4, 5, and 6) now we have the constant preparation to keep the podcast compelling, worthwhile, and active episode after episode. Just like in preparation for classes we teach, during the week we have folders, physical, or electronic, that my cohost and I use to "toss in" articles, books chapters, e-mails, Web sites, resources, news items, and so forth, that we find that apply to our podcast series in general and also to specific topics that we know we will be considering. This practice is one I have had for many years of teaching as I am constantly renewing the content of my courses and need a systematic way to collect that material *and* be able to find it when I want it!

Simply stated I have a file folder labeled with the name of each of the classes and each of the podcasts I am creating and recording. Therefore we have a constant source of new material. Additionally, when you have an active cohost, now you have twice as much material from which to select!

Planning. Next comes the planning, layout, or outline stage of the podcast design. In this case most podcasters develop some form of a predictable outline that you can expect from their show. You should be able to guess the three basic parts: introduction, body, and "outro." Because audio podcasts are just that, auditory, it is important to give your listeners some reliable clues about what is coming next in your podcast. Therefore writing a concise introduction and exit (outro) that will be used in closely the same format each episode not only signals the beginning and the ending, but also provides a consistent place for them to find vital information such as the name of the podcast, your name, the Web site, the podcast feed, and your e-mail address. Should they need that information and they can't find it *anywhere* else they can fast-forward to those spots and *know* you will have provided that information.

In addition, you will also find that having these consistent elements for the podcast provides a grounding and reassurance for yourself as you get used to recording, hear the sound of your voice, and get over the podcasting/broadcasting "jitters." Even this minimal framework will assist your planning process as well, because you can begin to "pick up your train of thought" or the "conversation" of your podcast as you use the same format and come back to the same intellectual setting so to speak. At the same time, surprises, creativity, and spark are always welcome in learning settings and the same with digital media. However having a reasonably predictable format will help your listeners anticipate the next step, retain information and reinforce the content. In the next section we will discuss the format of the podcast more, and start off with whether you have a closely scripted or outlined podcast or not, but here we will finish our discussion of planning first.

Planning the podcast will now entail deciding on a format that will fit your content and audience. Expecting that both of those are determined by your podcast in general, you may have one format you use all the time. For instance, Podcast411.com *always* has an interview format; that is the very purpose and essence of the show. However in comparison, while English as a second language podcast (ESLPOD) is always a tutorial format, sometimes it uses a dialogue conversational format for tutorial and sometimes it is a monologue. Additionally on ESLPOD they include activities, worksheets, and quizzes as other resources to support the learning to be gained from the podcast broadcast itself. These two examples illustrate the fact that in podcasting you have the opportunity to select formats for the podcast in general and then also for individual episodes; many variations may be used and educators can also use the medium to experiment with many new teaching formats and techniques for them—from interviews, to narratives, and dialogues, these might be new opportunities to develop materials *with* or *for* students.

Once again returning to the design elements of the podcast, format planning and materials should coordinate. Therefore the materials you collect and the materials you outline will eventually be the basis for your episode show notes, resource list, archive, and additional supporting Web-based materials.

Valuable Tip from Kathy and Mark: *Develop a plan early on to consistently collect and design your podcast episodes so that the development process will flow easily for you. If you collect the information, lay it out in an outline, and use the same information to plan and design your web materials you can reduce time, and increase your efficiency and enjoyment of podcasting for teaching and learning!*

Format Options. Among format options the two major areas we will consider are what we term script related models and then format designs. The **script-related podcast models** is a phrase we, Kathy and Mark, use to describe how closely a podcast follows a script. For instance does the podcaster layout an outline and then write a script for the podcast and read the script verbatim? This type of podcast would be a *fully scripted podcast.* In complete contrast an *unscripted podcast* would be one where the podcasters are entirely spontaneous and may not even have an outline; they virtually turn on the mikes, hit record, and start talking! The type of podcast that would be a balance of the two extremes would be an *outlined and moderately spontaneous podcast*; in this case the podcasters are using an outline as a guide and framework, but they develop the conversation or narrative as they podcast; that is, they are not reading a script.

While it may seem odd to think of someone reading a script into a microphone at first, perhaps for many school-aged students this is the easiest way to get them started. They have clearly defined lines they are reading, they have boundaries, and it is a format familiar to them in a traditional classroom and school performances.

Additionally, for instructional materials, a closely scripted podcast can provide a very tightly crafted, fully cited account of detailed material. Examples of fully scripted podcasts are any number of student broadcasts such as Radio Owl for K-8 students providing a report on Native America Research, their third episode (which we referred to in PFT Episode 44: King & Gura, 2006, July 7). In addition, to Professor Umbach of John Jay College in New York City provides independent, iPod-guided art history tours of museums in New York City for his art students (PFT Episode 54, King & Gura, 2006, September, 11).

In comparison an outlined and moderately spontaneous podcast provides more freedom for development, creativity and interest for the audience and is especially relevant when you have more than one person podcasting together because they have the synergy that can develop. *Podcast for Teachers* and *Adventures in Transformative Learning* (King & Heuer, 2006) are examples of two podcasts from this podcast format the first of course is about educational technology topics and part of the richness of the podcast is the dialogue and debate between the cohosts. *Adventures in Transformative Learning* is about coping with change in adulthood and later adolescence and provides an example of how Drs. Heuer and King share stories from their own lives and others, share interviews with adult learners, and discuss the theory and application. What has been often a highly theoretical topic becomes very conversational and applicable to every day life by using this method of an outlined podcast and spontaneous discussion. It is also important to point out that in both these cases the cohosts have worked with each other for a few years prior to podcasting together so there is a history and common ground, although different at end of sentence insert reference (King, 2005; King & Wang, 2007).

In the broader spectrum of educational podcasts, and taken from a strictly K-12 classroom context, Jeff Bradley's (2006a, 2006b) work with his students is an example of two podcasts that have outlines and yet moderate spontaneity (www.SlausonPodShow.com and www.WISEguy.com). The students do very well with the facilitation of the teacher to stay on topic and develop the podcast in interesting and yet relevant directions. Another point to be made about this format—content editing needs to be focused on because sometimes those "rabbit trails" or "red herrings" are just too far off track, or things get too giddy, and need to be deleted from the podcast during production.

In the unscripted format, pretty much anything can happen. There seem to be more podcasts out in the public domain in this format than in the educational realm, because many people started off with podcasting as audioblogging. Therefore there is a large group of people who turn on the mike and speak their mind, tell you about the sun or rain outside, what they ate for breakfast, and what color socks they have on. In educational settings you can see that such ramblings would not be entirely educationally beneficial except perhaps to study conversational language or foreign popular cultures. But some educators do produce audioblog format podcasts that rather verge on this side of the scale, Dave Warlick's (2006) Connected Learning is along the lines of stream of consciousness. He gives each episode a title. But it really is potluck as to where he is traveling and if he isn't traveling then it is going to be more of a blog entry via podcast.

Extremes of the unscripted podcast can be train wrecks and that is why educators usually steer clear of them unless they are ready and able to invest much effort in time consuming sound editing. It is better to have an outline and clear direction to focus thoughts and especially young minds; otherwise the editing alone will be unwieldy not to mention the potential problem areas that could be encountered from students mentioning things they shouldn't on a school-based podcast (i.e., maligning people, private information, foul language, etc.).

> ***Valuable Tip from Kathy and Mark:*** *While there is no FCC control on podcasting at this time, schools and parents will certainly have protests about certain topics. Considering the breadth of format designs that can be used in podcasting, there is much richer ground to sow and outcomes to gain using structured and moderately structured format designs with students can positively engage.*

Format Designs. After reading the prior overview of the script models and this section on format designs, the next step should be for you to actively seek out and listen to a variety of other media and podcasts, on many different topics—not just education. As you look through the podcast directories, go beyond education into the talk shows, tech podcasts, news updates, audio books, music podcasts, and whatever other interests you may have never explored. Take a listen and make some notes about what appeals to you and why. Also note what does not appeal to you and why. And make a master list of all the types of podcast format designs to which you listen. At this point, continue to reflect on different forms of media. As you listen to the radio, watch movies and listen to other podcasts in the future think about format designs and effective communication. Basically asking, what is new? What is the same? What works? And what doesn't? Here is an introduction to some of what you may see on that quest for format designs.

We have identified at least eight podcast format designs that educational podcasters might frequently use. To be certain you may use one or more of these in a single episode of your podcast, or your podcast might follow the same format every week. However a survey of these different formats will be beneficial in expanding the scope of possibilities that you may consider as you plan, design, and record your future podcasts. Just as we as educators use many different instructional tools to develop and teach classes, so too we as educational podcasters should consider which formats we want to use to meet the needs of the audience, the content and even the podcaster.

Interviews are the first example of a format where one or more people are invited to participate in the podcast and the podcaster will ask questions about that person. Today we can conduct podcast interviews in person, telephone, or via the Internet very easily. Therefore this makes an easy way to add a lively component to your podcast with interviewing guest visitors.

Another popular format in general podcasts is the *group talk*. In this format there are two or more cohosts who participate and may share leadership of the podcast. Group talk can vary from being closely outlined and guided to running rampant, but in educational applications the format can be used for teachers to create an environment of professional conversation, or it could be used among or with students to create discussion groups all very successfully once practiced and edited.

We chose to use the format topic *recorded events* to represent a variety of possible podcast content types that have the same format. These recorded events in educational settings might be a school play recording from the front row or sound booth (not performed specifically for the podcast), a guest speaker who visited the school, a lecture, commencement exercises, sports events that are just recorded "as is." As one can tell the fundamental common element here is that the event is recorded "as is" and no special accommodations are really made for the podcast—the delivery is not redesigned to address the technology.

Newscasts are another format type for podcasts akin to formal evening or daytime news to the school radio show of yesteryear that is now also broadcast on podcasts. This format is listed separately because a newscast is usually a distinctive format from other recorded events with news anchors, special reports, and so forth, being customary segments.

Educational podcasts can take great advantage of the application of *dramatic readings* as another form of student performances. Considering the genre of radio performances in years past, some podcasts have picked up this tradition and illustrate it vividly. If you need an example of this style of a dramatic reading, Decoder Ring Theater is a mystery show that is very polished and well done, while it is rather "old school." If your students like Batman, I suspect they will admire this series as well and educators can use it as a platform to teach about dramatic readings. Public speaking is such an important skill and audio recording can assist in providing exciting practice and opportunities for self critique for students. Dramatic readings provide a chance to make public speaking even more fun while learning many of the traditional skills as well as essential twenty-first century digital media content.

Another form of an audio reading could be an *audio guide*. Many people have experienced other forms of audio guides with cassette tapes and video guides as tours. The same could be done with podcasts as students describe places or historical events through an audio guide, that they research, write and then read. In these cases the podcast audio guide might also serve as a simulation of an event or place. Alternately an audio guide could be written and produced to be used in tandem with an activity. Therefore it could serve as an electronic museum docent, virtually, or actually, if listeners took it physically with them through the halls of a museum or other designated locations.

The final two examples are counterparts of one another: *monologues* and *panelcasts*. In a *monologue* only one person is speaking. In some cases this may be narrative, audioblog, or dramatic reading, but more specifically monologue is a term used to describe a specialized script written for one person to deliver. It is spoken by one person and usually delivered with the use of a carefully written script with a specific focus such as politics, comedy or satire. Applications in education of a monologue could be a critique of literary work, political opinion, or humorous perspective of their lives. Learning to research, write, and deliver such productions can build great self-efficacy in individuality, critical thinking, and confidence.

We also have had exciting experiences with a group recording format that we call a *panelcast* because more than a "group talk" this is a panel conducted with a live audience and recorded and announced specifically to be podcasted. Rather like an old fashioned radio show or a television show it is different because it is an academic panel as well. To hear an example of this format check out PFT Episode 33.

For this episode we invited educational leaders to be part of a panel of experts in person at a conference and we wired the auditorium so that the panel and audience would be recorded for the podcast panelcast event. The effect was tremendous as the audience was thrilled to be part of the podcast they were familiar with and to be in the role of a participatory television audience. We highly recommend looking for opportunities for audience participation and panelcasts.

Interview Tips

Related to podcasting formats is some friendly advice we offer on interviewing and including people in your podcasts. While you will become comfortable with the microphone and recording experience over time, your visitors and guests will find it new and probably daunting. One of the easiest ways we have found to overcome this hesitation has been to create an environment that is one of friendly conversation.

Several steps can be taken to help facilitate this experience including:

- Research your guest's background and interests before hand;
- Prepare general and specific questions to guide the conversation;
- Do not expect to use too many questions, as you do not want to overwhelm or barrage your guest;

- Send your guest brief instructions beforehand so he/she knows what to expect;
- Explain the recording procedure at the time of the event so your guest knows what to expect and ask if there are any questions;
- Build a welcoming climate of respect and friendliness by greeting them, and chatting with them before the recording starts;
- Be relaxed and supportive of your guests, they are likely volunteering time to be on your podcast;
- Give your guest time, probably at the end of the interview, to offer anything that they might feel had not been mentioned in the podcast;
- Be sure to have your guest sign a written release that allows you to podcast and release the episode; and
- Once you are ready to release the podcast be sure to contact your guests with the specific information and a brief description so that they can forward the information on to their network of people. This strategy will provide increased recognition and exposure for your guests and for your work as well.

Knowing Your Audience—Urgently Needed

As we consider the final sections of this chapter about *Talking to the World,* we want to emphasize the critical value of **knowing your audience and addressing your audience's interests.** What better place than the "clean up spot" in the batter line up? Why do we consider knowing your audience to be of such importance in a podcasting in education book? For two major reasons: one, it is a fundamental principle of sound instructional design to understand the needs and context of your learners, in this case your audience, and two, it seems to be one of the least recognized principles in podcasting.

We could list a multitude of variables we determine, assess and address in instructional design. However at the very least we want to understand as educators we would want to understand our learners' content level, prior learning experiences, learning expectations, and context in which they are learning. All of this information helps us craft instructional experiences that will most appropriately address their needs in ways that they can use learning best.

And yet in podcasts that are produced by teachers and students, there seems to be little recognition, understanding, or effort made to determine who the audience is, what their needs are and how to address them. Perhaps this is because we have to turn the process around a little bit.

Rather than looking at the students and assessing their needs, in podcasting and other digital media content creation, we have to consider our potential audience and *then* describe those characteristics. However that is not the end of the process.

Let me explain. Consider understanding our audience as applied to formative podcast development as we have described:

- Determine your podcast content area focus.
- Consider who your likely potential audience would be according to:
  - Content level you desire to address;
  - Prior learning experiences they may have at this level;
  - Learning expectations they may likely have;
  - Possible contexts in which they are learning; and
  - Motivations for learning.
- Create a description of your podcast that highlights these points.
- Design your podcast to address these needs.
- Design listener feedback opportunities so that you can:
  - Continually improve the podcast;
  - Address their learning needs;
  - Answer their questions; and
  - Create a vibrant, participatory learning community.
- Publicize your podcast in communities, online and face-to-face, where such potential learners and listeners will likely hear about it.

If we step back from these points and consider them, they are not that different from what we do in a face-to-face learner-centered classroom. Through such instructional design we incorporate active learning, learner participation, and context-sensitive content. The difference is that we are in a digital media environment, we are using asynchronous technologies and we are reaching people around the globe with the possibility of creating global communities. We can build on sound pedagogical principles and extend teaching and learning through technology, rather than pushing it backward and stifling it with one-way communication. Knowing your audience, and responding to audience needs can be the vibrant element in hitting a home run with your podcast for educational purposes.

SUMMARY

In this chapter, as we have worked through the elements of a podcast and many of the possible formats that podcasts can take. We hope that you have continued to see the vision of podcasting in education as a means to accomplish more than mere *transmission* of content. The power of podcasting for teaching and learning remains in the fact that it is creative, generative, and contextual. Podcasting and other forms of digital media content creation provides teachers and learners with opportunities to research, design, and communicate the content they are studying, with new voices, to make new connections across the globe and even within themselves. By understanding podcasting formats so more instructional tools may become available rather than just duplicating the status quo. We propose that this chapter is a starting point, a foundation upon which to build so teachers and learners can create different expressions of their knowledge and new innovations. Let us hear from you as you continue your journey in your development of podcasting in education.

Chapter Terms for Your Reference

Audio guide: Podcasts which describe places or historical events through a script or narrative which is written and then read. In some cases the podcast audio guide might serve as a simulation of an event or place. Alternately an audio guide could be written and produced to be used in tandem with an activity.

Fully scripted model: Podcasters layout an outline, write a script for the podcast and read the script verbatim.

Group talk: A podcast format where two or more cohosts participate and very often share leadership of the podcast. Group talk can be closely outlined and guided to being freewheeling, but in educational applications the format can be used by teachers, for teachers to create an environment of professional conversation, or it could be used among or with students to create discussion groups.

Monologue: It is spoken by one person and usually delivered with the use of a carefully written script with a specific focus such a political, comedic, or satire.

Outlined and moderately spontaneous podcast: Podcasters use an outline, but allow for spontaneous development of the details of the narrative, conversation, and so forth. They do not usually use a formal script or at least directly read from a script.

Panel cast (or Keycast): A panel conducted with a live audience and recorded and announced specifically to be podcasted. Rather like an old radio show or a TV show it is different because it is an academic panel as well. To hear an example of this format check out PFT Episode 33.

Recorded event: These recorded events occur in educational settings. They might be a school play, commencement exercises, or sports events for example recorded from the front row or sound boot, that is, it is not performed specifically for the podcast. Or a recorded event may be a guest speaker who visited the school, a lecture, or student speaker who is recorded "as is."

Script related podcast models: Refers to how closely podcast follows a script.

Unscripted podcast: Podcasters record entirely spontaneously; they may not use an outline. Imagine turning on the mikes, hitting record and starting to talk!

CHAPTER 8

THE WORLD IS LISTENING

Finding and Keeping Your Podcast Audience

TRANSCRIPT OF ANYSCHOOL PODCAST FROM MAJORS HIGH SCHOOL, BELIZE

Melrose: *Hi all, this is episode 25 of our weekly podcast from our sleepy little high school in. We have been podcasting 25 weeks about our school stuff, doing interviews with favorite teachers and students and students, and doing special events for our show. But me and my cohost, Pete, we just don't know if you are there. Hello???? Anybody listening?*

Pete: *Geez Melrose, yeah I don't know maybe we are talking out into the air and it's just disappearing.*

Melrose: *I know some of my friends click in on the Web, but other than that?*

Pete: *Hello??? Ya know, what is the use of 25 episodes? Who are we talking to? Couldn't we do the same thing with just a school newsletter? Why bother?*

Melrose: *Well, I like the tech gadgets ...*

Pete: *Yeah, Melrose, I know you do, but it would be nice to know if anybody listens and who listens. Too bad there is no way to know. It's not like we are a*

Podcasting for Teachers: Using a New Technology to Revolutionize Teaching and Learning, Revised Second Edition, pp. 125–144

big TV program with big money and advertising and marketing people who would find out.

Melrose: *Hello out there????? Anybody out there???*

TRANSCRIPT OF ANOTHER ANYSCHOOL PODCAST FROM LITTLEPEAK HIGH SCHOOL, NEVADA

Ella: *Hey folks, welcome to Anyschool Podcast from Littlepeak High School in Little Peak Nevada; Go Tinhorns! This is our 25th episode and we are so psyched up (whistles, whoops, cheers in backgrounds), because we have reached 10,000 listeners to our podcast.*

Jairo: *Hey Ella how do we know that?*

Ella: *Well Jairo it is because our podcast is listed in an Internet server that tracks how many times the episodes are downloaded and from where they are also accessed.*

Jairo: *What do you mean?*

Ella: *Well we know that 70% of our listeners listen to us on iTunes, but that the rest use other ways to find our podcast.*

Jairo: *Oh so maybe they are finding us on the school Web site?*

Ella: *Exactly, but we can also see that people from all over the world have linked to our podcast.*

Jairo: *Yeah, we also get e-mails through our special e-mail address and we read those on our show.*

Ella: *It's great to know that there are people who enjoy hearing about our school, plus we get to learn about them.*

OVERVIEW

The preceding school podcast scenarios depict drastically different situations. In both cases we have students dedicating a great deal of effort in creating and producing podcasts. But in the first, they do not have any indication as to who their audience is or whether they have an audience. In the second scenario, they have a clear understanding of how their audience is finding them, where they are from and have created ways to cultivate feedback with them. What a difference this information makes for the focus and commitment of the students to their work!

Based on our firsthand experience we know that it is not difficult to build in the means to gather this information. In addition it is not difficult to build in listener feedback mechanisms. However, both of these elements take thought and planning on the part of the podcasters (aka educators and/or students). In this chapter we present standard approaches that podcasters use to develop an audience, as well as some "out of the box" methods.

Readers will find topics in this chapter including:

- **tracking listeners** to your podcast to determine "what works and what doesn't";
- **finding your audience** including inside tips as to how to identify your topic with your professional expertise and audience in mind;
- using your existing network of contacts;
- using technology resources to help build an audience like blogs, and Web sites;
- where and how to "list" and "post" your podcast, and how to get media "buzz" about your podcast;
- **keeping your audience** with tips on how interactive elements of podcasts can build listenership through interactivity can assist in holding listenership; and
- how to use tracking statistics to serve your audience.

Podcasts do take time to plan, develop, produce, and publicize. With that said, it makes sense to get the greatest benefit from the work you and your students work. If you or your students have created good work, why not be sure that other people hear it and benefit from it? That is exactly what this chapter is about. We want to help educators understand, be prepared, and effectively build their podcasts by finding their desired audiences, reaching them and then easily gathering data about how effectively they are accomplishing those goals. The tools are *freely* available, let's take full advantage of them in order to model to our students how to transform teaching and learning and use technology to share their views!

TRACKING YOUR LISTENERS

It may seem a little odd to start with tracking your podcast listeners first, but there is a reason to this mathematical production madness! If one plans from the start to track listeners, it is very easy to do so, and yet the converse is true. If you do not plan to, you might end up having to set up a new URL address for your podcast feed and then having to redirect all your listeners to the new address, and that means losing some of them! Therefore:

> ***Helpful Podcast Tip from Kathy and Mark:*** *Choose a podcast host that provides robust tracking of podcast listeners. This information should include not only how many times each episode is downloaded, but also how many different IP addresses access each episode, what podcatchers or aggregators are used to access the podcast feed (i.e. iTunes.com, Podcastpickle.com, Odeo.com, etc.) and what Web site links were used to lead to the RSS feed (i.e., your specific URL, your home page, a blog that has posted your feed, your listing in another directory, etc.).*

Figure 8.1 provides a basic view of one of the popular podcast host's stats pages (libysn.com) which shows a portion of our statistical data about one of our podcast series. This first view provides a expansive screen (only a portion shown here), which shows the number of downloads, a chart which displays number of downloads per month, most popular directories listeners access your podcast from, as well as preliminary data about each episode. The bottom left corner of the screen shot reveals information about how people access the podcast. For instance do they go to a URL or do they use a podcatcher portal like iTunes?

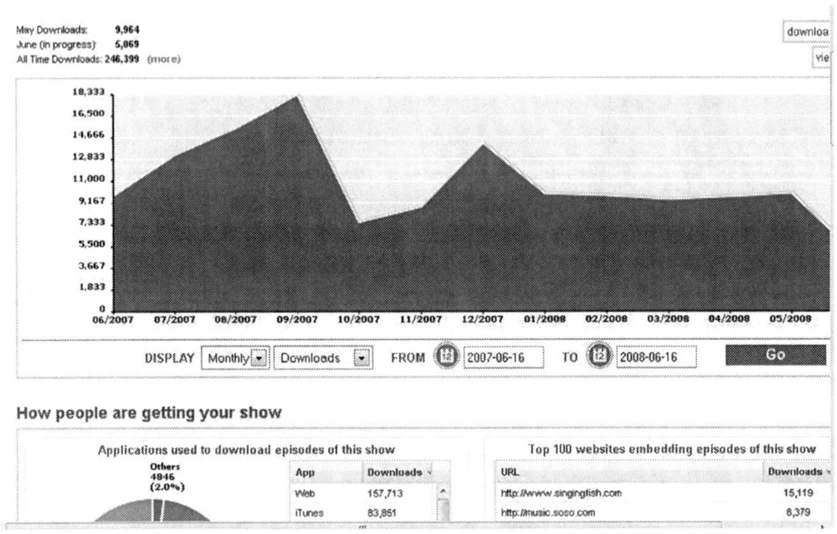

Figure 8.1. View 1 of tracking statistics page from http://www.Libsyn.com. © Libsyn. Used with permission.

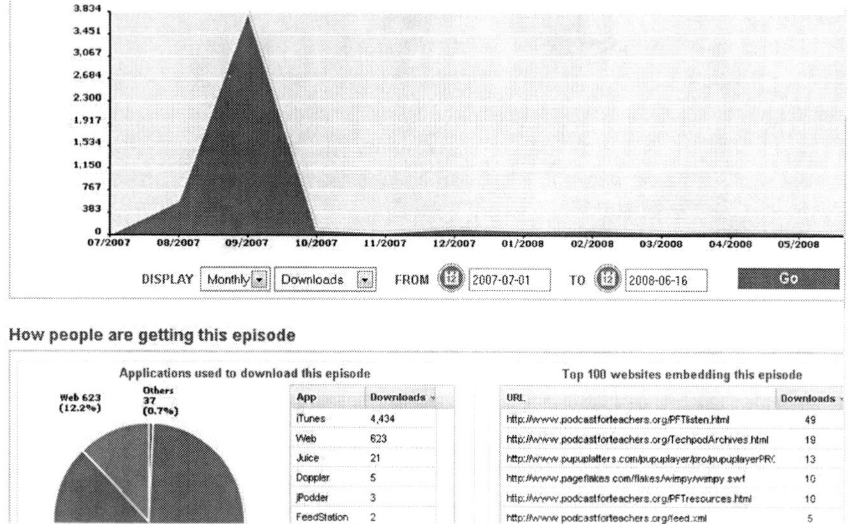

Figure 8.2. View 2 of tracking statistics page from http://www.Libsyn.com. © Libsyn. Used with permission.

However as seen in Figure 8.2, most podcast hosts provide even more information. For instance you can "drill down " to great detail for most of the data on the first page (Figure 8.1). Therefore when we select episode 101 of our first series, it reveals the same data about our individual episode that it earlier showed about the entire series. In this way we can easily and quickly review aggregate and disaggregate data.

The real power of these data then results not in their individual episode numbers, as fascinating as they are. However the value in these data is more powerful when looking at them across time within your series of podcasts with specific audiences, or among different audiences. For instance, think about what might change if you did the same or different podcasting with another group than you did comparisons among them. In fact, this is easy enough to do because with podcasting you can make changes from one week to the next and see if there are changes with the listeners. If podcasters set up their podcast from the beginning to track their audience per episode and across episodes, then they have a wealth of information to do comparisons among. If you start gathering the data later on, you will have lost some of your earlier information which could be valuable for your future planning.

Understanding your podcasting audience today will also help you keep track of their needs as they continuously change and you will therefore not be suddenly caught unaware that their needs have drastically changed. Audiences will want to interact with podcasters, and that is a vital part of your relationship with them. But it is also important not to bother your listeners to provide information which you can gather on your own via podcasting statistics.

A few major services that have been in the podcasting industry for a while are Libsyn (www.libsyn.com), Feedburner (www.feedburner.com), Podtrac (www.podtrac.com), and Podomatic (www.podomatic.com). However each of them is different and thereby offers choices for podcasting educators. Frankly we find that Libsyn, which stands for Liberated Syndication, is a very good, well-rounded choice for podcasters because they provide a very inexpensive solution for podcasting which includes hosting of the files, at only $5-10 per month (as of June 2008) with unlimited bandwidth and fully integrated statistical data.

Feedburner is a service which is freely available via a Web site. It will convert your podcast feed, the XML address, to an address which allows the statistical data to be tracked. However, Feedburner does not host files or account for bandwidth needs. In addition, Podtrac is another podcasting related service which emerged after December 2005. They provide statistical and marketing services tracking and have developed some innovative approaches to help podcasters try to increase their exposure. However some of the Podtrac services are expensive when considered for classroom K-12 educators; educators who use podcasts for other applications such as publishing, curriculum development, research, and development and the like may find this investment within their means.

Podomatic.com and Podbean.com are among those podcasting hosts which we refer to as an "all-in-one" podcasting solution and may be particularly appealing to some educators as they provide limited free accounts. Such "all-in-one" podcasting services include a convenient basic feature of being able to directly record online and this in addition to modest storage space, an automated podcast feed, hosting, custom e-mail address, and basic statistics. These features may enable teachers to "test-drive," explore and use many of the educational capabilities of podcasting with little startup, and little technical skills. However, as with all of the free and very inexpensive podcasting hosting plans the motive is to "sell the users up" to the next level and additional features.

FINDING YOUR AUDIENCE

Essential Concerns. When podcasters consider how to find their audience, they need to consider many concerns. However, we would suggest they keep their focus on these few concerns at first:

- **WHY?** What is the main reason you are creating the podcast series?
- **WHAT?** What is the current gap and need in existing podcasts and digital media?
- **WHY YOU?** What is your expertise and professional passion?
- **WHO? And WHERE?** Do you already have an audience? If not, where will you reach them?
- **LIMITS?** Do you have deadlines, costs, resources, or other restrictions?

Why?

These questions can assist in focusing your vision and keeping your attention on defining your podcast with your audience in mind. In turn, this will assist you in reaching your audience. For instance, as you consider **why** you are creating your podcast series, you will more specifically focus your message and identify your prospective audience from the beginning.

What?

In identifying the gap in existing podcasting content the concepts of professional expertise and niche content can be powerful. Visiting podcast directories and searching for podcasts on topics similar to your prospective options or preferences can assist in defining the scope of the need for your efforts. Ask yourself questions such as, **what** is missing? How will **your** past experience and **your** professional expertise stand out in this context? How can **you** build on current trends that fit the aspirations you have for your podcast?

In the first 2 years of podcasting we also experienced the emergence of *The Long Tail* (Anderson, 2006) theory in the popular literature. Both fields documented how specialized media develops a following, in this way we have experienced that what would seem to be very narrow topics have indeed developed significant podcast listeners. One of the many benefits of this digital media is that it allows for such focused concentration because the cost in production is so low in comparison to traditional paper-based publication.

Who and Where?

In defining their topic more specifically and understanding the existing audience, podcasters are also already discovering **who** and **where** their own audience will be. Building on your expertise, professional associations, existing specialty groups or clubs, online and in-person discussion groups, and your current network of associates and collaborations all provide opportunities to find, build, and energize an audience for the podcast. These groups of potential listeners can also be valuable people to speak with first-hand via online survey or focus group to determine what format, content and length for podcasts they would prefer. It is important to continue to have a vision of building and escalating the breadth of your audience. However, podcasters also need to carefully consider if they have any limits to which they need to pay close attention.

Limits

For example, your podcast may be underwritten by a budget or your time might be allocated through your fulltime position. If so, you need to carefully budget and track your time, resources, and expenses on this project in order to stay within your **limits.** Other limits may include content scope, deadlines, file storage, or bandwidth. Educational podcasters might need to stay within a specific scope of content in order to fulfill the requirements of their department head, school board, or publisher. Most successful podcasters are working on a schedule in which they produce their episodes on a routine time frame; therefore, they need to budget their podcast production management process to account for that end time and hit the time and date on target.

In addition unless you have established a podcast host account with a service which provides unlimited bandwidth, it will be necessary to keep a close eye on the bandwidth of your podcast series. Bandwidth is a function of the file size, popularity, and number of downloads of your podcast. If you are on a prorated bandwidth service, increased popularity can result in huge monthly bills or in the service disconnecting your feed because it overloads their network. (No kidding. This really happens!) File storage on the other hand hardly ever is unlimited, the best you can do is identify a podcast host plan which will provide more than enough space for you to permanently and reliably store your files and provide more than your expected bandwidth at a high reliability at a reasonable cost.

> ***Helpful Podcast Tip from Kathy and Mark:*** *When setting up your podcast don't assume you can post your podcast MP3 files and feed.xml file on the school's server. Talk to your school's or district's technical support staff and be sure to explain that your files will increase bandwidth needs. If this will be a concern for them, and it should be, get their approval in writing (or*

e-mail) to have the podcast hosted on an outside service in order to avoid overloading, or compromising, the resources of your organization.

More Technology Resources. In order to grow the podcast and find additional audience members it is important to have the podcast elements that we have mentioned in prior chapters, including an active e-mail address, Web site, and blog. Your blog will give you the opportunity post your show notes, show outlines, details about your interviews and guests, additional curricular materials, and additional Internet resources. Blogs are a social and viral technology; therefore, as you link to other digital media they may begin to link back to you. All of this activity increases your visibility and ranking in the Web-based search engines. You might want to experiment and not use your blog to just rehash the podcast. Instead you can post queries, discussions, and ancillary materials that listeners would not otherwise gain.

Such an approach draws your listeners to the Web site as you mention it in the podcast and you then have the opportunity to build more varied learning opportunities and interactions. From your Web-based resource list, to suggested links and educational resources, books, other digital media like podcasts, and the opportunity to host online conferences, you could be building a community through your podcast. In fact, this has been our experience with Podcast for Teachers, Techpod. We progressed from the podcast to many Web-based resources, articles, online virtual workshops, virtual conferences, and now book publication. All the while we have maintained and continued to advance the format and responsiveness of the original, core service, our podcast which reaches over 10,000 people per week through its various distribution formats.

In addition to posting the information about your podcast to the usual podcast-related sites, and there are over 100 podcast directories, consider also the many content-related sites where you may post information about your podcast. For instance, if you have a podcast about reading for K-12 education, a posting on the bulletin board at the IRA Web site would be a most appropriate strategy. Posting informative articles about your podcast's current and future content on your blog and then providing those articles to various educational news sources such as *e-School News* (http://www.eschoolnews.com) or *Technology and Learning Magazine* (http://www.techlearning.com/) are additional examples of how to cross promote sound educational ideas, content and your podcast.

In addition to providing valuable content articles, building online resources and/or communities, podcasters also have the opportunity to create a media buzz about their work through regular press releases. You can use press releases to highlight significant advances that you have made with the podcast.

Helpful Podcast Tip from Kathy and Mark: *When you reach certain key numbers of participants, interview notable guests, speak at conferences, have articles published, or begin distribution of your podcast through new channels (such as a new Internet radio station, syndication, etc.), use the opportunity to spread the word abut your podcasting work. Creating a media buzz through articles, fliers, school, Web, and conference announcements focused on that which is of interest to the general public is easy because our digital media loving society gravitates toward your dual emphasis on how you are supporting education!*

Getting Listed, or "The 411 on the 411." You remember this adage, if a tree falls in the forest and no one is there, does it make a sound? In the same vein, if you create a podcast and don't post it in the podcast directories, can anyone find it? Well, certainly they *can, but you are making it difficult for them!*

As of this writing there are over 100 podcast directories. And that means iTunes is only one of them. We have mentioned several of the other major ones, but they include:

- Happy Fish
- iPodder.org
- ipodderX
- iTunes.com
- Odeo.com
- Podcast411.com
- Podcast alley.com
- Podcastingnews.com—directory and resource site
- Podcasting-Station.com—general podcasting directory
- Podcastpickle.com
- Podnova.com—directory combined with aggregator for one-click subscription
- PodOmatic
- PodZinger.com
- Singing Fish—audio/video search engine
- Women in Podcasting—podcast directory for female podcasters
- Yahoo Media Search—from Yahoo's new search feature of all media types
- ZENcast—Creative Zens' podcast directory

For a current list which is kept very up to date, visit Dave Walch's *Directory of Directories* at *Podcast 411* http://www.podcast411.com/page2.html (Podcast411.com, 2006) and Podcastingnews.com.

How do you get included in the lists? The answer to this question is the sad news, at this point in time, that podcasters still have to enter their podcast information into each directory. What does this mean? The reality is that although you have registered your podcast in iTunes it does not mean that you are listed in the 100+ other podcasts directories. Therefore, when people go to the other directories looking for podcasts they will not necessarily find yours.

How does a podcaster handle this situation? One strategy is to gradually submit your information to all the directories; the other is to make strategic choices as to where your listening audience will most likely be found. For example, for most educational podcasts about K-12 education, I would not bother submitting mine to the hunting and fishing podcast directory (yes, there is one).

The process of submitting your podcast to the directories varies widely based on each directories' individual format. There are perhaps three general scenarios we can describe: A, B, C, from easy to detailed.

- **Podcast Directory A:** Submit your feed URL and the directory will extract all the necessary information from your feed file. You will receive a confirmation e-mail when your podcast has been added to the directory.
- **Podcast Directory B:** Submit the name of your podcast, your e-mail address, your Web site and your feed URL to the directory. And the directory will extract all the remaining necessary information from your feed file. You will receive a confirmation email when your podcast has been added to the directory. The time frame for the addition can range from 24 hours to 2 months!
- **Podcast Directory C:** Register with the Web site and wait for confirmation email to start the submission process. Submit about 10-15 fields of information to the directory (see Figure 8.3) including, but not necessarily limited to: the name of your podcast, your e-mail address, short description of your podcast, **long** description of your podcast, keywords, your Web site, your feed URL, one to three topics for your podcast, webmaster, and/or cohosts to the directory. The directory will extract all the remaining necessary information from your feed file. You will receive a confirmation e-mail when your podcast has been reviewed and added to the directory.

This submission process to the podcast directories is all part of the setup process. Once you start podcasting you can also better assure that directories know your podcast is alive, well, and active by using automated pinging services. A *ping* is an Internet function which sends a message from one computer to another (most of the time through many intermediaries) to let them know they are on the other end or that information is updated. Web sites and services such as Pingoat (http://www.pingoat.com) and Ping All! (http://www.allpodcasts.com/PingAll/Default.aspx) provide easy ways to send a quick message out to many podcast directories and search engines every time you post a new episode on your podcast.

For example when I post a new episode of *Podcast for Teachers Techpod*, I go to Ping All! (see Figure 8.4). Then I enter http://www.podcastforteachers.org/feed.xml in the dialogue box, click on **Ping!** and it sends out a message to several major podcast directories and search engines that new information, a new episode, is on our feed. In turn, the search engines will then scan the feed and gather the new information.

Finding your podcast audience has many dimensions to it which span from the stages when you are still dreaming about your podcast, to when

Figure 8.3. Sample podcast directory registration form from Podcastpickle.com. © Podcastpickle.com. Used by permission.

you have been producing your podcast for months and years. However another critical aspect of podcasting is *keeping your audience.* The next section of our chapter will discuss guidelines and suggestions we have found especially helpful in this regard.

KEEPING YOUR AUDIENCE

You have worked hard to research, design, write, record, edit, and produce your podcasts. You have built your audience. A looming question remains: how do you keep that audience coming back to you episode after episode? As educators and also constant consumers of digital media we have the opportunity to apply our professional training, insight and many of our experiences to answer this question in not only effective, but also creative ways.

In this chapter we have been addressing this major question already by building a podcast that will address the needs of the audience you serve. As described we have laid the groundwork for you to:

- identify the gap in the existing field of education, digital media and podcasting,
- explore where your audience is and what their needs are,
- prepare so that you can track their interest through their listening patterns (podcast statistics),
- design podcast resources to provide educational content that serves their needs (i.e. Web site, blog, discussion board, etc.), and
- spread the word about your podcast, its value and focus.

Now this chapter will address some of the high points about building a podcast **format** that will address your audience's needs. Such a compelling format includes interactivity, feedback, reliability, brevity, and convenience.

Interactivity in a podcast can span many formats, from

- e-mail responses which are sent in and privately responded to,
- on-the-air "shout outs" to the e-mailers,
- discussion boards where listeners can interact with the podcast host and/or build a community among themselves,
- live podcasts where listeners participate in the podcast recording.

In our experience as both podcast hosts and listeners the reading of the weekly **e-mail bag** and **"shout outs"** is a very effective way to interact

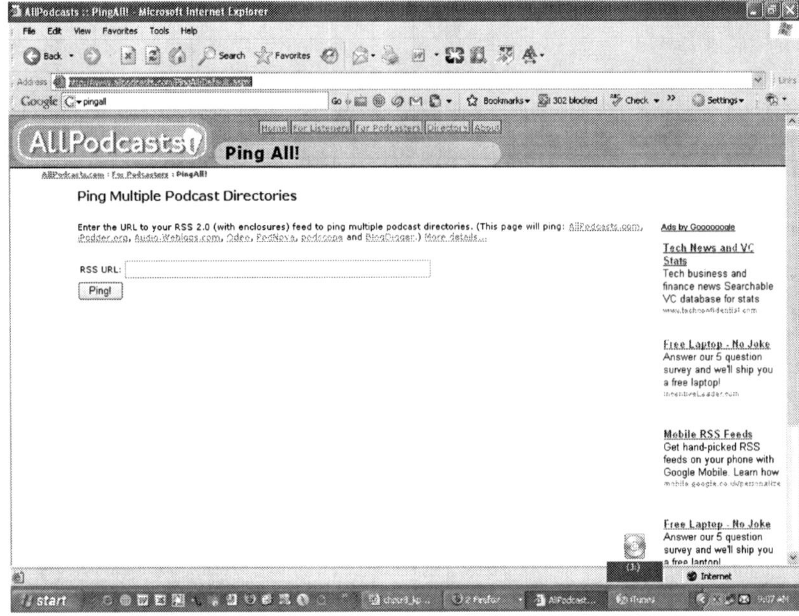

Figure 8.4. View of Ping All! (http://www.allpodcasts.com/PingAll/Default.aspx). © OpinionatedGeek Ltd. Used by permission.

with the podcast audience. People enjoy hearing their name on the show and it also helps listeners hear that there are other listeners that are in similar or different situations to their own. Do not think of this process as self-lauding, it really is a time where you are recognizing your listeners and they appreciate your taking the time to think of them in your busy celebrity status life (yes, you!).

Discussion boards, bulletin boards, or **wikis**, can be another way to not only build interactivity but also build community *among* participants. While these are common among general podcasts, we do not see nearly as many in educational podcasts. In part this phenomenon is because educational podcasts often are focused on a specific class and the educator has other opportunities to interact with the class. But also there has been a tremendous backlash in schools and community against the use of public forums in K-12 education for fear of outsiders. This fear does not need to take over in this setting however.

Discussion boards can be setup so that only users who have registered, received permission from the moderator or have the password can post messages. Therefore there are several levels of security that can be put into place. The opportunity for rich interaction, creative thinking, critical evaluation, and expanding perspectives and worldviews is just keystrokes away through discussion boards and wikis. We really encourage educators to explore the possibilities of these applications with their technology specialists and determine if there are any available through their school or organization, their podcast host, a free service (e.g., www.wikispaces.org or www.pbwiki.com) or open source (www.phpBB.com).

Live podcasts are much less common in educational settings and can be a bit tricky. However they really are worth a look at for special occasions. Perhaps two schools or classes could meet online and have a cooperative podcast, or you could interview a guest from a remote location. Using a remote tool such as a virtual classroom podcasters can have an easy to use virtual environment where people around the world can meet, chat, and talk synchronously and record the conversation, with no long-distance phone charges! In addition, through special configurations you can also set up voice over IP (VOIP), such as SKYPE, to record remote conversations with high quality without cost.

An example of a podcast which is recorded in a live format, with a participatory audience is one cohosted by Paige Eissinger and Kathleen King, Transformation Education LIVE! (http://www.transformationed.com/podcast) is a podcast about lifelong learning and technology. Paige Eissinger has worked with school systems on occasion to provide technical support and you will find her and Kathy's topics and dialogue always informative and interesting.

Statistics. When we guided you in researching your podcasts and designing them we included setting up features to track statistics about the listeners. At this point this information becomes really important in keeping your audience.

Be sure to check in on those numbers each week and examine them. They are not complex. Look through the details before you jump to conclusions though because each service is set up a little differently. Parse out the difference between unique downloads, subscribers, and Web page downloads. Each of these pieces of information is named a little bit differently in each service, but has important information about, for instance, whether your listeners use a podcast directory to reach your podcast, go to your Web site, and/or whether the numbers you are looking at may be from an automated service or individuals (unique downloads versus repeated).

Now go back to those questions we had for you earlier in the chapter and consider what is working with your podcast episodes and perhaps what is not? What podcast topics and formats seem to get more traffic? And what delivery systems do your listeners prefer? You can use this information to customize your podcast, educate your audience, identify additional listeners, and *keep your audience.*

Reliability. A critical issue in keeping your audience is that of reliability. Within this one term we mean to encompass not only that you produce your podcast on a regular basis that you let your listeners know about, but that you also have consistent quality content and a fairly consistent time length for your podcast. You can imagine that it would be difficult for your listeners to keep track of you and be faithful as followers if they don't know when your next episode will be, or if it will be 15 minutes or 60 minutes long. Therefore providing a reliable format schedule, quality content, and production length will go a long way in enabling your listeners to be able to return time and again.

Brevity. Building on this point about the recording length of the podcast is that of brevity. Research regarding podcast listener habits is that most people listen to podcasts on their commute or while they are occupied on other tasks such as during their workout or during their work day. By far the most popular time is their commute which averages 30 minutes. Thereby indicators are that podcasts are recommended to be from 20-40 minutes long. For educational purposes a 20-minute podcast might be a bit short. If a podcast is created by middle or high school students and/or for that population or older and has an educational purpose certainly the 30-40 minute timeframe provides a more substantial block of time to delve into a topic, develop it, and provide a closing. In contrast a podcast created by or for K-6 students might gear toward a 20-30 minute time frame with shorter attention spans.

> ***Helpful Podcast Tip from Kathy and Mark:*** *At the same time, an hour is too long for a podcast as we must remember that in this audio medium podcasters need to keep the listener's attention. Keys to success for timing include frequent change of action and using the 20-40 minutes to the maximum, by planning it out, packing in your information in a sequence that builds to your objectives, reinforcing them and providing action points. These elements will bring the educational value to a quick closure and garner a greater amount of attention from your podcast listeners.*

Convenience. As we near the end of this chapter on "The World is Listening" the final section on keeping your audience resonates with one of the major appealing factors of podcasts: convenience. The reason that podcasting has risen in rapid popularity is that it enables people to be in control of their choices of content and time. If you continue to build on that strength you will maximize the opportunity to keep your audience. Some of the ways to increase the convenience of your podcast is to make the continuous "delivery" of your podcast to the listeners as transparent and painless as possible!

In our experience we have found that podcatching software can be difficult for novice technology users. They have difficulty figuring out they need to download the software, find the podcast and subscribe. Here are some other options:

- "1-click": iTunes, Podcastpickle.com, Yahoo.com, and other podcast directories have icons that you can put on your Web site and users just click them and it opens (or downloads) the software and subscribes to your podcast. In order for this to work podcasters have to do some setup work. They have to enter their podcast into that specific directory, configure the button for their podcast and include it on their Web page, and then count on the user to click on it. The downside is that a podcast Web page could end up with 1-15 of these "1-click" icons on their Web pages which can be a little confusing to beginning listeners.
- BlogTalkRadio (http://www.blogtalkradio.com): This Internet podcasting, online community and radio station hosts and plays only podcasts. Building on the familiarity of call-in radio show format, it is an unusual delivery system and concept. You can record your podcast from any telephone, and while it is being recorded it is streamed through the online interface. Once completed the podcast is saved and processed, it is then posted automatically to your own blogtalkradio feed.

  Several benefits of the blogtalkradio interface include listeners not having to download special software, the personal connection side of podcasting is promoted, series are each given their own space, logo, feed, blog, etc., and listeners always have many podcasts available to listen to live/streaming or archived. In addition, community is emphasized as one can easily participate in the production of a podcast by calling in or being in the chat room with the hosts while they are recording.
- E-mail podcast delivery—Feedblitz (www.feedblitz.com): This option converges podcasts with e-mail. Once it is setup the user clicks on the podcast Feedblitz icon on the podcast Web site and then every time a new episode is released it is directly emailed to their inbox. This is a great option for those who don't want to check in with a podcatching program or who want to be able to forward podcasts to friends and colleagues. To set this delivery up all the user has to do is enter their e-mail address at the Feedblitz address for a particular podcast. For example if you go to http://feedblitz.com/f/?sub= 50046 and enter your e-mail address you will receive every new episode of Podcast for Teachers in your e-mail

box. This Feedblitz system, others like it, also has subscription services available for podcasters to be able to track how many people receive the episodes in this manner.

- Mobile phone delivery—Mobilcast (http://mobilcast.com/) and Voiceindigo (www.voiceindigo.com/): This option allows podcasts to be delivered to user's cell phones. The podcast has to be setup for delivery—they have to register and may need configuring. Additionally at this time, the listener usually needs a data plan for their cell phone and might incur extra cell phone charges for their data plan.
- Blog and Web site: Of course you should have a well-defined Web site and/or blog where users can always find the latest episode. They should be able to easily find these sites. Good sources to look at for blogs include Wordpress (www.wordpress.com), Live Journal (www.livejournal.com) and Google's Blogger (www.blogger.com). When the corresponding blog and Web sites are created be sure to use names that are related to your podcast and easy to remember.

SUMMARY

With this chapter we have laid out numerous steps to find and keep a listening audience for your podcast. Included in these strategies are not only what you need to do after you create you podcast, but very importantly, how you should plan and research from the beginning. From data gathering, to podcast directory research, content review, instructional methods, podcast formats to ensure robust content and interactivity, and how to spread the word about your podcasting work within the educational community and beyond, it should be evident that quality podcasting which accomplishes and serves teachers and learners is not happenstance. Our experience and understanding has been that innovative technologies build on solid pedagogy, reach further through technology opportunities and resources, and need to be guided by educators who have a vision to transform teaching and learning. Podcasting is another opportunity to reach learners far beyond the walls of our physical classroom, let's listen to them, grow with them, and see how we can reach further to develop the field.

RESOURCES MENTIONED FOR DEVELOPING PODCASTS

- Blogger. http://www.blogger.com/start
- Blogtalkradio. http://www.blogtalkradio.com/

- Directory of Directories. http://www.podcast411.com/page2.html
- Doppler. http://www.dopplerradio.net
- *E-School News.* http://www.eschoolnews.com
- Feedblitz. http://www.feedblitz.com
- Feedburner. http://www.feedburner.com
- HappyFish. http://happyfish.info
- Ipodder. http://www.ipodder.org/directory/4/ipodderSoftware
- IpodderX. http://ipodderx.com/
- iTunes. http://www.itunes.com
- Libsyn. http://www.libsyn.com
- Live Journal. http://www.livejournal.com/
- Odeo.com. http://www.odeo.com
- PBwiki. http://www.pbwiki.com
- phpBB. http://www.phpBB.com
- Ping All! http://www.allpodcasts.com/PingAll/Default.aspx
- Pingoat. http://www.pingoat.com
- Podbean. http://www.podbean.com/
- Podcast.com. http://podcast.com
- Podcast 411. http://www.podcast411.com
- Podcast Alley. http://www.podcastalley.com
- Podcast for Teachers. http://www.podcastforteachers.org/
- Podcasting Station. http://www.podcasting-station.com/
- Podcast Pickle. http://www.podcastpickle.com
- Podnova. http://www.podnova.com
- PodOmatic. http://www.podomatic.com
- Podtrac. http://www.podtrac.com
- PodZinger. http://www.podzinger.com
- Singing Fish. http://search.singingfish.com/sfw/home.jsp
- SKYPE. http://www.skype.com
- Teachers' Podcast. http://www.teacherspodcast.org
- *Technology and Learning Magazine.* http://www.techlearning.com/
- Transformation Education LIVE! http://www.transformationed.com/podcast
- Voiceindigo. http://www.voiceindigo.com/
- Wikispaces. http://www.wikispaces.com/
- The Women in Podcasting Directory. http://www.womeninpodcasting.com/

- Word Press. http://wordpress.com/
- Yahoo Media Search. http://search.yahoo.com/
- Zencast. http://www.zencast.com/

PART III

BECOMING A PODCASTING EDUCATOR

CHAPTER 9

TEACHING WITH PODCASTS AND PODCASTING EDUCATOR'S LEARNING CURVE

WHO SHOULD TEACH WITH PODCASTS AND PODCASTING?

Podcasting has potential value for teaching and learning across the curriculum. Because podcasting is a recorded word product, it has obvious connections to language instruction. As is discussed in depth elsewhere in this book, podcasting can help English Language Arts (ELA) facilitate learning in areas that are often not given much attention—speaking and listening. Although these are stated goals of ELA instruction, they are often not given as much attention as part of the instructional program as they should get. Podcasting can help address that.

Programs for English as a Second Language (ESL) have been some of the earliest and most successful adopters of podcasting. ESL students have a natural need to consume content that is rich in listening to spoken language and instructional programs designed for them require constant acquisition of new content to satisfy that need. Podcasting has proven a boon to educators in this area and is increasingly becoming popular with those involved in foreign language instruction as well. And of course, music instruction, an area that has a built in need for recording and shar-

Podcasting for Teachers: Using a New Technology to Revolutionize Teaching and Learning,
Revised Second Edition, pp. 147–158

ing student performances as well as content to support learning has an obvious connection to podcasting.

What may be less obvious is podcasting's applicability to other areas like math, science, social studies, business, and art history. In many of those subjects students currently do reports, make presentations, engage in panels and debates, and are involved in a variety of focusing activities and proving behaviors that involve relating, although most often through the written word, what they are studying and learning. Furthermore, in classes in those subject areas that alternatively rely on tests for these purposes, it is often the case that such projects and activities are avoided because their far ranging benefits aren't understood or they seem too difficult to prepare for, provide with necessary resources, or implement. Podcasting changes that equation. It is a very easy and practical body of practice to bring into the instructional program. Seen from the angles presented below, it is not a drastic departure from well-established practices that educators traditionally rely on to produce results in student achievement. However, with a little imagination we can also see that podcasting has the potential to offer benefits that exceed the immediate need to teach a specific curriculum.

Like other digital technology innovations, the World Wide Web for instance, podcasting is flexible and has something to offer all teachers no matter what the subject or grade level.

TECHNOLOGY SKILLS AND FAMILIARITIES

Is it a Podcast?

The increased prominence that podcasting has given the production and consumption of audio content continues to interest teachers and students alike. In the excitement of embarking on this journey however, many fail to reflect adequately on the approach to "publishing" audio content they will opt for, how the purposes, goals, and objectives of their content relate to that approach, and how the two influence each other.

It's often the case that teachers and classes see Podcasting as the only dimension to what is really a continuum of applications and approaches. The result of this is either that they don't use the term *podcasting* properly, in effect, naming audio applications that aren't truly podcasts by that name, or they do true podcasts, but do so in a way that is not their most appropriate possible choice.

The term "podcast" connotes audio content provided to an audience through the use of an RSS feed that "pushes" the content continuously to subscribers. There are other, related uses of audio though that is distributed or provided to audiences, but they should more accurately be called, and more to the point understood, as other than true podcasts.

CONTINUUM OF DIGITAL AUDIO CONTENT AND STUDENT LEARNING PRODUCT TYPES

Non-Web-Distributed Audio Content

It may suffice for some simply to produce audio and then distribute it over a school LAN network, through disks or other portable media, or simply by e-mailing audio files. The purpose of the content and the type, scope, and location of the audience are the factors that will determine whether or not this approach is sufficient, desirable, and effective. Most schools have the capability to do this already and would simply be putting resources already in-house into use. For instance, early elementary classes might make good use of a shared, low-cost digital audio recorder to record class season's greetings messages. To publish this, teachers may find it sufficient to burn a disk for each student to take home. This type of activity might even preclude the need for all of the pre-K through third grade teachers in the school from direct involvement with the technology. One or two might handle the recording sessions while the majority concentrate on writing the class messages and rehearsing and managing the performances. If the recording is distributed as an MP3 file on the disk, parents might transfer it from disk or e-mail to an MP3 player that they can carry with them and share with friends and relatives as they might a wallet fold-out portfolio of their youngsters.

Web-Distributed Audio Content

- Audio Post: Single audio files are produced and posted on a Web site. These are available for audience consumption when needed.
- Audio Blog: an ongoing series of audio files are produced and posted in anticipation of audience use. This is done periodically, but continually. (Note: blogging resources generally do not host audio files, but provide a prominently marked place in which the URL of a hosted [elsewhere] file may be embedded in an accessible and user-friendly interface.)
- Podcast: an ongoing series of audio files are produced, posted, and "pushed" to subscribers via an RSS "'feed." In this sense podcasting is like broadcasting, however contemporary technology actually

> makes it a more effective and efficient manner of communications. In fact traditional radio or television broadcasting does not involve subscriptions of content that are delivered as soon as they are produced.

An example of the advantage that can come from understanding the above continuum of publishing approaches can be inferred from the podcasts listed on the Feedburner Web page created by Porter Middle School (http://feeds.feedburner.com/PorterMiddleSchoolPodcast). At the time of this writing the two most recent podcasts were posted in late May and mid February of 2006.

While it may be considered a nicety, truly this group did not need to expend the effort or expense involved in establishing a feed for their work. Simply posting the files would have sufficed. The school's podcast page on its Web site (http://www.austinschools.org/campus/porter/about_podcast.htm), in all likelihood served the purpose sufficiently of providing a "go to" place for those interested in accessing this content.

Furthermore, individuals who may have gone to the effort to formally subscribe to these podcasts might have been disappointed or confused as this group didn't follow through with what may be looked at as the implied promise of offering a true podcast, the posting of regularly scheduled content on an ongoing basis. Of course this is understandable in a public school in which so many activities vie for attention and manpower. In this case less might have been more, a better solution. And then again, perhaps this was the correct solution for reasons that only the school understands. The point though is to be clear about options, choices, and the reasons for making them. As a general rule, schools would be better off using technologies for real, demonstrable purposes and not to simply use them for their own sake.

HOW MUCH OF A GEEK MUST A TEACHER BE?

Teachers need not be or become hardcore techies in order to adopt podcast-based learning activities as part of the instructional program. The section below presents the skills that are needed and indicates the relatively low level of technology mastery required in most cases.

Using Podcasts

The following may be considered some basic prerequisite skills for those interested in getting their feet wet with digital audio as part of teaching and learning. This section covers skills for the use of already produced podcasts in teaching and learning, not the production of original podcasts.

- **Browser**: In addition to launching a browser and using it to navigate the World Wide Web, there should be some familiarity with search engines and conducting searches. Beyond these very, very basic skills, because podcast-using teachers are likely to be downloading and uploading a variety of resources on a regular basis, it may prove useful to understand the differences between a few of the more common browsers and develop a simple awareness about the capabilities and drawbacks.
- **Plug-ins and associated downloads**: Podcasting teachers and their students will likely try a variety of podcatchers and directories, media players and other digital "tools." A familiarity with the concept of identifying, downloading, installing, and managing these will prove very helpful.
- **Familiarity with the computer's sound/audio functions** (speaker preferences and settings, volume, etc.).

MORE HELPFUL UNDERSTANDING FOR TEACHERS INVOLVED IN PODCASTING-ENABLED INSTRUCTIONAL PROGRAMS

- **Audio File Formats:** WAV files, AAC files, MP3 files, or others, there are a variety of formats to the files that carry digital audio content. While in most cases, a teacher will be dealing with MP3 files, a degree of understanding about the variety of types and the characteristics and pros and cons of the more common ones likely to be encountered and used as part of the new digital audio content in classrooms will be useful.
- **Media Players:** There are a handful of common downloadable media players all of which vie for attention. Familiarity with these and their pluses and minuses is worthwhile background knowledge for audio using/creating classes.
- **RSS Aggregators:** What makes a podcast a podcast, as opposed to simply a Web posted audio file? Answer: an RSS feed. RSS (or Really Simple Syndication) is a technology that "pushes" content to subscribers rather than waiting for content consumers to chase it down and request it time and time again.
- **Podcatchers and Podcast Directories:** These online resources represent ways of locating and acquiring podcasts that are developed specifically for this purpose.

Creating Podcasts

Many of these items are discussed in greater detail in the second section of the book.

- **Audio Software:** Familiarity with various audio software offerings will prove useful. There are free downloads, free trials, and "for purchase" software that runs the gamut from simple to professional level. Choosing the right one for a given school or class situation will affect the ultimate success of a classroom podcasting project. Many teachers and students start with Audacity, a relatively simple, free download.
- **Audio Editing Techniques and Effects:** Related to the entry above, there are a number of essential techniques required: recording the original sound items, editing out superfluous or intrusive elements like silent pauses and ambient noise, editing in ancillary elements like interviews recorded separately, as well as layering music or other sounds under voices, fading volume in and out of the recording, and so forth. Converting files from one audio format to another, exporting as MP3 (or other) format, and saving are processes performed with audio software, as well.
- **Uploading:** Finished sound files need to be uploaded to a host server. This involves the use of a type of software called FTP (File Transfer Protocol). Traditionally, this is a separate piece of software. However, some services that provide podcasters with a "complete solution" may incorporate this into their Web-based interface.
- **RSS Feeds and Listing Podcasts With Directories:** You will need to create a feed that "pushes" your content to subscribers who locate your podcast on a podcast directory. There are numerous approaches to the above that are covered in much greater detail in the first section of the book as well as how to get your podcast listed.

Additionally, those teachers who want to pursue a non-Web distributed approximation of publishing audio-based student work will need familiarity with converting files from one format to another, exporting, and saving audio files. The more basic skills of transferring files to portable media (i.e., CDs) and attaching to email are necessary as well.

Pedagogical Understandings

Podcasting represents an opportunity for many teachers to explore areas of teaching that are appealing, but which few teachers actually manage to make part of their practice. Artistic and creative activities, or more accurately in the case of podcasting, activities that take advantage of formats developed in the arts, can become the types of things that enliven and enrich learning in every class. Podcasting-based learning activities also take advantage of formats developed in the field of journalism, a dimension that can enrich much subject area learning.

While many teachers are intimidated by what they believe to be a need for talent or artistic or technical training in the areas of creative expression, the use of technology can make such activities something that all can handle. Furthermore, there are a number of with foundational understandings that speak to the legitimacy and importance of approaches to instruction that easily connect with podcasting and its capacity to make the instructional program offered more relevant and aligned to overarching, if seldom achieved, goals of education. Teachers interested in podcasting-based learning will benefit greatly from familiarizing themselves with the following four concepts that will aid in understanding, explaining, planning, and implementing learning activities that involve podcasting.

Instructional Foundations

1) Authentic Learning Activities. Authentic learning involves instruction that focuses on "real" connections between student activities and products and the world beyond the school in which they have a clear and apparent application.

The School Board of Tomorrow section of The National School Boards Association Web site spotlights an Education Leadership Toolkit item titled Authentic Learning (n.d.) as part of its Curriculum and Assessment section. This document states "A crucial aspect of curriculum is to base curricular goals on authentic, challenging tasks." These are characterized by:

- All students practice advanced skills;
- Multidisplinary curriculum;
- Collaborative learning;
- Heterogeneous groupings;
- Interactive modes of instruction;
- Student exploration;
- Teacher as facilitator;
- Performance-based assessment; and
- Extended blocks of time.

2) Project-Based Learning. On the simplest level, acquired podcasts may be used as "content" within the context of traditional and established teaching practices as an alternative to the type of print content found in texts and educational trade books. Other than accounting for the technology required to present the content, and managing the classroom to establish an environment in which listening can be accomplished comfortably, the conceptual differences between using recorded and print material are not overwhelming. However the creation of audio recordings invites teachers and students to embrace project-based learning as a conceptual basis for the use of this medium as an instructional resource.

Project-based learning (PBL) is a student-centered teaching and learning strategy which enables students to acquire new knowledge and skills in the course of designing, planning, and creating a product or performance. It provides students an opportunity to develop higher order thinking skills through hypothesizing, questioning, and analyzing.

Seven features have been identified as key components of project-based learning (Dunlap, McInnis, Wiggins, & McCarthy, n.d.):

- Core curriculum content,
- Multimedia,
- Real-world connections,
- Student decision making,
- Collaboration,
- Varied and frequent assessments, and
- Extended time frame.

3) Differentiated Instruction—Differentiated Learning. Differentiated Instruction involves using a range of instructional approaches that address the varying learning needs of students. These student needs become the prime consideration in designing instruction. According to a number of conceptual models students fall into learning style types reflecting their dominant learning needs, such as visual learners, auditory learners, or kinesthetic learners. The Sacramento City Unified School District conveniently defines the practice as follows (What Is Differentiated Intruction? n.d.):

> Differentiated instruction is based on the following beliefs:
>
> - Students differ in their learning profiles
> - Classrooms in which students are active learners, decision makers and problem solvers are more natural and effective than those in which students are served a "one-size-fits-all" curriculum and treated as passive recipients of information

- "Covering information" takes a backseat to making meaning out of important ideas.

> The key to a differentiated classroom is that all students are regularly offered CHOICES and students are matched with tasks compatible with their individual learner profiles.

Differentiated instruction approaches teaching by engaging students in activities that cater to their particular learning needs, strengths, and preferences. It is challenging to develop such engaging tasks but project-based instruction supported by technology is an approach that makes this much easier to accomplish.

Auditory Learners. Auditory learners are individuals who learn best through listening. They achieve best when instruction involves lectures, discussions, conversational exchanges, and instructional resources that involve sound and listening.

Auditory learners are very receptive to subtleties of information carried by the tone and timbre of voices. Print material is best learned by auditory learners when they hear it read or spoken.

Podcasting-based instruction is an opportunity for teachers to become sensitive and responsive to the needs of auditory learners and to the auditory needs of all learners.

INSTRUCTIONAL PRACTICALITIES

Classroom Management Concerns

Adopting, Growing, and Evolving. The above approaches to instruction have all earned a track record of success in a significant number of school settings over the years. However, adopting these approaches involves a learning process that may best be described as learning by trial and correction. Inevitably, implementing this type of instruction implies an improvement process by which the practitioner, perhaps in partnership with a supervisor, evaluates activities formatively, adding and dropping dimensions as he sees how they play out first hand and fine-tuning the program over a period of time.

Planning. The simplest level of podcasting-based instruction involves the presentation of ready to use podcast content to students in class to perform a similar function as a text. There is a difference though to the feel and pacing of content presented this way. Students respond to audio content differently, as well. For instance, they may want to look about the room or leaf through a book as they are listening—behaviors that would indicate they are not paying attention if they were tasked with reading a passage from a book. This is not necessarily the case though when they listen to a podcast.

Classroom routines change as well. The entire class must be in place and ready to listen when the podcast is started. In a whole-group listening activity there is no opportunity to get a student who comes in late caught up.

A level or two beyond the above scenario may include assigning listening to podcasts as part of homework, or as an extra resource for homework. Also, availability of a class set of computers and headphones, or MP3 players yields the capacity to have a class, or part of a class, listen to individual podcasts during class. Planning for these aspects involves familiarizing oneself with new classroom routines and student behaviors.

Above all, plotting where within the course of or unit of instruction to integrate a podcast-based activity or project involves seeing possibilities in handling segments of a curriculum differently. Learning to judge the duration of a project is crucial in fitting it in with the scope and sequence, as well.

Many teachers who want to assign portions of the technical aspect of a podcasting project directly to the students will be reluctant to give up instructional time within their specific subject to the teaching of technology skills. Learning to assess the skills that students already have is necessary to avoid that and alternatively, learning to collaborate with the school computer lab teacher will allow classes to overcome that obstacle.

Implementing. Podcast using teachers will have to acquire an understanding about how to best set up the classroom to accommodate listening to and recording audio material. This includes developing an instinct about securing equipment, keeping laptops charged, and arranging the classroom to take advantage of acoustics and power outlets.

Listening to podcasts, whether ready to use or student made, involves teaching listening skills to students, something that teachers will need to learn to do. How does one structure questions and conversations about subject matter in order to encourage and support students in effective listening? How does one structure follow up activities to those based in listening to or producing podcasts so as to reinforce learning accomplished this way?

Teachers who have not assigned learning projects, whether they be oral presentations based on research reports, the production of works of art, or class theatrical performances, will have to develop an understanding about how to present such learning activities. How does one make the connection between content learning and the production of a performance easy for students to see? If examples are played for the group, how then do you encourage students to produce original work rather than simply imitating the examples?

There are new classroom management skills and understandings involved, too. Managing students in the use of tech equipment, even if it is just a set of headphones for a desktop computer and configuring seating for collaborative group projects are a couple of shifts in running a classroom that teachers who have not done this sort of instruction previously will have to get themselves up to speed on.

Above all, the management of time is something that requires much adjusting. Most teachers will find that a podcasting project is a long-term unit that must be broken up into clearly defined subtasks. Allocating sufficient time for each of these is crucial so that students do not fall behind, as is accounting for what early finishers will do during class. How does one handle students who are absent and miss classes? Often teachers discover that teacher-created checklists and project timeline handouts facilitate things immeasurably, although learning to create and use these with students takes a little learning in and of itself.

Is it best to have the students concentrate primarily on the content learning, planning, and scripting of a podcast, or should they be involved in the actual recording and editing? Is it best to have the students each contribute their portion of spoken content in turn as part of a class "live performance" style podcast for which the teacher functions as stage manager, recording engineer, producer, and editor, a highly manageable scenario for teachers who have the requisite skills—or is it better to have the students in groups around the room, noisily recording in pods of three to five with a laptop and microphone assigned to each group?

Assessing. How does one assess podcast projects? The creation of a performance rubric is something that many teachers doing this sort of instruction find supports and enhances it greatly. This involves its own learning process as does the implementation of the rubric when the time to assess comes. Should the rubric be distributed at the beginning of the project in order to inform the students' planning? Do the students assess their work as well? Assess one another's work? Should accountable talk, a process in which the student explains the decisions made in the creation of a work or performance as part of the social aspect of the learning process, be part of the assessment process? Performance assessment requires time and experience to become comfortable with.

And a Few Other Things. Additionally, the production of podcast-based learning projects involves some degree of contemporary media sophistication. Learning to teach these understandings is important as the students are not just presenting their learning project, but growing up in a world in which similar media items are produced by the billions continually. Figuring out their place in a student's life as well as the place of the student's work in the world is a confusing new understanding of the way things are. It is important that teachers prepare themselves to support their students in this.

Publishing, sharing, and promoting student, class, and school podcasts is a logical end to the process. This involves a raft of informed decisions as well as a few simple skills. Furthermore, there is security (of student well-being) and intellectual property issues to contend with.

While the volume of skills and understandings involved with podcasting-based instructional activities may seem very large, the good news is that it need not all be learned at once or in advance of beginning to introduce podcasting into the classroom. There is a wealth of information available and while there are many individual skills involved, the great majority of them are not especially difficult to acquire.

CHAPTER 10

HOW TO CREATE PODCASTS AS TEACHING RESOURCES

TEACHER CREATED PODCASTS

Understanding that podcasts can be used to enhance, enrich, and extend the scope, reach, and efficacy of classroom activities, podcast content that is *just right* for a given instructional situation becomes a resource of exceptional potential. Teachers, accordingly will acquire instructional content in podcast form a number of different ways.

As the medium catches on no doubt podcast content will simply be provided to teachers. Just as it is currently unquestioned that a standard textbook will be provided to science teachers as basic equipment, this practice will likely include podcast content eventually as well. It is likely that school district curriculum coordinators will provide or suggest reviewed and vetted podcasts for use by the teachers they guide and support. It is quite likely that this will be done by the subject area professional organizations, as well, many of which are likely to produce podcasts of their own. Furthermore, content producers often adapt their production goals to accommodate trends and new developments, and it is logical that text and educational trade book publishers will produce podcast content. Textbook publishers could make a great contribution by producing podcast material that is ancillary to their hard cover offerings. By providing podcasts that enhance the use of their texts and make their comprehen-

---

Podcasting for Teachers: Using a New Technology to Revolutionize Teaching and Learning, Revised Second Edition, pp. 159–168

sion easier, they would avoid the conflict of setting up a choice between text or podcast, and reinforce the information age understanding that various forms of content can meld into a synergistic mix that is better than the individual items on their own.

In addition to podcasts that are provided as part of the general program of professional support, teachers will find and appropriate podcast content on their own, whether it be originally intended as general content or produced specifically as an instructional material. There is already a great deal of content prepared as podcast to be found through search engines or podcast directories. Many eventually will come to understand too, that content that would be most useful is content they need to produce for themselves.

FORMATS AND USES

A popular motto among architects and designers is "Form Follows Function," a saying that has much to offer teachers contemplating designing instructional podcasts, as well. A podcast done for the sake of doing a podcast will be an interesting discussion piece for a short period of time and be forgotten soon afterward. The existence of a real need should drive the creation of instructional resource podcasts. This need, which relates to the way it will be used, informs the shape and format a podcast ought to take. As can be seen from the following list, teacher-created podcasts take numerous forms to address a variety of uses.

Review and Prep Materials

Preparing students for tests is considered by many teachers to be an important part of their job. Producing "take home" study guides is a practice with a long track record of acceptance. Podcasting can be used in the same way as these traditional print materials although its dimension of sound offers some new and previously unexplored characteristics of this type of material. For instance, foreign language teachers certainly can make good use of podcasting as a way to provide students with material that helps with pronunciation, a type of learning that requires imitation of sounds. Music teachers, as well, can provide samples of the way a piece of music or the tuning of an instrument is supposed to sound, something that can't be provided by print materials. A science teacher in New York City produced a student written rap song on the theme of protein synthesis as a content review aid. This is a good example of using digital audio to create a device that students will find appealing, that conveys content well, and that fosters recall.

Audio Guides

Audio guides are a handy way to provide important information when the act of reading may get in the way of other important activities or when the quality of aural content conveys more than print can. An interesting resource used in global studies is the culture trunk, a box packed with objects and artifacts that convey meaning through their aspect as primary sources and sensory and aesthetic repositories of meaning. In experiencing the contents of a culture trunk, many of which are provided by museums and other cultural institutions who have access to authentic artifacts with which to stuff them, reading print material is a distraction as it requires use of a set of skills divorced from those used to apprehend the objects, as well as requiring students to break eye contact with the subject they are examining. Podcasts prepared by the teacher can support the students in avoiding this issue and assure that the information about the objects the teacher wants to convey is explicitly stated.

Activity Prompts

Numerous learning activities across the curriculum involve student response to content items presented to them to elicit a reaction, provide food for thought, or establish context. Podcasting is a convenient way to produce, store, and disseminate these to students. Online writing prompts for students are becoming an increasingly common support. The Port Angeles School District for instance, provides weekly math writing prompts on its Web site.

It is a short distance from these text-based writing prompts to the podcast prompts offered by The Mad Libs Podcast which promises to select the best written essay response to be read by the writer on its following podcast show. Music teachers, too, might podcast a musical prompt to spur improvisation skills or improvised response skills.

Direction Narratives

A public school band teacher in New York City, as a response to his frustration at having to explain essential chores, like how to disassemble, clean, and reassemble brass instruments, something that all players must do, produced his own narrative procedural sets of directions to students using digital media. Such resources can save valuable class time better spent on other items as well as supporting students by allowing them to have a detailed set of directions delivered to them with the reassuring voice of their teacher whenever and wherever they need it—including on the bus to a band performance where the narrative conveyed through an iPod makes the procedure far less intimidating. This might also be used by visual arts teachers to provide step by step directions in mixing colors and science or computer lab teachers who routinely must recount procedures to students who are obliged to follow them closely to benefit from the class.

Teacher Read Texts

There are points in instruction for which it is desirable for the teacher to read a text to the students. One of these instances is Shared Reading an important facet of reading instruction for emergent readers that encourages and supports them. This practice may include echo reading in which the students repeat the words after the teacher, choral reading—reading at the same time as the teacher, and "supply the missing pieces" reading where the teacher reads the bulk of the book and pauses while students suggest rhyming words or other predictable words that would fit in the book. Clearly having the teacher's performance recorded can extend her reach and enable parents to continue the learning at home.

Sample Content Applications by Subject and Type

The following are real examples of teacher-created, instructional-resource podcasts with potential to satisfy some real classroom needs.

1. English Language Arts

Mrs. Wenzel's podcast on the theme of What is Poetry? is a complete, well thought out lesson. It demonstrates that areas of literacy are open to interpretation and enriched by it. Students are actively asked to shape the lesson by offering opinions and sharing them with others. It begins with the teacher interviewing numerous other teachers in the school asking their opinion about What is Poetry?, and gives the students a feel for the variety of responses. The podcast next asks students to reflect for a minute and then give their own answer. A very rich source of podcasts created by a group of writing instructors at the Center for the Study and Teaching of Writing at Ohio State University offers good insight into podcasting's potential. Included in the group are some instructional podcasts structured as interviews by writing instructors with accomplished writers (http://cstw.osu.edu/podcasts/).

2. Social Studies

History According to Bob is a podcast by a college professor. It is a frequently updated lecture on a variety of history related subjects. While podcasting a scripted lecture may not be everyone's favorite application of this technology, this teacher's engaging style, and brief and to the point content makes this a worthwhile way to present material to students. Teachers might use this "as is" but based on this model, might produce their own content that is enhanced through humor based on insider's knowledge of school and class culture.

3. Science

With her podcast Science Lab Equipment, Mrs. Murchison (Bryan Independent School District, Bryan, Texas) presents material essential to her students' experience in her lab. By using a podcast like this the teacher can be relieved of presenting and repeating basic information in class and free up valuable instructional time for more in-depth learning. It also enables absentees to get caught up and functions as a useful review item.

4. Health

Mrs. Borchert's Health class (Lincoln-Way Community High School) is enriched by the podcasts she's produced as teaching materials for it. The downloadable worksheets that are posted on the Web site that accompany the podcasts makes them somewhat interactive, requiring students to listen for information and provide it on the worksheet. For students unable to attend classes that cover this material in person, the podcasts can be a very engaging way to keep up with class work and stay connected to the class.

5. Parent Outreach

Podcasts can communicate to parents the breadth and richness of the program their youngsters are experiencing at school or carry specific information designed to bridge the parent/school gap. For example, using a podcast enhanced with a few digital photos, Mrs. Lehman. a teacher in the Central York School District, captured and shared with parents and the extended community a field trip her class of young elementary school students made to Brown's Tree Farm, a local attraction.

TEACHER MADE PODCAST INSTRUCTIONAL RESOURCES: PLANNING CONSIDERATIONS

Why do teachers create their own resources? While the current norm seems to be for teachers to function as implementers of standard curriculum materials prepared for them by experts in the field, there are advantages to teachers producing their own materials.

While on one hand, the use of uniform materials provided by publishers and reviewed and adopted by school or district instructional supervisors assures that the appropriate content is covered, many teachers desire materials that for a host of reasons they feel will be more accessible to students. For example, teacher-created materials have the advantage of:

1. Addressing specific cultural characteristics that may make the materials more relevant to students;
2. Embodying language subtleties that allow students to better engage with and absorb content;
3. Offering alternative and supplementary content that allows material to be presented in addition to standard material;
4. Presenting content outside of the strict linear sequence that print materials establish;
5. Addressing "intelligences" and learning styles other than those addressed by traditional text materials; and
6. Offering a favorable affective dimension to instruction as the effort and sense of humor a teacher invests in producing materials contributes to student/teacher rapport.

Teacher created podcasts may aid directly in classroom logistics and management, and indirectly, but importantly, contribute to learning by virtue of helping to establish a better classroom climate and smoother functioning learning environment. Teachers who wish to save valuable instructional time may create podcasts relating classroom rules and regulations, or detailing activity procedures, or simply explaining the purpose of a unit of study. These are the types of things that can burn up endless precious student teacher contact time, but that need to be stated repeatedly. A podcast can be the most effective way to handle this.

While the act of podcasting in many cases is intended to reach a broad audience continually, for a classroom it may have other goals. Podcasts, once posted, are available anywhere—anytime. A teacher who podcasts a narrative procedure for a home kitchen science experiment is making that material available to the student and his parents or others who may want to monitor or help with assignments. It will be available anywhere an Internet enabled computer is available or wherever an MP3 player on which it has been downloaded is taken. This includes the home or home of peers or others, on vacation, anywhere. Such materials can not be lost, are available for instructional supervisors to review, and are archived and ready to be referred to and perhaps recycled down the road. Furthermore, a structure for updates, as assignments are updated, refined, or revised as progress in the classroom dictates is provided.

As an example, a chemistry teacher may come to realize that memorizing sections of the periodic table of the elements is a necessary foundation for serious discussions and problem-solving-based projects. Simply giving the students a chart to memorize does not produce the desired result. By writing a little song as a learning aid in which the elements are given names and personalities and posting this as a podcast, students may access and use it directly form their computer at home or in the school media center during study period, or they may download it to their MP3 player and listen to it on the school bus before and after school, thus turning fallow time into a productive learning opportunity. The teacher might even elicit student feedback during class and record it on a portable digital recorder thus the memory aid is refined by student input and then uploaded periodically as an update to the original podcast.

Looking at the planning table below, we can see that in this case the need addressed and rationale for creating this podcast is the need for content that covers the material in the text, but that presents it differently. In this case, the teacher might actually play the podcast in class once or twice to familiarize the students with it, but understands that students will use it primarily during their personal study time. He has a good idea of the type of access to the technology needed that the students have. The connection to the curriculum is clear; he has produced an alternative, ancillary material for teaching a core body of knowledge.

The pedagogical advantages are many, the podcast takes advantage of its motivating characteristics as students enjoy and are engaged by music which also addresses the needs of auditory learners. Furthermore, the need for memorization, a necessary, but frequently off-putting chore that represents a foundation for higher order, thinking-oriented activities, is handled in a way that supports the students in accomplishing it. Finally, the teacher, having had the opportunity to exercise his imagination and creativity feels satisfied and is motivated to create more materials for the class. Because of the fun and out of the box dimension to this part of the class, student/teacher rapport is strengthened.

We might chart the planning considerations as follows:

Need or Rationale for Podcast	Manner it will be accessed by or presented to student	Curricular Connection	Pedagogical Advantages

Each of the considerations contributes to an overall understanding of how the podcast produced will contribute to and function within the instructional program.

As a more detailed example, a teacher of visual art who wants to demonstrate to students how the Old Masters mixed the colors on their palate decides that the best way to teach this is to have each student go through a complex formula and process for mixing it in a step-by-step fashion. He will demonstrate the procedure for the class once and students will take notes of his demonstration. In the past though, he has had to repeat the steps over and over, reminding students and loosing valuable instructional time and spontaneous teachable moments in the process.

By recording a podcast and posting it, students may download it before class and begin experimenting with and preparing themselves for the difficult process ahead of time. In class, the students follow the directions played to themselves individually on MP3 players. Each can stop and start the recording at will, moving ahead in the experience at a pace most comfortable for himself.

In this instance podcasting addresses a real and significant instructional need, the need to provide detailed, sequential instructions on an on demand basis. The students each need an individual player and so the manner of accessing the content is clear. Additionally, those who care to download the material on their own time and on their own devices can get a head start on the project at a place and time other than that overtly allotted for learning this material.

The curricular connection, the color theory portion of the visual art curriculum, was a prime determinant in using podcasting for this instructional activity.

As a follow up to the color mixing exercise, this teacher decides to send his students to the art museum for a weekend experience in observing first hand the range of colors used by Old Masters. When they get to the museum they play another podcast created for them by their art teacher. In this podcast they move through the painting galleries stopping at each of 20 works that the teacher directs them to look at and analyze the colors employed to create them. When they get to each station they turn on their MP3 player and listen to the teacher explaining where to look and how to view it now they have learned about color theory. The pedagogical advantage is significant, as the way the Old Masters created their colors is a real world application of what has been learned in class. Quickly showing the students a few reproductions is a poor substitute for directing them to do an extensive survey of master works at the museum and without this experience the full weight of what they learned would not be possible.

THE TECHNICAL SIDE AND CONCLUSION

The second section of this book covers the background knowledge needed by teachers to handle the technical side of creating podcast teaching resources. Podcasting for teachers has progressed to the point that there are now available numerous services, many of them free or low cost, that make the technical side of this practice infinitely easier than when it first emerged a short while ago. In almost all of the examples given in this chapter very rudimentary equipment was used in relatively simple techniques. In many cases a single microphone connected to a single laptop computer (one that the teacher or school had already before the issue of podcasting arose) and Internet access were all the technology resources required to produce their podcasts.

Listening to a range of podcasts made by other teachers before setting out to do your own will give a clear and reassuring idea of the modest level of technical proficiency and artistry that is needed in order to produce a podcast that functions as a valuable instructional resource. Creating their own instructional materials is something that teachers have always done when the right item hasn't been available or when their own expertise outstripped that of the publishers and the specific needs of their own students is an important consideration. Podcasting makes this easier and more effective in many respects. The prospect of a substantial library of teacher created instructional podcasts available through the Internet is an exciting possibility that is eminently attainable and that would contribute to teachers' gaining far more control over their own profession. The means of achieving this are available right now.

RESOURCES

Central York School District. http://www.cysd.k12.pa.us/education/components/docmgr/default.php?sectiondetailid=6439&catfilter=112×tamp=116299447

History According to Bob. http://www.summahistorica.com/

The Mad Libs Podcast. http://www.podcastdirectory.com/podshows/793528

Mrs. Borchert's Health Class. http://www.lw210.org/central/departments/InsTech/InstructionalTech/Site/M.%20Borchert/M.%20Borchert.html
Mrs. Wenzel's Podcast. http://www.ci.bryanisd.org/1vision/Teacher%20Podcasts/AD661DA5-D5CA-4886-ADC3-17B3DDE1DCC0.html
Podcast for Teachers, Techpod. http://www.podcasatforteachers.org
Port Angeles School District, http://www.pasd.wednet.edu/school/mathwasl/
Science Lab Equipment. http://www.ci.bryanisd.org/1vision/Teacher%20Podcasts/04A32B1B-DAFB-4629-B4FC-077C79168D17.htm
The Teachers' Podcast, http://www.teacherspodcast.org

CHAPTER 11

HOW TO SET UP THE CLASSROOM FOR PODCASTING

Podcasting can be done in the classroom with little investment of funds. In addition to a laptop computer, one needs a microphone, and audio software. Other than Internet access, and possibly a pair of headphones, that's pretty much all that's required. Of course this can be become more elaborate, involving the use of several microphones and a mixer. However, with the addition of a simple, inexpensive USB microphone to a more or less up-to-date laptop, something already common in our classrooms, beginners or those who wish to keep it simple need not make any further investment.

Once the podcast content has been recorded, the rest of the process involves online resources, or resources that can be acquired online, but these need not affect the classroom set up. The session's audio file can be transferred to other computers via a variety of portable media and worked on later wherever an up-to-date, Internet-enabled computer with a broadband connection is conveniently available.

In most situations, the teacher will do the uploading of files that marks the end of the podcast creating experience. In many instances, the teacher will also do whatever editing is needed as well. For those situations in which students are to handle editing, the same or similar laptop

Podcasting for Teachers: Using a New Technology to Revolutionize Teaching and Learning,
Revised Second Edition, pp. 169–179

used in the recording part of the process can be used. This can be a class set of laptops or a shared cart of laptops that have audio software installed. During the editing portion of the project, there will be repeated playback of what's been recorded. The sound function on the laptops will have to be enabled and adjusted and perhaps, a set of inexpensive headphones should be added to each laptop used for this purpose.

SETTING UP FOR VARIOUS TYPES OF PODCASTS

The type of podcasts you will be doing will directly affect the type of classroom set-up you'll need to establish. However, in simplest form a microphone with a tabletop stand connected to a laptop via a USB connection is all that's needed. These can sit on top of the regular classroom furniture. You may wish to run a power cord to the laptop instead of running it off its battery, depending on the battery life and amount of time anticipated for recording. If that's the case, then the number and location of electrical outlines are considerations in how you set up the classroom.

One of the best aspects of this simple type of set up involving a minimal amount of equipment is that it is portable, storable, and sharable. The sole component that represents an item of great value is the laptop computer. Preparing this for podcasting involves only the installation of a single piece of software, examples of which can be downloaded free. Consequently, the teacher will have to plan for this download and installation on multiple laptops if having a number of computers makes for a more practical program.

Access to a USB thumb or jump drive makes it easy to back up, store, and transfer the sound files produced for podcasts, some of which may be large files.

Storing and securing the laptop when not in use for podcasting is likely a matter of complying with established laptop procedures that most schools already have in place. If a lockable cart is not part of the school program, a secure closet or storage locker is generally easy to find. The microphone and stand are relatively inexpensive and easily stored. Because a very good deal of podcast-based student activities involve planning, research, and preparation, the actual amount of time in which the equipment is needed represents only a portion of the total. Consequently, a number of groups of students or classes may share the podcast equipment set up which can be moved from room to room, rather than the school needing to purchase multiple sets.

The recording part of the process does not require Internet access. Those *post* recording portions of the process can be done later on using another Internet-enabled computer inside or outside the classroom.

THE SOUND FACTOR

There's no way around it, the ambient noise of the classroom will affect the nature and quality of the recordings you produce. As has been stated already, the type and purpose of an educational podcast project will determine the conditions needed to produce it. The podcasting classroom need not be as perfectly free of all sound as a professional recording or radio or television studio. Even commercial broadcasters have found it acceptable, even useful, to include ambient noise that can't be eliminated. Sometimes it actually adds flavor, character, and authenticity to the show. News reporters on the street include ambient noise there to good effect, broadcasts from traffic helicopters include the engine noise, and broadcasts from sporting events include the sound of large audiences reacting to the action on the field. This has become so much an accepted thing that at times one can detect that some of these broadcasts are actually enhanced by the inclusion of such sounds artificially. It is important to understand this when determining the level of extraneous noise to consider acceptable in school-based podcasting, as well as how it will actually affect the outcome of what is being attempted.

The guiding principle in all of this is clarity. Extraneous sound should not impede the audience's understanding of the principal audio content you produce. Such sound is noise and has to be controlled or eliminated. However, if the content of your classroom podcast is supposed to communicate that it is being produced in a typical classroom, then a level of classroom sound is either acceptable or perhaps, desirable. Again, the content dictates what is workable and what is not.

While sound drifting in from outside the classroom window or from the school corridor, at reasonable levels, may be fine to leave as is, conversations that are competing for listener attention will not be. For this reason even though classes of students may be organized into small collaborative groups to plan a number of podcasts within the class, they may not be able to do the recording portion of the work simultaneously. A good way to handle this situation would be to set aside specific times, after the individual group podcasts have been planned and are ready to go, to record groups one at a time. This would be true for solo or duo recordings, as well.

When the time for recording has arrived, the classroom can be set up as a theater. A single table toward the head of the class can hold the equipment needed and a student or two may sit at the table alongside the performers to function as recording engineers or helpers. In this way, those involved in delivering whatever type of performance is called for will have their attention freed from these chores. The teacher's role will be to facilitate and manage the flow of the class and the bulk of the students who at this point are not directly involved in recording the specific podcast being produced can function as an audience. Their reactions to the performance going on at the head of the class may be planned as part of what is recorded. It is also their opportunity to learn from observing and analyzing the experience and efforts of peers, a valuable dimension to learning.

Alternately, depending on a broad range of factors, some teachers may opt to do the actual recording at a time other than during class, after school perhaps or during a preparation period, pulling a small group of students away from other, whole group assignments.

WHOLE CLASS PODCAST CREATION ACTIVITIES

During the great days of radio programs were produced following the format of live shows one would see in a theater. A notable difference however, was the focus on audio content produced and broadcast, rather than the content being a visually oriented item like a play or vaudeville show. The other important difference is that the audience rather than being the recipient of the content produced in radio shows, was actually part of the production process and its applause and other responses were part of the content produced. This last point establishes a context for effective whole class content projects.

The whole class approach to producing podcasts, if structured so that it emulates the classic live radio program format of the 1930s and 1940s, can be a highly valuable and easily managed activity for classrooms. As with the classic radio programs, much of the work involved in producing the show has little or nothing to do with the technology or act of recording or broadcasting. Planning, writing, rehearsing, and so forth all are essential and wonderful platforms for a variety of authentic activities across the curriculum.

In this whole class approach, after the group has planned and written its podcast, it is convened as it would be for whole group exercise. In this case instead of simply using a chalkboard or interactive whiteboard as the repository for brainstorming or whole group notes, there is a central area for the microphones where the "action" will take place. This is little different than bringing in an item for a science demo or other special activity in which the class's attention is focused on a centrally located spot in order to get the benefit of whatever resource is being used.

The teacher, or a designated student(s), facilitates the flow of the activity by keeping the class on its (pre) scripted or outlined plan. Of course, unlike the experience of those who produced "live" radio, the class's audio content is to be recorded and then edited. This is a relatively low risk situation in which items that are not done satisfactorily can be done again until the desired result is achieved.

The whole class podcasting center can be cobbled together from a spare table, a few chairs, and a microphone or several microphones. In its simplest form, one microphone will sit in the middle of the table between the moderator, or announcer, and the two or three class members who may be called to sit at the table to "perform" during any given segment. In the case of a Q & A format in which class members or guests offer questions to be answered, the podcasting center should be set up to accommodate the questioner's brief presence at the table, so that he can speak to the microphone and the question can be well recorded as part of the session.

MODIFYING THE CLASSROOM LAYOUT

For the whole class podcast production the standard classroom layout of furniture will suffice so long as all members of the class can easily hear the flow of conversation from their individual seats. If that's not the case, perhaps having all members move closer to the podcasting center will improve the situation.

As guests are likely to be part of the content of your podcast sessions, placing chairs for them near the center would be wise. Minimizing movement within the room and the noise it generates will prove helpful and having guests seated near the podcast center until they are instructed to move up to the microphone will help.

Once you begin making whole class podcasting sessions part of your class routine the need to eliminate distractions that tend to creep in continually will make itself felt. Classroom routines must be established so that class members do not need to move about the classroom or in or out of the classroom during recording sessions. Perhaps a 45 minute moratorium on lavatory breaks will be useful. A sign posted on the door to the classroom clearly indicating that none are to enter during the podcast session is another very useful way to eliminate distractions.

SMALL GROUP AUDIO CONTENT ACTIVITIES

An important variation to the approach above involves small group podcasts. The teacher facilitated whole group approach models how the production of something authentic and important relies on leadership and organization. The small group podcast approach is a wonderful opportunity for students to learn about collaboration, team work, and spontaneous independent problem solving.

Producing projects in groups of four is a practical and meaningful way for teachers to structure such an activity. In this model, each group of three to five students (four on average) produces its own podcast, sharing not only the project, but a single set of equipment. Each group should have a laptop computer, a microphone, and at least one set of headphones. Also, they will need portable media, preferably a thumb or jump drive, with which to back up, store, and transport their work. If the laptop used for this project is to be used for other activities and/or by other students, this is essential.

For this approach to podcast activities, the aggregate amount of noise produced by the entire class will prove to be a great challenge. Each group should have a table they can share, gather around, and set up their equipment. Because of the noise factor, many will find that moving these tables to the far corners of the classroom helps. On the other hand, moving furniture is time consuming and distracting in and of itself, and assigning the groups to tables roughly in the spot where they will be used is better than having the youngsters move tables across the room each time they are to work on their project.

With the typical class being comprised of 30 students the set up for this approach will likely involve six or seven groups of students each at an individual table. Small collaborative projects done in such groups in many areas or the classroom has been a standard feature of the instructional landscape. The planning and writing portions of the group's podcasts present little that is outside the parameters of typical collaborative group projects. The noise and sound factor, however, will require some classroom management beyond that. Depending on the unique physical set up of each classroom and the character and sophistication of each group of students, the aggregate noise generated, may represent a serious impediment to the successful completion of the projects, which require a clear recording as an end product.

It is hard to predict the results for any given classroom as the acoustic properties of the space and the audio qualities of the hardware and software used include so many variables. A test should be undertaken to determine what challenges will be presented. If it turns out that allowing all groups to discuss their work and record their projects simultaneously is problematic, then through classroom management the project can be made to happen. Groups will simply have to take turns. While one group is allowed to record its session, the others may have to be involved in activities that contribute to a relatively quiet and supportive environment for them. There are other types of activities that can be implemented while the recording group has the floor.

INDIVIDUAL AUDIO CONTENT ACTIVITIES

Based on the success of whole group or small group podcasting projects, it may appear that individual podcast projects are the logical next step. In many respects this is true. With a few projects completed the technical side will seem familiar and manageable. However, setting up a typical classroom to support 30 odd students all podcasting at once is difficult in the extreme. Teachers who feel the need for this, bless their hearts, might consider letting the students do some of the recording at home (assuming they have computers available there, or with portable digital recorders if they don't) and having individual editing chores done in the school computer lab, assuming this is available and or the lab teacher is amenable to collaborating on the project.

POST RECORDING

The issue of ambient noise is less crucial during the editing or post recording portion of the project, assuming that students are to be assigned to handle some of these chores directly. Because this involves a number of tech skills that the students may not have acquired, teachers early in their podcasting experience may opt to handle this part of the process on their own.

If collaborative groups are the organizational principle used, allowing each group to play back its content with desktop speakers at low volume as they work on editing and enhancing it may be reasonable, so long as each group can hear what it is doing clearly and not interfere with the work of others. A scenario like moving the groups to corners of the classroom or taking advantage of alcoves, offices, or spare classrooms, may help if this approach is taken. An alternate approach is to use a splitter box or Y-adapter that allows the sound from a single audio jack to be distributed to several headsets (Y adapter available at Radio Shack).

Assuming students have the ability to take laptops home, some of the editing process may be best assigned as homework or extra credit. Similarly, depending on the school and organization, podcast projects begun in subject classrooms may be continued during this portion of the process in the school computer/media lab with the collaboration of the technology teacher. Schools and classrooms vary so widely in their physical challenges and advantages that it is impossible to do more here than point out the factors to take into account and suggest some strategies with which to respond.

REVIEWING AND LEARNING FROM DRAFTS

After the podcast has been produced, or after benchmark or draft versions have been produced, it may be advantageous to hold a session, in which it is played for the group and they respond to it, giving feedback and suggestions. This may take the form of mid production sessions in which the group listens to its work to make mid course corrections to brain storm new ideas and fresh content, or simply to admire and understand what they've done before they send it out into the world and begin work on the next project.

This may take the form of classic whole group instruction; the teacher plays back the audio that's been produced and conducts a brain storming session to get a consensus of reactions from the students. Playback for the whole group will require a set of ancillary speakers that plug into the laptop the file is played on. There are many serviceable speakers that can be purchased at a very low cost if the classroom does not already have a set.

This part of the process is essential, as involvement in the planning and editing parts of the podcasting continuum give a very different understanding of what's been done than simply listening to a playback of a finished product.

This can be extended to post broadcasting as well, with students assigned to come in to class to report on and discuss reactions they've gotten from a broadcast that has gone out to the community, or beyond. To bring the process full circle, they may interview listeners, recording the interviews digitally with an inexpensive digital recorder, and then bring those in to class to share and discuss further. The particular emphasis on using these recorded reactions could be as the jumping off place for planning future podcast projects down the road.

SCHEDULING CONSIDERATIONS

Sticking to a schedule that all know and agree to follow is a useful routine to establish as part of podcasting projects. Nothing will make for greater difficulty than the absence from school of a key interviewer or guest for a class podcast activity. If these are possibilities, then having key roles covered by "buddies" understudies or doubles who can relieve each other is wise.

Making scheduled sessions part of the routine will help. However it is useful to understand that podcasting is at least as challenging on focus and concentration as any other classroom activity and should not be scheduled for an amount of time longer than any other sort of activity could reasonably be expected to hold the attention of a group of youngsters. If anything, once the novelty has worn off, the pressure to get it all right may indicate that podcasting be scheduled for a slightly shorter session than other activities. Furthermore, there is a fair amount of preparation, set up, and break down that is part of the activity and the times these require should be accounted for in the activity's time planning.

Again, minimizing distractions is essential and coordinating with the school administration so that PA announcements, fire drills, and the other seemingly unavoidably endless "time outs" are at any absolute minimum will help.

THE VISUAL

While simple podcasts (excluding the possibility of vlogs or video blogs) are purely audio there are some visual aspects of the overall process for students. For many podcasters promoting their show involves continually informing potential audiences about it and enticing them to listen and share their knowledge about it with other potential listeners. Once the class's podcast has acquired a name, it may prove effective to have the students produce several signs announcing it to the world and identifying the class as the producer. This will serve both to inform others about the podcast and to deepen the class's esprit de corps and commitment to and identity with the show. You may wish to post a sign outside the classroom that will serve as a billboard informing all that a podcasting class is being conducted and another inside the classroom establishing the podcast as a point of pride and a focus for class activities.

Establishing a bulletin board or posting area within the classroom will allow the class to maintain its identity as a podcasting class during those times when it is not involved in creating podcasts. This area may hold photographic documentation of the class's podcasting efforts, schedules, e-mail from listeners, "how to" information for the podcasting students, and so forth.

As is indicated by other areas of this book, podcasts are often done best as part of a broader effort that can involve other sorts of online information dissemination. Podcasters generally use Web sites, blogs, e-mail lists, and other digital information media to expand the efficacy of the podcast. These can be enhanced at times with digital photos and making the shooting of digital photos part of the overall podcasting program is a good enhancement. In line with this, setting up the classroom mindful of the fact that there will be graphic record keeping accompanying efforts to produce audio content, is a good idea. Photos taken may enhance the podcast's Web site, but they may also be posted in the classroom or just outside it and this should be considered part of the classroom set up for podcasting projects.

ORGANIZED LISTENING

Listening to podcasts, whether it be the group's own podcasts or those of others is an important part of the overall podcasting program and the classroom needs to be set up in order to make that happen well.

Listening is likely to happen as an instructional activity in several modes. Certainly, part of the time the group will want to listen together to a piece of audio content as a whole group activity. In this case the need will be for the content to be played through speakers powerful enough to ensure that all members of the class can hear it clearly. The fact that the class is generating this level of noise calls for ensuring that it not interfere with other activities going on in the school beyond the classroom.

At other times the entire group, or large portions of it may be called on to listen to podcasts, or individually. In those instances either an MP3 player will be needed for each student, or a laptop, and optional headphone splitters. In the case of the laptop, depending on the physical and acoustic set up of the classroom, the audio content may be listened to over the laptop's built in speaker or through a set of inexpensive headphones.

As mentioned previously, if using laptops, storage and security, distribution, and power are factors that must be accounted for. In this instance of individual listening as a whole group activity, many will find the use of MP3 players more practical, as they allow the students to sit without regard to any sort of connection to the Internet, hard wired or wireless, or power source while in use. MP3 Players do have their own requirement, generally needing to be tethered to a computer briefly to be charged and to have the desired content downloaded or transferred to them. Their low cost is a factor in their favor, while their small size will require efforts to keep them secure from theft or loss.

LOBBY DISPLAYS

Podcasting will draw attention to itself. As it is a performance, a type of activity that is well understood and appreciated within the culture of schooling, it has a special quality. Consequently, even though podcasts are not live performances, they are things that invite being shared and shown off. Many will find it worthwhile to extend the classroom, in a sense, so that the podcasting program (not just the podcasts themselves) can be taken out into the school and displayed much the same as would be a student art exhibit. This might take the form of posters announcing the podcast posted in the school or perhaps, a kiosk-type exhibit in which a school computer is made available in a public spot inviting listeners to sit and sample the podcasts. Parent night exhibits done this way would be well appreciated.

Podcasting is a practice that can be aligned with a school's instructional goals and need not represent a digression from them. In fact, in many respects they can be a valuable enhancement to teaching and learning. While setting up the classroom to accommodate the needs of podcasting does require thoughtful and informed reflection and effort, and in some cases minimal expenditure of funds, it will pay big dividends. The relevance that podcasting adds to the instructional program, its ability to excite, motivate, and engage youngsters, and the pride and esprit de corps that it will establish for school communities are tremendous benefits. Podcasting, because it is a medium of communication, brings people together in many respects. In this sense it is a practice that can strengthen the school as a community of learners, an important aspect of schooling, although a difficult one to achieve.

CHAPTER 12

WHO'S USING PODCASTING IN EDUCATION AND HOW

APPROACHES TO USING PODCASTING FOR TEACHING AND LEARNING

As podcasting matures, the number of educators adopting it continues to grow very rapidly. This large number, however, tends to sort itself out into an ample, but finite number of approaches and practices. This chapter provides a survey of these. However, it should be kept in mind that teachers who embrace podcasting are often creative types and tweak the practice to suit their specific needs. Consequently, a Web search will turn up a great number of examples; many of which may not fall into a specific category perfectly or that may combine approaches. Additionally, because podcasting has been adopted from the pre-K through graduate school levels, this chapter offers examples across grade and ability levels.

COURSE CASTING

Course casting is the practice of recording a live class or lecture and then offering that recording as a podcast. Although this was one of the first applications of podcasting for education and has become a popular practice, it has severe limitations. This artless use of technology produces a

Podcasting for Teachers: Using a New Technology to Revolutionize Teaching and Learning,
Revised Second Edition, pp. 181–197

truly *catch as catch* can product. Generally what's captured, in addition to any content of real value, are long periods of "dead air," spaces in which nothing of interest is recorded, paper shuffling, calling the class to order, as well as students and filing out of the classroom. Usually no effort is made to edit course casts to eliminate any of this. The quality of the podcast is very low from a production standpoint. The sound quality is often poor with inaudible elements, vast differences in volume from moments when the speakers are near the single microphone set up in the classroom or far away. Also, no effort is made to clean up the sound or enhance it with the functions designed to do this included with much of the software available for podcasting.

Worse than the considerations discussed above are the ways that course casts are fit into the instructional program. While instructors often point to these "captures" of their lectures as having value for review, or for make-up in the case of students who miss a class, students very frequently feel that if the class is provided as a podcast, then there may be little point in actually attending in the flesh, as listening to the podcast is more convenient than actually going to class. As will be seen below, when this approach to podcasting is compared to others, what's clear is that course casters miss the point of producing podcasts as extras and enhancements; more content provided through a different modality in order to provide a richer educational experience.

COMMON PODCASTING FORMATS OF VALUE FOR EDUCATION TODAY

Here are some common ways that podcasting adds real value to contemporary education.

"Good to Go" Podcasts: Using Podcasts as Acquired Content

Many podcasts are produced for a general audience that simply requires listeners access them for use. These podcasts can be appropriated as instructional resources, often providing wonderful content not available through other means. Bringing authentic materials into the learning experience has long been a favored practice of teachers and podcasting is one way that technology makes this previously difficult to achieve practice infinitely easier.

We are approaching a point at which print publishers and producers of broadcast content reflexively provide much of their material in podcast format as part of the continuum of media they utilize. Because so much material is produced, surveying this body of content is likely to turn up numerous items appropriate for students across a wide spectrum of subject areas and grade levels. Even a simple search engine-based Web search will facilitate this type of effort greatly.

A good example of this is RD Out Loud from the perennially popular print magazine, *Reader's Digest*. The Web site for *Reader's Digest* proudly announces: "*Expert advice, celebrity interviews, fun facts, and dramatic true stories-whenever and wherever you want*" (Reader's Digest, 2007a, para. 1). As it clearly anticipates that podcasting is new to a great many of its readers, it offers further:

> Q. What is RD Out Loud?
> A. RD Out Loud is a weekly podcast from Reader's Digest, hosted by Editor-in-Chief Jackie Leo. It's a weekly audio show that has celebrity interviews, health and fitness advice, food and nutrition information, dramatic true stories, family and relationship tips, and more. (Reader's Digest, 2007b, para. 1-2)

Among its sections—People, Health & Fitness, Food & Nutrition, Dramatic True Stories, and others—are to be found many items that clearly align with subjects currently taught in our schools.

Another of this type of podcast with very clear connections to the classic curriculum offered in schools is Learn Spanish—Survival Guide. This podcast's Web site states:

> The information in these podcasts is for those people who travel to a Spanish speaking destination and are looking for a language survival guide. It's also for those people who would like to brush up on their Spanish or learn more for communication in general. (Spencer, 2006, para. 1)

The experience that this podcast can bring to a traditionally organized class represents an opportunity to vary the types of material and activities offered students while staying within the general parameters of the curriculum.

One interesting example of this is the episode titled Learn Body Parts with Simon Says in which a party game format is employed to educate and entertain.

Teacher Generated Podcasts— Creating One's Own Instructional Materials

"Good to Go" podcasts are also produced by teachers for teachers and their students, although at this time in lesser numbers than those produced by organizations set up to provide content. Here are a few worthwhile examples.

Audio Guides

John Jay professor, Greg Umbach, created a podcast as an audio guide for a museum visit he assigned his class. This professor of history created a podcast as a gallery guide to enhance the assignment and facilitate viewing an exhibition of historical artifacts. While he might have assigned this activity in the more traditional way of having the students read a variety of items he either identified or wrote personally for them, he used the podcasting technology to provide a greatly enriched experience for his students.

The resulting podcast audio guide was tailored specifically for the students in his course, and not a general guide as any visitor to the museum might listen to. This one was created specifically for the class, steering the students to particular items on display and providing commentary purely from the perspective of the members of the class.

This is becoming an application of podcasting in which the technology is distinguishing itself as the very best way to carry out a significant use, the gallery guide. It also makes the production of such guides far easier and more inexpensive, thus inducing the production of a great many more such guides for a great many more exhibitions.

Content Items

- The Bobby Bucket Show is a lively, spirited podcast that informs youngsters about books, gives perspectives on their meaning, and generally makes them and their significance accessible. A talk show format is used with engaging conversations between Bobby Bucket (the adult book guide) and Little Bucket (the child fellow traveler) who read excerpts and trade insights, all to the benefit of young readers.

  The Bobby Bucket podcasts are accessible through a blog that reads "The Bobby Bucket Show!—Bucket of Books!—A Podcast for Kids, Parents, and Readers of all ages! Celebrating READING with Books, Music, Author Interviews, and more!"

  In this podcast Bob, accompanied by a young student side kick, presents a potpourri of ideas, tips, resources, and commentary on the experience of being literate.
- The Singing Science Teacher is a podcast produced by Rick Charles, a seventh grade science teacher. Rick provides middle school level science content as songs. His podcast Science on the Wild Side can be accessed at http://www.podfeed.net/podcast/Science+On+The+Wild+Side+Show/9279

- Dan Bach, a mathematics teacher at Diablo Valley College produces Dan's Mathcast, a podcast intended as a math instructional resource. This informative, instructive, and entertaining podcast can be found at the Web site http://www.dansmath.com/pages/podpage.html
- Mr. Langhorst teaches eighth grade American history at South Valley Junior High School in Liberty, Missouri. He produces the podcast Speaking of History which can be found at the Web site: http://speakingofhistory.blogspot.com. This blog's header reads:

  > History—Speaking of History podcast and blog is maintained by an 8th grade American History teacher in Missouri who attempts to use technology to enhance the curriculum. They are teaching about George, Thomas and Abe using the latest technology. (Langhorst, 2006, para. 1)

Student Generated Podcasts (Student and Teacher Podcasts)

- Global Issues Initiative. Student-conducted interviews tackling pressing global issues (http://globalissuesinitiative.podbean.com/) produced by The Woodside Priory School is a series of podcasts in which students interview professionals in the San Francisco Bay area. The issues are identified by students, as are the invited professionals. Covered issues include environmentally responsible entrepreneurship, activism, and perspective.
- Great Gatsby Reports. An interesting example of podcast as student report can be found at the Web site of Vineland North High School (Vineland, NJ) on the page Podcasts by Ms. Woodruff's 7th period—College English II classes http://www.vineland.org/vhs/north/English/index.gatsby2.html

  This podcast and Web site is based on *The Great Gatsby* which is set in the 1920's. *The Great Gatsby* is a novel of great suspense and controversy. It emphasizes aspects of love and romance in different ways while focusing on a man's unwillingness to let go of the past. It is a novel in which people's morality and integrity are tested in the American struggle to gain power and stature by any means possible.
- Performances: Student performances, especially those that are fully auditory, are a natural connection for the use of podcasts. Perfor-

mances are an established instructional practice, providing both focus and culminating activities for extended learning experiences. They are also an established format for alternative assessment of student learning.

Schools are beginning to use podcasts for this purpose. One clear example is the Cranbrook Middle School of Bloomfield Hills, MI.

The School's Cranbrook Composers' Podcasts Web site states, "When school is in session, we will post 2 podcasts per week featuring student compositions created, produced, and podcasted by students in music triarts class at Cranbrook Kingswood Middle School" (Ruthmann, 2005. para. 1).

- Reflections on learning and life: The Caracas International School in Venezuela has established a Web site as a part of its podcasting program which provides students an opportunity to report to an audience on their reflections on learning activities. One interesting example is that of a 12th grade student discussing the art work she has produced while a student there. In this video podcast episode Neudis Abreu, a senior at CIC, discusses the importance of art in her life. She also comments on some of her paintings.

Class Casts and School Casts

Just as the school newspaper has been an educational institution that serves a great many goals and purposes within the context of school, to a lesser degree the school radio station is a longstanding tradition. It has been increasingly more challenging for educators to provide opportunities to do school radio as the technology resources required have been, with the exception of a very small percentage of fortunate, well funded schools, beyond the reach of the average public school. For the most part, those school that have been able to engage in this wonderful activity have done so by appropriating the school's public address system for mock broadcasts. These however, are limited in where, how, and when they can be produced and listened to. Furthermore, one of their most serious drawbacks is the inability for students to record their shows easily and effectively.

Podcasting changes this, giving schools the opportunity to produce a very professional type of content that offers great flexibility in scheduling and availability to listener. This is so much so that with podcasting, schools not only can provide a school radio experience, but can do so on such a broad basis that individual classes, clubs, and departments can have their own podcasts.

A good example of class casting podcasts can be seen in activities done at Jamestown School in Arlington, VA.

Here's a sample class post from the site. It illustrates, among other aspects of class podcasting, how podcasts can be used to archive special events for on-demand reference and sharing

> *Jamestown Settlement Field Trip "Talk Show" javascript:player* ('http://m2.slapcast.com/mp3/Jamestown/Jamestown-2006-12-01.mp3')
>
> *Posted on: 2 Dec 2006*
>
> *Ms. Cronin's fourth graders went on a field trip to the Jamestown Settlement in October (a 3 hour bus trip from Jamestown Elementary in Arlington). Here they discuss what they learned in a talk show format. (Jamestown Elementary School, 2006, para. 5)*

The Radio Popcorn podcasts produced by the students of the Kowloon Junior School are group efforts involving varied student work from interviews with adult experts, book reviews, narrated humor, and more. (http://clc.esf.edu.hk/GroupRenderRSS.asp?GroupID=410&ResourceID=73239)

School Casts. School radio is a very well established practice. A Wikipedia article titled "High School Radio" states "High school radio within the United states is almost as old as radio broadcasting itself." It outlines a great many difficulties in establishing and maintaining this rich body of student activities, citing among the most challenging "the expense involved with maintaining broadcast equipment," "Instructors or faculty involved with initially establishing the radio station leave or retire and the school is unable to find replacements," and "a general perception that radio technology is no longer as exciting to high school students as newer technologies such as the Internet" (Wikipedia, 2006, School Radio, para. 3-4).

The recently emerged podcasting technology addresses all of these challenges by virtue of its low cost, relatively easy learning curve, and relevance for youngsters due to the fact that it is Internet-based, being part of a body of technology applications currently much in vogue among digital natives. Furthermore, it makes radio an activity that can be done in schools in lower grades, as well. School districts no longer have to invest hard to come by resources in one or two large secondary schools.

School casts can be used to perform a variety of community building and performing functions. At Albermarle High School in Charlottesville, VA (part of Albemarle County Public Schools), for instance, the Albemarle High School Podcasts Web page carries podcasts of the principal's state of the school addresses, his way of getting a high priority organizational message out to the broad community involved with the school.

Beyond these purely functional school podcasts, increasingly common are school productions that convey the richness of student interest and enthusiasm. One example is FOOCast, produced by the students of Otautau School in New Zealand.

On their first episode a group of students introduce the school and the podcast, give a book review, and introduce the principal who gives a sincere, off the cuff interview to students in which she talks about her job and life. The podcast can be accessed at its Web site Otautau FOOCast.

The Coulee Kids Podcast is a good example of how a podcast can help a school community leverage a focusing activity to communicate to the greater world the depth and breadth of intellectual and social activity at a school. It is produced by teachers and students at Coulee School program of Longfellow Middle School in La Crosse, Wisconsin.

Another wonderful example is from the Chatham Middle School in Chatham, Massachusetts. A recent episode includes school news, interviews, coverage of the geography bee, a schoolwide event, reviews of school dramatic performances including specially recorded audio clips that illustrate by providing on the spot reflective interviews with student performers. Yet another good example is the News and Announcements from Dixie Heights High School (http://dixie.podbean.com/), from Kenton County school district in Kentucky.

Podcasts as Part of an Extended Package of Content

No matter how thorough or creative a teacher and those who support her instructional efforts, there are limits to what can be presented to students in terms of contact time, variety of activity, and volume and type of content available. Podcasting can help teachers who want to expand the body of what they set before their students find numerous ways to give more.

Another example of how podcasting can provide additional content presented in form and format that is different and that will add greatly to the overall instructional experience is the Classic Mistake podcast. In this example, real mistakes by math students are presented as the prompt for and focus of a wide variety of math problems. The producer, Nevil Hopley, currently head of math at George Watson's College, Edinburgh, Scotland, offers these as effective and out of the box ways to foster student engagement and promote alternative entry points for learning this difficult subject.

Capturing Appearances by Special Guests

Special guests have long been an important enhancement to instruction in schools. Unfortunately, these appearances, as rich as they may be, happen infrequently and are short of duration. Furthermore, often not all members of the school community can attend and take advantage of them. Recording and podcasting the appearances of special guests are a wonderful practice that enables a school to take full advantage of these windfall experiences.

The Baylor School of Chattanooga is a school that has made good use of this approach to podcasting. Through the school Web site the entire world can benefit from appearances and presentations made by guests, many of whom are alumni. One of these is Jamy Wheless, a digital animator at George Lucas's Industrial Light and Magic production company. The podcast's Web site states

> *Jamy Wheless '82 is a digital animator who has worked at George Lucas's Industrial Light and Magic for the past 10 years. He has created digital characters (for example, the Hulk and Yoda) for several recent blockbusters including Star Wars, Pirates of the Caribbean, Chronicles of Narnia, and many others. Students enjoyed hearing from Jamy about his craft. Here is some additional information about Jamy and his career. (Baylor School, 2006, para. 1)*

CASE STORY—LANGUAGE LEARNING, GLOBAL REACH, AND MOBILE CONTENT

One of the ways that podcasting enhances teaching and learning is to free the learning experience from the classroom and school, even from the home where homework and studying are done, making it a truly anywhere, anytime opportunity. Podcasting makes it possible for students to remind connected to the school, their teachers, and their peers, but untethered to even the Web, computers, wireless, and networks while they are off on their own.

A good example of how podcasting can positively impact learning this way is ESL Podcast. This podcast provides practical English lessons for those in need of intense, quick, and authentic content to promote the acquisition of English. It can be listened to on demand, repeatedly on the go. ESL Podcast is developed, written and produced by Dr. Jeff McQuillan and Dr. Lucy Tse. Their collaboration illustrates how an educational podcasting can also include students. Dr. Tse scripts story ideas and records many of the dialogs. Dr. Jeff serves as the host and reads scripts and provides explanations (ESLPOD, 2006)

The background information on their Web site provides good insight into purposes and processes in podcasting for teaching and learning:

> ***Why are you doing this podcast?***
> *For many people around the world, learning English is very important. Unfortunately, there are very few useful, effective sources for learning English. Most people take English classes, which help them up to a certain point. ESL Podcast is designed to help you continue to improve your English.*
>
> ***What's so different about ESL Podcast?***
> *Well, first, all of our podcasts are free to anyone who wants them. Second, ESL Podcast uses a very different approach than other courses or Web sites.*
>
> *We believe the fastest way to improve your English is to listen to conversations and discussions you can understand. Many people try to improve their English by listening or reading things that are too difficult. They understand only 40-50%, which means they are wasting half of their time!* (ESLPOD, 2005, para. 3-5)

Another example is the Authors in Your Pocket podcast which gives discussions about books, writing, and related aspects of literature.

> *We provide a weekly podcast that includes the latest book news, insightful one-on-one interviews with your favorite literary personalities, and monthly book club Q&A sessions with the authors themselves......*
>
> *With the emerging popularity of podcasting we have expanded our services to envelop this new "audio on demand" technology, giving our listeners the control they are becoming increasingly used to in the digital world. The best part is ... they have total control over when, where, and how to listen to our shows.*
>
> *The iPod frenzy doesn't stop at music! What better way for our readers to really connect with their favorite or emerging authors than to hear them talk about writing, their books, and their lives. (Tricom Podcasts, n.d., para. 1-3)*

CASE STORY—CAPTURING—ARCHIVING—SHARING: A KINDERGARTEN TEACHER USES PODCASTING

Numerous teachers at the Creek View Elementary School in Alpharetta, Georgia engage in podcasting and related tech-supported activities.

Kindergarten Teacher, Kathy Shields describes her efforts as follows on her blog titled Small Voices.

> *Small Voices podcast is produced by Kathy Shields, Kindergarten Teacher in Georgia in order to encourage literacy skills by providing a wider audience for students—small voices, where being small is a BIG deal! (Shields, 2007a, para. 1)*

Ms. Shields, uses podcasts (some of them enhanced with video) at times in a somewhat traditional way, to capture and archive student performances that represent proving behaviors of learning. But she and her colleagues also use them as a way to capture special activities that are part of the general instructional program at the school. This approach to educating young children is a well-established practice that goes a long way toward developing school esprit de corps, well socialized students, and an appreciation for learning.

A good example is the podcast blog entry below from the event WRAD Day (Write and Read All Day)

> *I met Congressman Price in my PJs! He visited CVES on WRAD day; a day of writing and reading all day in pjs. Students stretched out on slippery sleeping bags wearing fuzzy slippers. Favorite stuffed bears took flight and we all snuggled together to hear a stream of storytellers. Tom Price must have been surprised to see how the students were able to shift gears and demonstrate a typical reading center rotation using technology in the midst of mayhem. (Shields, 2007b, para 1)*

Another interesting dimension to the way this group of educators uses these technology tools, and those of Podomatic, their podcasting resource of choice that provides these, is the social networking functions associated with podcasting.

While creating and serving an audience for these very young students is as much an issue as it is for their older peers, their content is not of great interest to the world in general (other than to educators who may want to reflect on these activities as foci and models.)

Pushing this small, highly specialized groups' content by an RSS feed is probably content distribution overkill for this group's needs. These episodes truly are produced episodically, not with predictable regularity or great frequency. However, their audience building needs are real and Podomatic offers them a blog function under each blog posting that encourages audience members to email individual episodes to parties that may be interested in them: parents, district administrators, classes with whom they may have an agreement to swap content they produce, and so forth.

Furthermore, inspecting the "friends/add a friend," "fans of this show," and "favorite links" functions encourages networking among colleagues and colleagues of colleagues, a word of mouth, grassroots type of function that works well and may even encourage viral aspects of dissemination eventually.

Case Story Podcasting for Professional Development

Podcasts as professional development can take various forms. This book provides an entire chapter on this subject, but for completeness of this chapter, a number of examples are included below.

In many instances the shape of a podcast created for this purpose is something like that of other distance education-based formats for professional development, relating somewhat to the format of a traditional live class. In others podcasting takes the audience to real world professional development events allowing those who could not attend the opportunity to benefit. Finally, in still others the professional development is provided much as a standard radio program.

Because time is one of the very most limiting factors in delivering professional development, podcasting's ability to make content available during periods of time that educators have traditionally not been able to take control and advantage of, is likely to make it a very significant medium for this very important purpose. Following are a few examples of podcasts for professional development.

Teachers Teaching Teachers

The ADHD Podcaster can be found at its Web site *which describes it as*

> *The premier podcast on the Internet giving the truth about ADHD. Live updates of the latest developments in the field of psychology neuropsychology and nutritional medicine that will help eliminate ADHD. Turn ADHD into an advantage not a disability.* (Lo, 2006, para. 1)

Using podcasting to provide professional development (PD) in this area, and others like it is very significant. While few teachers, others than the minority who receive special needs specific training as preparation for work with a special education population of students, will ever receive any in-depth ongoing PD in how to work with students who demonstrate Attention Deficit Hyperactivity Disorder, the vast majority of teachers will have to work with such students during some portion, if not during the bulk of, their teaching careers. A general classroom fifth grade teacher for instance, will likely have to dedicate those few PD opportunities on developments in general literacy and mathematics instruction, for instance, without the luxury of devoting time to ADHD or any of the myriad of other items she might benefit from.

Professional Educators who Podcast Professional Development *On Demand*

Our popular weekly series Teachers' Podcast, geared for K-12 educators and their educational technology learning needs, curricular applications, and educational research and news, is an example of a professor and a seasoned educational administrator and teacher who provide professional development "on demand" via podcasting (http://www.podcastforteachers.org).

In addition, we also offer a less frequent Transformation Education Live with many of the same content areas, but the focus is on higher education issues, higher education teaching and learning and distance education. This series is hosted primarily by Dr. King and Paige Esissinger, but they are frequently joined by guests and other colleagues on Transformation Education LIVE! (http://www.transformationed.com/podcast).

A third podcast done in this same vein of professional development is Adventures in Transformative Learning (Dr. Barbara Heuer and Dr. Kathy King) where we serve the needs of both adult educators, workplace trainers, and administrators in understanding adult learning, organizational issues, leadership, adult development theory, and practice. This series has the same emphasis of portable, practical, and *powerful* content, which is selected based on the specific audience and by gathering experts in those fields (http://www.podcastforteachers.org/atl).

Schools That Podcast

Once the practice of podcasting has been adopted by a community of educators/learners, it often becomes a schoolwide initiative with podcasting adapted for a variety of purposes. Grandview Elementary School's (Monsey, NY) "Top of the Fold" site is a good example.

In fact, the school librarian is interviewed in an audio/video post in The School Library Journal's SJU.com, an online journal, in which she explains the program at the school in detail with embedded media examples.

Podcasts are used as instructional materials here. In a unit, explained and highlighted on the school's storytelling Grandview Library Blog about the Japanese inspired literary form Kamishibai Storytelling it gives examples of folktales read and offered as podcasts which offer a polished reading by an experienced reader guide, on demand whenever, wherever desired.

There are many examples to be had on this site of audio and graphic enhanced podcasts of student reports. Some of these are individual student work (The Cat), some are class presentations of compilations of individual student work (nine related individual third grade book reviews titled 5 Star Books), and some are of group or team reports (2nd Graders Learn About Sea Turtles in which various individual students contribute to a single group recording).

There is also professional development, a good example of which can be seen in the librarian's own piece titled "Where's My Sock" which is a carefully narrated and illustrated report on a series of related prereading exercises to prepare youngsters to read this book and to extend their learning about it and the experience of reading a book and its significance. This can also function as a window into school activities for parents.

OUT OF THE BOX PODCASTING

While the above categories give insight into common ways that podcasting can be well put at the service of education they are not intended to be viewed as definitive. Categories often are most useful for practitioners at the beginning of an involvement with a resource or a new technology. As experience is accrued, the use of such resources becomes more spontaneous, something that is reached for as a solution intuitively, when the practitioner's sense of tapping the right tool to satisfy a specific need suggests that one among many tools and practices is best.

The use of podcasting or "keycasting" to quote a term coined on the fly to describe it is a good example. Our first "keycast," "panelcast," "participatory podcast event," podcast came about as a convergence of a number of prominent needs for a large community of educators in the New York City area. Tech-to-Go! was a series of annual technology conferences for K-12 educators held on Saturdays as free events for those teachers interested in attending on a day off in order to walk away with a handful of new (for them), free tech integration practices and resources to support them. At the fifth of these conferences, which was held at Fordham Preparatory High School, located on the Bronx campus of Fordham University, a traditional, guest speaker-centered keynote address delivered during a

Take AWAY Activity—E-mail it, Write it, or Podcast it		
If you have ideas about educational technology and education and podcasting …		
If	*Then*	*E-mail Details*
If you have ideas about educational technology and education and podcasting …	E-mail to us and become a TTPOD SPOTLIGHT entry on for The Teachers' Podcast	Subject: **TTPOD Spotlight Idea** Teacherspodcast@gmail.com
You have a podcast for consideration in the Who's Using Podcasting List	E-mail your podcast URL and feed to us Who's Using Podcasting	Subject: **Who's Using Podcasting** Teacherspodcast@gmail.com
You have seen a good article about podcasting, blogging, wkis, and more uses or new media	Email your podcast url to us Who's Using Podcasting	Subject: **Who's Using Podcasting** Article Teacherspodcast@gmail.com
YOU want to write (or have written) an article about ed tech, podcasting, blogging, wikis	E-mail your article and permission to use it to Teachers Podcast for possible posting in the new Reflection Corner Teacherspodcast@gmail.com	E-mail to: Teacherspodcast@gmail.com Subject: Article for TTPOD Reflection Corner
In order to keep the word current and out there about what is happening in the field we need people like you be sharing with us and to have places to share that work! So keep in touch with Teacherspodcast@gmail.com		

Figure 12.1. Take AWAY Activity—E-mail it, Write it, or Podcast it.

traditional morning plenary session was replaced with a "keycast." In addition to the organizers' inability to locate an appropriate keynote speaker to address the population of attendees, the community needed a rallying event, a public forum in which it could recharge its spirit as it evaluated its progress and state at the moment. Furthermore, the technology of podcasting was just emerging at that moment as an important item that all technology using teachers (the precise profile of those who would attend the conference) ought to have had good insights into. For those reasons, having all in attendance participate in a panel informed and community forum podcast was the perfect format with which to break from the traditional.

The resulting podcast distinguishes itself from other incidentally recorded and uploaded conference events in a number of ways. To begin with, this event was planned as a podcast. Attendees were invited to attend it knowing it would become a podcast and invited to participate in the community forum section of the program as participants to be included in the podcast that would result. Furthermore, pains were taken in the planning of the event and the setting up of the physical space in which it took place to support the best quality sound capture possible, and the recording was edited carefully before the podcast was considered finished and posted. The result was a very satisfying out of the box live experience and podcast.

Elements of the Tech-to-Go! keycast certainly fall into the categories listed in the chapter above. And as is also true for numerous examples included in the chapter, there is inevitable crossover between categories, as well. The overarching point to be taken from this example, however, is that a group of educators with some experience in making use of podcasting as a possible solution for real education needs, as well as the technical "how to" dimension of this technology, adopted and adapted podcasting in a freeform way to establish a practice on the spur of the moment which was highly significant and meaningful for those involved.

CONCLUSION: AS EDUCATORS CONTINUE TO EMBRACE PODCASTING

We hope this chapter has sparked many ideas for you about how you might broaden the circle of educational podcasting. The field of podcasting in education is at the infancy of this digital implementation and we know that teachers and students will take us new places in months and years ahead. One of the resources Mark and I endeavor to continue to provide on a reasonably updated, and selective, basis is a list of exceptional uses of new media and podcasting in education at the Teachers' Podcast web site (http://teacherspodcast.org/resources/), hence the idea for this chapter. You can always check in there for your own benefit, to see what else has emerged or submit your ideas (see Figure 12.1).

RESOURCES

The ADHD Podcaster. http://www.theadhdspecialist.com/adhdblog/podcast.html
Adventures in Transformative Learning. http://www.podcastforteachers.org/ATL
Albemarle High School. http://web.mac.com/rcairnes/iWeb/Albemarle%20High%20School%20Podcast/Albemarle%20High%20School/Albemarle%20High%20School.html
Baylor School Podcasts. http://www.baylorschool.org/podcasts
Bobby Bucket. http://www.bobbybucket.com/blog/B96573213/index.html
Chatham Middle School New Podcast. http://feeds.feedburner.com/cmspodcastsClassic Mistake
Cranbrook Composer's Podcasts. http://cranbrookcomposers.blogspot.com
Dan's Mathcast. http://www.dansmath.com/pages/podpage.html

ESLPOD. http://eslpod.com
FOOcast. http://podcastnz.com/index.php?main_page=product_music_info&cPath=4&products_id=27
The Great Gatsby. http://www.vineland.org/vhs/north/English/index.gatsby2.html
Jamestown Podcast. http://slapcast.com/users/Jamestown
Learn Spanish—Survival Guide. http://www.switchpod.com/cats.php?a=3171
Podcast for Teachers, Techpod. http://www.podcastforteachers.org
RD OUTLOUD. http://www.rd.com/openContentCategory.do?contentCategoryId=685
Science Lab Equipment. http://www.ci.bryanisd.org/1vision/Teacher%20Podcasts/04A32B1B-DAFB-4629-B4FC-077C79168D17.html
Science on the Wild Side. (n.d.). Retrieved January 9, 2007, from http://www.podfeed.net/podcast/Science+On+The+Wild+Side+Show/9279
The Singing Science Teacher. http://www.podfeed.net/podcast/Science+On+The+Wild+Side+Show/9279
Small Voices. http://kinderteacher.podomatic.com/
Speaking of History. http://speakingofhistory.blogspot.com/
The Teachers' Podcast. http://www.teacherspodcast.org
Transformation Education LIVE!. http://www.transformationed.com/podcast
Prof. Umbach. http://web.jjay.cuny.edu/~history/umbach/worldspring06/
York River Academy Podcast. http://scarpenter.libsyn.com/index.php?post_id=63159

CHAPTER 13

HOW TO PLAN PODCASTING-BASED ACTIVITIES FOR STUDENTS

Planning podcasting-based activities with students need not be difficult. In many respects the organizational and classroom management dimensions involved are highly similar to common practices for schools already. There is nothing new about project-based learning and the related phenomena of student performances and learning products are convenient ways to understand podcasting's connection to pedagogy. In many respects the production of podcasts will call for students to be organized for collaborative learning, and that too is established practice.

Hopefully, however, podcasting will attract some of the very substantial numbers teachers who haven't as yet had much experience with these approaches to instruction. This will call for podcast using teachers to enter what is for them, new and unfamiliar territory. Exploration of new teaching practices and approaches can be exhilarating and inspiring and can produce wonderful personal and professional growth.

For the students there are wonderful benefits, too. Podcasting-based activities offer enriched learning opportunities for those whose intelligences or whose particular learning styles may be served better by instruction that is not text-based exclusively.

Podcasting for Teachers: Using a New Technology to Revolutionize Teaching and Learning, Revised Second Edition, pp. 199–210

SUGGESTED PLANNING PROCESS

Like any unit of instruction, planning podcasting-based activities involves juggling many factors. Everything from instructional mandates, to the time available to produce required learning outcomes, to the resources available to support activities impacts the capacity, practicality, and desirability of a given approach or practice.

This chapter covers various factors to take into account in bringing podcasting into the classroom.

CURRICULUM

Podcasting has a natural fit with several of the overarching goals of language instruction areas (English language arts, English as a second language, and foreign language instruction). Furthermore, it has particular relevance and applicability for those areas that might be described as language across the curriculum, in other words the communications that are required to learn and demonstrate learning within the context of social studies, science, math, and other subject areas. Additionally, podcasting is a wonderful focus for students as they satisfy needs and requirements of technology skills learning.

The wise curriculum coordinator or teacher will see that there is a unique opportunity here to accomplish numerous goals simultaneously through the same project. Obviously, this opportunity is most accessible to elementary teachers who often have the responsibility of delivering instruction to youngsters in all or most curriculum areas. It is also often the case for such teachers that technology is one area in which there is a specialist teacher who teaches their class in the school's computer lab. These "computer lab teachers" are often highly interested in seeing their class, which is frequently considered a "minor" subject of lesser importance, brought into the mainstream instructional efforts of the school as it addresses its most high priority items, like literacy. A little effort to coordinate the lab's efforts with those of the core academic instruction classes can pay big dividends. This is also true of middle school, where coordinated efforts between discreet subjects like English language arts and science or social studies, which appear appealing and obvious on the conceptual level, are difficult to accomplish on the practical level. These connections can be made to happen through an intermediate activity or subject area like visual art or technology.

A full chapter devoted to plotting podcasting's connections to curriculum appears later in the book.

PEDAGOGY

Podcasting-based activities fall into three principal areas:

1. Podcasting can be used to support a traditional approach to instruction in the core academic areas. It is a relatively simple matter for an informed teacher to search and acquire podcast content to be presented to the class. Such audio content can be played easily to the class in a whole group instructional activity, substituting the digital audio items for textbooks or supplementary hard copy items, which make up the mainstay of such classes.
2. As was discussed in chapter 10, podcasting can also be used by teachers to produce the instructional content and materials they would like to use, but which they can't locate through other sources. Such podcast material is not intended to take the place of teaching but rather to extend the reach and availability of the teacher's voice to times other than class time.
3. Podcasting makes wonderful projects for students. These projects are highly motivating opportunities to produce an authentic product/performance to be presented to a real audience.

Because podcasting-based projects are a tremendous departure for many teachers from traditional-style lessons, it is worthwhile to touch base with basic principles of teaching and learning to ensure a firm pedagogical foundation as activities are planned. One highly valuable body of work that can help in this regard is The Principles of Learning (n.d.) developed by The Institute for Learning, a project of the Learning Research and Development Center of the University of Pittsburgh

The institute established a framework based on eight principles: clear expectations, fair and credible evaluations, recognition of accomplishment, accountable talk, socializing intelligence, self-management of learning, and learning as apprenticeship. While practically any progressive student learning activity will embody all or most of these, there are several that are particularly relevant as guideposts for podcasting-based activities.

Clear Expectations. In adopting podcasting it is essential that student activities do more than "involve" youngsters in an exciting new technology, that curriculum-based objectives for podcasting-based activities are set, and made known. Furthermore, podcasting is perfectly suited to capture, store, and disseminate examples of student work that meet those objectives.

Academic Rigor in a Thinking Curriculum. As active uses of knowledge, podcasting-based activities should be structured to provide a focus for learning core knowledge and provide opportunities for students to exercise high order thinking and problem-solving skills.

Accountable Talk. As part of podcasting-based activities, students should be able to defend and explain the decisions behind their work. Furthermore, podcasting provides an excellent opportunity to focus and capture this talk.

Socializing Intelligence. The authentic nature of student podcasts' real-world presence before an audience creates a learning context for which the responsibility for "intelligent" work is clear and focused.

PROJECT-BASED LEARNING AND AUTHENTIC ACTIVITIES

As mentioned in a previous chapter, student activities that produce recorded digital audio content fit squarely in the pedagogical philosophy of project-based learning. What focuses and guides such projects is that the student voices will really be heard and considered by a real audience, a distinction that makes it an "authentic" learning activity.

These two interrelated concepts have become very popular goals of progressive educators in recent years. Although the implementation of such approaches is still not the norm in our classrooms, the following passage taken from the Web site of Edutopia (2006), an influential publication put out by the George Lucas Education Foundation, illustrates their appeal to educators.

In project-based learning, students work in teams to explore real-world problems and create presentations to share what they have learned. Compared with learning solely from textbooks, this approach has many benefits for students, including:

- Deeper knowledge of subject matter;
- Increased self-direction and motivation; and
- Improved research and problem-solving skills (Edutopia, 2006, para. 1).

Furthermore, the following passage from the North Central Regional Educational Laboratory defines Authentic Learning in brief.

> Authentic learning is simply learning that takes place in a context similar to the context in which the knowledge might be used in the real world ... Authentic Learning simply means that learning must include both content and context if it is to be useful in the real world." (NCREL, 2006, para. 1)

It is establishing this context that is often challenging for teachers hoping to plan activities that vary from the traditional teacher-centered lecture and class discussion format. The production of a performance that will be offered to and heard by members of an invited and/or self selecting audience interested in specific topics is a path to accomplishing that, one that podcasts accomplish easily.

Those planning podcasting-based activities for students should maintain focus on them as the products of ongoing projects structured to support and culminate with the podcast as proving behavior or learning product. These products and performances should be authentic activities and products, having a real world connection and presented to a real world audience.

CLASSROOM PRACTICES

Presenting Podcasting-Based Activities to Students

A first experience with podcasting for a class might well be presented as a variation on an oral report or a group presentation. Both are traditional activities commonly done in our classrooms. By using these activity formats, for which podcasting has obvious and clear connections, much of the confusion that might happen by other approaches can be avoided. Furthermore, once a culture of digital audio and podcasting has been established in the school, variations and differing approaches will prove easier.

While students are likely familiar with MP3 players and downloaded music, many may well be unaware of the "report" type of podcast they will be producing. Podcasts intended to educate on specific issues, whether or not they are produced for school or student consumption or for a general audience, are a type of downloadable content that is far less popular than the music or comedy items today's students are actually likely to know first hand.

Regarding the activities, a complete and clear set of all expectations should be laid out for the students before they begin any aspect of the work. Similarly, a useful tool for the teacher to create to support students in doing the project would be a check list of all the elements they will need to do to finish the project, indicating due dates and other significant items involved.

Part 1

A logical place to begin a class podcasting project would be by having the students listen to the type of podcast they will be assigned to produce.

This might be best accomplished by the teacher locating and downloading a few samples of podcasts. Educational, informational, and commentary bearing podcasts now abound on the Web and a modest search using either a popular podcast directory like iTunes or a search engine like Google will turn up a great deal of material. It will also be useful to download some student produced podcasts. These are also found via the Web in abundance now, as well.

These sample podcasts can serve well as the focus of worthwhile whole group lessons in which the group listens to them together, and/or reviews them as reflective audience and analytical critics. Class brainstorming processes done during these listening and responding activities will establish specific likes and dislikes, do's and don'ts, favored types and approaches, and so forth. All of this will establish a valuable foundation for activities that follow.

An extension and variation on the above might be to have the students search and download their own examples which they can share with the group as they present their own critical analysis and recommendations, much the same as a good book report might do.

Part 2

Now that the class is clear on what a podcast is, and the type of podcast they will be producing, it can shift its attention to the process of producing its first efforts.

Subject

Selecting the subject of the podcast will require the imagination of both teacher and students. In order to support the students in completing this activity successfully, very clear objectives and parameters should be laid out for them.

As the class will be producing numerous podcasts (or numerous segments of a group podcast), and considering that at the end of the process they will be shared beyond the class, a degree of uniformity of subject matter will keep the project easily understandable for all—creator and audience alike. A broad theme like, *the impact of volcanic activity on the lives of people* (in the Earth science class), *battles of the Civil War* (in the social studies class), or *poets and their influence on popular music* (in the English language arts class) will establish relevance to the curriculum and allow enough room for students to narrow the theme down to a specific subject that interests them personally.

Project-Based Activities That Translate Well to Podcasting

The following is a list of traditional instructional activities that translate well to podcasting-based learning projects. Part of the value of these is that they are all items that have a long history and precedent in the instructional culture of schools. Podcasting will make them more relevant, fresher, and more motivating and engaging for students.

- **Book Report.** This can include any book report elements the class requires. It can be enhanced beyond the simple reading of a written report by editing in sound effects, dramatic readings of quotes taken from the book (perhaps by a different voice than that of the student doing the report), sound bites of the author's voice mined from the Web or taken from other digital media resources (if available), interviews of readers, and so forth.
- **Position Paper (persuasive essay).** For this project the students take a position on an important contemporary issue (or may do it as a time traveler from a previous or future period, if applicable), and makes a case for that position, backing it up with citations, statistics, snippets of recorded interviews, and so forth. Subjects like gun control, immigration, global warming, and student curfews will engage and produce spirited podcasts.
- **Debate.** This involves two students who have taken opposing positions on a common theme and produce a joint position podcast (see above). This can be extended to several students on each side, or can be done as a panel presenting several related position.
- **Research Report.** This type of podcast is a reporting of student findings to an assigned or self assigned research topic. The report can be made more dramatic as a radio/audio report, incorporating a variety of sound effects, music clips, interviews, and other sound resources to enhance the basic body of the report.
- **Dramatic Reading.** A valuable dimension to learning a work of literature is to prepare a reading of it to present to an audience. This kind of podcast will record this type of reading and may include various types of sound enhancement to heighten the dramatic effect.
- **Narrative Procedure.** How to make a peanut butter and jelly sandwich, culture a pearl, dissect a frog, and so on. The student is required to detail the steps of a process in order to produce a product or effect. Audio will allow students to communicate subtleties that are near impossible to produce by text alone.

- **Oral History.** Getting the subject of an interview to reveal important knowledge acquired by dint of direct experience is a difficult undertaking that requires a number of skills. Oral history is an essential skill for historians and digital audio not only makes for a more natural and relaxed interview process, but produces a more dramatic and compelling product. The report will include the recorded interviews but may involve the student editing out superfluous material, recording an introduction and summary as well as intermittent narrative to explain the recorded oral history segments. The piece may be enhanced by music and sound effects as well.
- **News Piece.** This project is an opportunity for the student to take charge of the media and create the type of piece that is commonly presented on radio and television. Students may try their hand at joining professional broadcasters in reporting national and international news, or they may produce news pieces specific to the school and local community.
- **Public Service Announcement.** Sometimes it's harder to make an important statement in 30 seconds than it is in 30 minutes. The problem of getting the listener's attention and making a convincing argument to stop smoking, don't drink and drive, report crime, look before crossing, and so on, is a worthy exercise in communication for students.
- **Critique.** This is a review of a movie, play, musical performance, restaurant, and such. This type of piece embraces direct research, reportage, humor, and so on.
- **Format Crossover.** Many of the above will become blends of several types in one podcast. For instance, a movie review of *All's Quiet on the Western Front* may include a book report as the movie is based on that work, research into the factual background of the theme, a movie based on (WWI), as well as others from the list above.

INCLUDING INSTRUCTIONAL—LOGISTICAL FACTORS

A decision will have to be made early on whether or not students are to be assigned individual or group projects. From the point of view of logistics, particularly regarding the use or sharing of technology equipment, group projects have advantages. The point here though is that this decision will influence a great deal of what follows and should be a central consideration in the planning process at this stage. Before the research and writing portions of the assignment is set in stone, the teachers would do well to have a good idea in mind of the actual production scenario of the project:

- Where and when will the class have access to the technology needed for the production portion of the project?
- Where, when, and how often will the class have access to Internet enabled computers to do the background research part of the project?
- Will they need and/or have a one-to-one ratio of computer to student for this project?
- Will you assign this as part of regular class time? In class? In the school's computer lab or media center?
- Will you assign all or part of this as after school homework?
- Do the students have access at home or at a public or school library for this out of class assignment?
- How many computers, microphones, and headphones (these may or may not be needed depending on a variety of factors) are available?
- How will the noise factor be handled?
- Will the classroom allow for individuals and groups to be recording and speaking simultaneously?
- Will you need to have individuals or groups take turns speaking and recording?
- Are there spare spaces that individuals or groups can be sent to with equipment to afford them the quiet they'll need to produce an acceptable recording?

Research

This part of the project is similar to other research oriented projects traditionally done in schools. One notable exception is that in addition to finding "information" for their reports the students may download items that are digital audio recordings. In fact, there are online repositories and search engines to locate them, specifically devoted to this type of content. Furthermore, if the students are going to download items recorded by others, they may have to familiarize themselves with the legality of using them (see section below) (Creative Commons, 2006; Electronic Frontier Foundation, 2006).

Writing and Editing

In may respects the writing and editing of a script or outline for a podcast project is similar to other writing-based projects currently done in schools. One important departure however is the factor of time. One of the parameters the teacher should set for these projects is the run time of the final project. Part of the writing process here then, has to do with the duration taken to read the student writing project during the recording process.

Recording

Many of the considerations involved with this part of the project are covered in the previous chapter on how to set up the classroom for podcasting. Because the techniques of recording are relatively simple, it is the classroom management and set up of the space in which recording will take place that requires the most planning. As with any other new classroom practice, there is a learning curve involved and the second experience will go much easier and quicker than the first. In addition to set up and classroom management dimensions to planning for this part of the project, it is essential, as is the case with any project that involves students using equipment and producing products, that the teacher really be familiar with it directly and can do the things that the students will be expected to do. If the plan however, involves coordinating this part of the project with a colleague, a tech specialist for instance, this dimension obviously changes. Furthermore, it would be wise to devote a separate class session (or part of one) for demonstrating recording, a little relaxed student experimentation, and trial and error. Time is an important planning factor and becoming familiar with recording as well as having a cushion for trial and error and second takes should be factored in while planning.

An additional factor that must be taken into consideration is storing student files. If the class will be engaging in whole group podcasting activities as described in the how to set up the classroom chapter, the recording will done and saved by the teacher directly. If, on the other hand, the students will be working in collaborative groups at their own computers, a mechanism for storing the files that result from the recording will need to be identified. This can be accomplished in a number of ways, the use of a thumb or jump drive probably being the easiest. The point is that this must be planned for ahead of time. Simply saving the files on the hard drives of laptops that are shared with other students in other classes may result in lost work.

SINGLETON OR GROUP PODCASTS?

Projects may be done as either singleton or collaborative group projects. Some items, like book reports, are generally done by individual students when done as text and may translate best this way as podcast as well. However, there is plenty of precedent for group research reports and team debates or panel discussions.

The factors to consider when deciding on how many students will produce the podcast or segment of a whole group podcast involve (a) which structure will foster the greatest learning for the student and (b) which will define a situation that is manageable in terms of time—resources (classroom setup and available technology)—and student maturity and behaviors.

It is better for teachers attempting their first project of this type to take baby steps than to attempt to run a marathon. Organizing a group podcast in which groups of students, as well as individuals, present their material sequentially as a single unified performance is an effective method that numerous podcasting teachers have adopted. In this case a single recording is made and the teacher has control of the process. The success with this type of project is a perfect launching pad for experiments with more elaborate and complex activities.

PULLING THE PLANNING FACTORS TOGETHER

When doing lesson planning for a podcast-based learning project, a chart similar to Figure 13.1 will be a useful addition to the standard lesson plan or activity guide that identifies the segment of the curriculum that the lesson or unit of study will address and the learning outcomes to be achieved. In many cases, producing the podcast is only a segment of an extended unit. Preparatory work, presenting, reflecting on, and responding to finished work, as well rating the podcasts are all parts of a complete process. See the upcoming section on assessment that also contributes to planning.

ASSESSMENT OF PODCASTING-BASED PROJECTS

Like other forms of project-based learning podcasting projects can employ a rating rubric to good effect. This will be used to rate the final product, but should be shared with the students from the early stages of the project as it will cue them as to what is expected and the weighting and prioritizing of criteria.

An effective example from Mary D. Bradford High School (Kenosha, WI) can be found online at:

Example: Middle School Life Science Project: This podcast-based project would fit well into a performance based science unit in which the production of a product or performance is used to indicate the level of learning achieved by the student.					
Project Title	**Subject Area**	**Project Type**	**Standards Addressed**	**Length of Audio Product**	**Number of students to be recorded**
Owl Pellet Dissection	Science–Life Science	Narrative Procedure	Life Science Concepts: • Structure and function in living systems • Populations and ecosystems	10	3
Project Description:	A running narrative (edited) of the process of dissecting an owl pellet and the reconstruction of the skeletal remains found within. An explanatory introduction is given first, outlining the rationale for the procedure and expectations of what will be found based on background reading done prior to the dissection. Also, a summary of conclusions is included at the end in which the student(s) states the inferences made from the procedure and explains why they were made.				

Figure 13.1. Podcast-based learning project planning chart.

http://sblogs.writingproject.org/filer/yvpBawpManilaWebsite/ejmaterials/schoolInTheCouleePodcastRubric.pdf

The final dimension to the planning process involves deciding who the extended audience of a podcast is and the approach to take in sharing it with the world beyond the classroom. In many cases the podcasts that students do will really be of interest to few other than school-based peers and parents. On the other hand, the Web currently abounds with student created content that has value to the general population of the world. Podcasting has set a new bar for students work. That few will hear the student voice no longer represents a limit to students who truly can be heard around the world. It is a wonderful opportunity and challenge.

CHAPTER 14

CURRICULAR CONNECTIONS

Using Podcasts and Podcasting as Resources for Teaching and Learning

"How you use technology in education is more important than if you use it at all."

—David Thornburg (1999, *Technology in K-12 Education: Envisioning a New Future*, p. 1)

The above quote is, taken from a white paper published on a U. S. Department of Education Web site titled "White Papers on the Future of Technology in Education." It frames an understanding about the place of podcasting in teaching and learning properly. Understanding that change in the classroom comes slowly and often with great resistance, those of us who promote such change through the adoption of technology have come to understand that the choice of resources and related practices is crucial. A misstep forward in attempting to "integrate" technology can result in several steps backward. Teachers, and those who supervise and support them, have little patience for experiments that take them down paths leading away from the very traditional results they are expected to demonstrate. Consequently, technology practices that are likely to offer significant impact and staying power in our classrooms need to be practical from a great many points of view (cost of acquisition and maintenance, ease of use, requiring only reasonable amounts of profes-

Podcasting for Teachers: Using a New Technology to Revolutionize Teaching and Learning, Revised Second Edition, pp. 211–230

sional development, etc.) as well as offering clear and significant advantages in the teaching and learning of the curriculum that educators see as central to their mission. Podcasting is one of the very best examples of this type of technology resource and practice available to our schools currently.

Further along in this paper Thornburg makes a second major point, that "Unless our thinking about education is transformed along with our continuing expansion of telematic technology into classrooms, our technology investment will fail to live up to its potential." Reflecting about the value that podcasting can bring to our classrooms, he reveals a very important dimension of it by stating "We used to live in a world where content was king. That world no longer exists. Content is abundant, and is, therefore a poor basis on which to base an educational system. What is scarce today is context and meaning. It used to be the mark of an educated person to have a vast reservoir of facts on which to rely. Today this skill is of much less value" (Thornburg, 1999, pp. 2-3).

Whether it is done with technology or not, making context and meaning a greater part of what is learned in our schools is an essential element of how education must change in a world that has been altered, and continues to be altered ever further, by the advent and run away success of digital information and communication technologies. Podcasting, and the body of practice that is developing around it, is an area of technology integration that can provide this context establishing brand of learning in our educational programs.

This chapter will illustrate some of the great potential that podcasting, and related practices, hold for today's classrooms. Encouragingly some educators enthusiastically gravitated toward podcasting as an exciting new resource very early on. Furthermore, now that a year or so has passed since its appearance, ideas about solid practices and pedagogy involving podcasting continue to emerge.

CREATIVITY, ENTHUSIASM, AND THE NEED FOR STRUCTURE

Educators with a thirst to push the envelope a bit often become greatly enthused by the possibilities an innovation like podcasting suggests. With a little imagination it is easy to imagine exciting ways to bring technology into the classroom. Consider the following passage taken from the Web site "The Center for Teaching History with Technology" (http://thwt.org/historypodcasts.html).

> Podcasting could be used to record a teacher's lesson or a student conversation. It could be used to create a homework assignment or even as part of a test. Students could use podcasts to interview each other about what they

learned during the week. They could create a newscast, hold a debate, or run a radio show. Schools could use podcasts to make announcements via their Web site. Students could read their own poetry or stories. Podcasts could also be used to record guest speakers and make their presentations available online.

Here are some specific ideas for the history/social studies classroom:

- Students interview relatives about their life histories, and then combine the audio interview with family photos in an iMovie project.
- Students write a radio drama based on a historical event and record their show (complete with commercials) using an iPod and a voice recorder.
- Students learn about a different country by interviewing a recent traveler. They record the interview and then create a digital travel album.
- Students use an iPod and a voice recorder to interview sources for articles for a class newspaper.
- Students write and record short stories and add music and sound effects.
- Teacher records a tutorial that students listen to on their own.
- Present student writing through a class radio drama or a poetry slam.
- Teacher records and broadcasts group discussions.
- Using an iPod and a voice recorder, the teacher records each student telling a story and then saves the recordings in iTunes for assessment purposes.
- On a field trip, students use an iPod with a voice recorder to take notes and a digital camera to take photos. They then create a guided tour in iMovie." (The Center for Teaching History with Technology, n.d., p. 3-4)

This passage demonstrates the kind of enthusiasm and creativity that a technology like podcasting can interject into teaching, a field that is far too often bogged down in lock step tradition and adherence to concerns other that what will motivate and inspire youngsters. The above ideas are good ones. However, before we list these alongside a great many others of equal promise, considering a pedagogical framework and foundation will prove valuable.

FOUNDATIONS FOR PODCASTING IN EDUCATION

Currently, a variety of formally adopted standards is a prime touchstone used to validate what is taught as well as to plan comprehensive, balanced programs of instruction. Entry points into the work of teaching and learning that can be demonstrated as aligned with these standards are a useful beginning from which to establish a solid foundation for the instructional use of podcasting. It is useful, also, to note that while there are a great many sets of standards currently in use by the myriad of school districts in the United States and beyond, the vast majority of these bear great similarity to one another. This is due, in part, to the fact that many of these standards documents originated in the work of national or international professional development organizations who involved themselves with the establishment of standards before state or more local departments of education undertook that task, and logically drew on their work in the process.

Analyzing and comparing these documents is an exhaustive subject. While space in this chapter doesn't permit this, a few clear and significant connections are listed below.

Language Arts

The California State Board of Education lists the following among its content standards for all fifth grade students:

> *1.0 Listening and Speaking Strategies*
> *Students deliver focused, coherent presentations that convey ideas clearly and relate to the background and interests of the audience. They evaluate the content of oral communication.*
>
> *Organization and Delivery of Oral Communication*
> *1.4 Select a focus, organizational structure, and point of view for an oral presentation.*
> *1.5 Clarify and support spoken ideas with evidence and examples.*
> *1.6 Engage the audience with appropriate verbal cues, facial expressions, and gestures.*
>
> *Analysis and Evaluation of Oral and Media Communications*
> *1.8 Analyze media as sources for information, entertainment, persuasion, interpretation of events, and transmission of culture (California State Board of Education, n.d.).*

Mathematics

The New York State Department of Education's Core Curriculum in Mathematics lists a Communication Strand that states

> *Students will:*
>
> - *organize and consolidate their mathematical thinking through communication;*
> - *communicate their mathematical thinking coherently and clearly to peers, teachers, and others;*
> - *analyze and evaluate the mathematical thinking and strategies of others (New York State Education Department, n.d., p. 24)*

Science

As part of the Illinois Learning Standards in Science, the Illinois State Board of Education lists the following areas of importance:

> ***Communicating***
>
> *Express and interpret information and ideas.*
>
> *Scientists must carefully describe their methods and results to a variety of audiences, including other scientists. This requires precise and complete descriptions and the presentation of conclusions supported by evidence. Young science students develop the powers of observation and description. Older students gain the ability to organize and study data, to determine its meaning, to translate their findings into clear understandable language and to compare their results with those of other investigators.*
>
> ***Using Technology***
>
> *Use appropriate instruments, electronic equipment, computers and networks to access information, process ideas and communicate results.*
>
> *Technology is invented and improved by the use of scientific principles. In turn, scientists depend on technology in performing experiments, analyzing data and communicating the results. Science students learn to use a range of technologies: instruments, computer hardware and software, on-line services and equipment, primary source data and images, and communication networks. They learn how technology, in turn, is the result of a scientific design process that includes continual refinements and improvements. (Illinois State Board of Education, n.d.a, pp. 7-8)*

These documents merely scratch the surface of pointing to even the most obvious connections between podcasting and established standards for what all students must learn and be able to do. The above connections to the communications dimensions of language, math, and science facilitate learning across this short list of subject areas as well as through the rest of the curriculum. For instance, language and specific mathematical and scientific approaches to language are useful and necessary in doing and reporting the work and learning in the areas of social studies and arts, as well. Furthermore, beyond this obvious connection to communication, other connections in the delivery of content and facilitation of the myriad of ways that students process content are strong as well.

As Thornburg points out "The effective use of technology in education requires though, experimentation, and a willingness to spend the time needed to develop and refine strategies until they are proven to be effective" (1999, p. 1).

PODCASTING IN PRACTICE

This chapter will offer numerous examples and models of how such experimentation is playing itself out in our classrooms as teachers begin to wrap their professional minds around podcasting's possibilities and refine ways to bring it effectively into our traditional classrooms. At the same time podcasting educators need to maintain the important balance between inspired innovation and standards-based educational goals.

Language Arts

As podcasting is so closely associated with various aspects of language, language arts is a curriculum area that it impacts easily. Beyond the obvious process skills of listening and speaking, it has deep implications in content areas like literature, as well. The following case story of a unit of study in a college literature course may serve as an illustration of podcasting's potential for this type of instruction, as well as a model on which teachers of various grade levels may craft similar units.

Using Student Podcasts in Literature Classes is a course that was given at Swarthmore College. A case story about the course states

> *The students received two sets of instructions for making podcasts. One, written by the professor, stressed what kind of content was expected. The other, written by Liz Evans of Swarthmore's Information Technology Services in collaboration with the professor, gave step-by-step technical instructions for recording and posting and subscribing to podcasts. (Evans, 2006)*

The course instructor, Peter Schmidt, describes the course as

> *a survey of important novels published by U.S. authors since World War II. Shared themes include war, peace, complex personal and family histories, U.S. state power, border-crossings, and the use of fiction to narrate crises in individual and national identities. Students learn to vary their interpretive techniques so as to appreciate tragedy vs. comedy, satire, and farce. (Evans, 2006).*

With the current availability of e-Books in MP3 and other easy to manage digital formats, such a course might simply make use of recorded versions of works of literature, recorded reflective discussions by critics and experts, and similar passive applications of podcasting with the student playing the role of passive consumer of podcast content. However, in this instance these practices were supplemented by learning activities that involved students in conceiving and creating their own recorded content. The instructor explains that

> *This podcast project tied in very well to a literature course, because in addition to teaching students about particular works of fiction, the key skill modeled when students quote and expand on each other's words is that thinking about cultural works is a collaborative process that happens in dialogue, not only in isolation. Cultural objects (including novels) are not static; they circulate, they are events. We may receive them privately, as when we read or work on a computer, but the process is not complete until we take the next step, which is to re-connect with others. We get ideas about interpretation from others, improve them (we hope) on our own, then place these ideas back into the cultural stream. (Evans, 2006)*

To make this sort of application of a new technology practical and effective from the instructional and classroom management point of view requires a good deal of instructional design, planning, and trial and error. The instructor further explains that

> *Each podcast assignment consisted of a "podcast pair" (two podcasts); students made a five-minute reading of a passage from a novel, coupled with a five-minute discussion of that passage: why the student chose it, what details were most important, what themes and issues the passage raised, and how the passage related to the rest of the novel. These podcasts were posted on a server and all students in the class were required to listen to selected podcasts on what they were reading before coming to class discussions. (Evans, 2006)*

Melbourne Case. Another interesting approach to using podcasting in the teaching of literacy is embraced by materials produced by Ms. Jo McLeary a high school English Literature teacher in Melbourne who shares her work through the blog she authors titled The Open Classroom. In October of 2006 she posted an item with the headline Podcasts for revision in which she reflects "I have made two episodes that are just me talking about Henry Lawson's *Short Stories* and Mark Haddon's *The Curious Incident of the Dog in the Night-Time* and plan to do two more this week which I will record with other Year 12 teachers at my school discussing their readings of the texts. The students can download these podcasts onto their iPods, as some have already done, and listen to them while walking to school without being considered 'nerds,' a sad reflection on school life today—if you are to succeed, you must make it look as though you did no work; being a nerd is one of the meanest things to say to a student. My dream would be to make regular podcasts of Year 12 texts next year throughout year 12 and involving the students (and possibly teachers at other schools."

In her podcast on the Martin Guerre book, for instance, she and a colleague offer highly insightful discussions about the texts that are being read in class. This appears to be a customized study guide to foster increased understanding. By listening to two masterfully reflective readers opine and discuss the points they feel students should pay particular attention to, illustrating understandings they feel the students should walk away with, youngsters can benefit form the sort of customized content that until recently was near impossible to be obtained.

Authors' Web sites. Still another very promising use of podcasts, one that makes use of podcast content is in the area of author studies. The use of children's author's Web sites, which are rich repositories of materials that make the experience of reading and enjoying the work of a writer come alive is a growing use of technology in elementary language arts instruction. Some authors are beginning to produce podcasts, which give young and beginning readers a further and more in-depth opportunity to know their favored authors on a personal level. A good example is posted on the OPAL (Online Programming for all Libraries) Podcast blog, which in September of 2006 featured a post with the headline "Book Discussion of Grandfather's Journey by Allen Say." Mr. Say is a famous and much beloved author for elementary through middle school students. Interestingly, he is one of the few high profile authors of this publishing niche who ordinarily doesn't rely on the Web to promote and enrich the experience of reading his books (http://opalpodcast.blogspot.com/2006/09/book-discussion-of-grandfathers.html). This podcast is part of a program funded by the National Endowment for the Humanities in conjunction with the American Library Association run by Alliance Library System of central Illinois, offering a number of important book discussions with a focus on books for children to encourage reading for pleasure.

DOWNLOADABLE LEARNING GAMES

"Who Said" is a literature trivia game offered to the general public as a podcast. The game's Web site states:

> *Every other day or so, I'll make an audio recording from a novel. It will be a short passage, always something a character says. Your task will be to guess the character, book and author.*
>
> ***Two ways to play**: on the Web site, and as a podcast."*
>
> *I'll post hints on the discussion forums.*
>
> ***To find out who won** and learn the answer, go to the discussion forum or wait for the next audio passage. Or sign up for notifications.*
>
> *There's no prize, but I will mention who got it right in the next recording. Maybe we'll have a prize sometime when the game grows a bigger audience and is more interesting to a sponsor like an online bookstore or an audio book publisher.*
>
> ***What kinds of books?** I'll begin with novels I like but will welcome suggestions for passages. My taste runs to Brit lit, but doesn't stop there. (Who Said Amy, 2005)*

This resource suggests ways that students can be kept engaged in activities that teach and extend subject matter. In participating in this particular activity, literature students are placed in a reflective milieu in which they are exposed to works other than those assigned in their own classes. This reveals for them similarities and commonalities to all literature and gives them the benefit of an extended learning community far beyond the parameters of their school.

FROM THE PUBLISHERS

Harry Potter on Tour

It should come as no surprise that publishing companies have seized on podcasting as a way to grow demand for their products. From this activity many useful podcast instructional resources have been developed and are offered to the educational community.

One very interesting item is the Harry Potter podcast material from Scholastic, the distributor of Harry Potter books. These are found and can be downloaded from the Scholastic Web site titled Let's Talk About Harry. The site greets readers with the descriptive introduction "In these unique podcasts hosted by Scholastic, three Harry Potter 'experts' talk about the world of Harry Potter, how it changed with Book Six, and what they think might happen in Book seven" (Scholastic, n.d.) These podcasts keep the excitement of the Harry Potter series going. Publisher's staff members who are associated with the series tour the country, visiting groups of young readers at book stores and presenting ideas and asking questions about the series to them. The questions were made known in earlier podcasts, allowing reader/listeners to prepare themselves for the face-to-face exchanges ahead of time. The podcasts are recordings of their interactive live presentations to these readers.

Nancy Keane provides podcast book talks through her Web site. These short "teaser" type overviews of the gist of books are read in a very friendly and inviting voice and might easily entice youngsters into reading the books she describes as well as giving them a bit of a positive and informative mental starting point before they begin the book.

Podcasts can foster the love and understanding of books and writing. While some may think that the audio nature of podcasting puts it at odds with the teaching of books, this is actually far from the case. In many respects podcasts foster a greater appreciation and understanding of print books than would be the case without them and related technologies.

AUTHOR PODCASTS ARE NOT JUST FOR STUDENTS

Reading Rockets "a national multimedia project offering information and resources on how young kids learn to read" offers numerous podcast interviews with prominent writers of books for young readers. It creates and disseminates information about reading through major projects, which include PBS television programs, online services, and professional development opportunities. The Web site states "See a list of our exclusive interviews with top children's book authors and illustrators that you can download as video or audio podcasts through Google Video, iTunes, OMN, and others." Their list of authors includes such notables as: R. L. Stein (Goosebumps), Niki Giovanni (Rose), Laurence Yep (Dragonwings), and many others. These interviews give the authors' personal reflections on their works, the act of writing, and on books. They can serve well as professional development items for teachers who present the authors and their works. They generally are spoken in an adult to adult type of voice. However, in many cases they, or portions of them, can be presented by teachers to their classes, as well.

Math

The Michigan Department of Education has published on the Web a sample technology-enhanced lesson plan as part of its educational technology implementation materials. This document titled Podcasting Math carries a descriptive abstract stating

> *Students access content specific math lessons via podcasting targeted to math standards. Podcasts are audio/video files delivered directly to the student's computer or portable music/video device. Lessons delivered via podcasts provide on-demand access to the student, the opportunity to review and repeat the lessons, and to skip ahead on content they already have mastered. Lesson describes accessing podcast lessons addressing 9-12 MET and Math standards. (Bennett, Salmi, & Moyton, n.d.)*

The document further illustrates how this podcasting-based practice will satisfy a variety of the state's educational technology standards (i.e. "Students use emerging technology resources [e.g. podcasting, Webcasting, compressed video...] while addressing a number of 'Content Expectations" in Mathematics including: Polynomial equations—A1.1, Complex numbers—L2.1, Quadratic Equations—A1.2, etc."

- A Podcast like **Dan's Mathcast** can add a great deal to a math class. By downloading the periodic episodes a new, expert voice is brought into the community. This show offers problems to students, who understand that they can work on a solution and tune back in for the following podcast to get a solution and an explanation. The podcaster invites listeners to email in questions or comments, offering a degree of audience interactivity. There are "math jokes," a math or myth segment, study tips, conversation and a degree of personality. The show could make a worthwhile whole group activity as the teacher plays it for the group, stopping to discuss ideas, have the students work on the problems the podcast offers or perhaps, modifying them for his group's specific learning needs and abilities. Or the podcast could be used as an extra credit-listen on your own enrichment to the class.
- The **Joseph H. Kerr School**, a member of Canada's Network of Innovative Schools and a participant in the SchoolNet GrassRoots Program, which promotes the effective use of information and communications technologies in Canadian classrooms, posted a number of mathematics podcast resources on the Web. In these media resources students take the role of instructor to provide math lessons, an interesting blend of teacher created resource and student performance which can be used as content for other teachers to present to their classes.

While math is currently one of the curriculum areas that has still not produced an overwhelming number of podcasts as content for students, there are a number of others worth mentioning.

- **Is All About Math (Video Podcast):** The Is All about Math VideoPodCast discusses a variety of topics in elementary mathematics using animations and a digital blackboard to help explain concepts.
- **Math for America**: Math for America is a not for profit organization with the mission of improving math education in U.S. public schools lists several math podcasting resources on its Web site. Among these is The Math Factor, which is aired on KUAF 91.3 FM in Fayetteville, Arkansas, the University of Arkansas NPR affiliated radio station. The Math Factor podcasts are found on the Web site http://www.podcast.net/show/83323. Math for America describes this podcast as "A brief weekly math conversation and puzzle."

  Also listed by Math for America is the BBC's **In Our Time**, this program on science offers numerous episodes with a very strong mathematics theme. They can be heard via podcast subscription or downloaded from http://www.bbc.co.uk/radio4/history/inourtime/inourtime_science.shtml. These programs are highly produced and very professional, as one would expect of broadcast BBC material.

Science

In his article "Globalizing Education One Podcast at a Time," Randy K. Yerrick (2006), a professor at San Diego State University's Center for Research in Math & Science Education, opines that

> "Podcasting can enhance science teaching by:
>
> - Bringing science experts and other resources to teachers and students;
> - Providing opportunities to replay significant scientific events and instruction;
> - Sharing data and data analysis anywhere and at any time;
> - Giving every student virtual access to pristine research facilities and state-of-the-art science demonstrations and simulations;
> - Facilitating supplemental instruction through multiple languages;
> - Extending the everyday classroom lab experience beyond the classroom walls, and promoting science equity by giving this access to every student; and
> - Sharing science teaching artifacts and events for the assessment of excellence in science teaching and learning."

Many of the practices and the resources with which to implement them mentioned in this list are already in use. We can find ample evidence of this in the following initiatives:

- **The Science and Society** Web site, http://www.scienceandsociety.net/#stock, offers recorded conversations on a variety of themes in science including; medical breakthroughs, energy and the environment, space exploration, nanotechnology, and K-12 science education.
- **Wild Chronicles (video enhanced),** is one of numerous podcasts National Geographic makes available. Its Web site carries the description "See the natural world like never before with adventurers, scientists, researchers, and the eye-opening Crittercam."
- **NPR's (National Public Radio) Science Friday**: **Making Science Radioactive,** which can be found at its Web site which states "Introducing a podcast of Science Friday from NPR—audio files you can download and listen to on your own time, on your computer or portable player. Using free software, you can automatically download the latest audio files and import them into many audio players, including iTunes and Windows Media Player" (National Public Radio, 2005). Recent episodes include: Brain News Update, Memory and Smell, and Mars Water Update.
- **Acorns** is an engaging science oriented podcast by Marion Owen a resident of remote Kodiak Island, Alaska. This bestselling author shares her insights into organic gardening, recipes, and the role plants play in keeping us clothed, fed and in good health. Recent episodes bear the titles: Charles Darwin's love affair with earthworms, what national resource are we wasting? And What's That Creepy Bug on Your Houseplant?

While one important dimension of the study of science reflects the way it embraces pure fact, on the other hand science is inextricably enmeshed in the products of the human imagination. Dreaming important ideas that are supported by fact is also the stuff that makes science important. Some science educators understand the need for instructional activities that capitalize on the drama in imagining new worlds to explore and conquer. A good example of how podcasting has been tapped for this purpose is the first NASA 21st Century Explorer Podcast Competition, which presented students with the challenge to create a podcast on the theme of how space exploration will benefit their lives in the future.

The NASA Exploration Web site states:

"Exploration provides the foundation of our knowledge, technology, resources, and inspiration. It seeks answers to the fundamental questions about our experience, responds to recent discoveries and puts in place revolutionary technologies and capabilities to inspire our nation, the world, and the next generation. Through NASA and its partners, we touch the unknown, we learn and we understand. As we take our first steps toward sustaining human presence in the solar system, we can look forward to far off visions becoming realities of the future.

The 21st Century Explorer Podcast Competition is an Education and Public Outreach project designed to inspire and motivate the next generation of explorers and to compete effectively for the minds, imaginations, and career ambitions of America's young people.

Students will create an audio recording or video short to answer the question:

"How will Space Exploration benefit your life in the future?" (NASA, n.d.)

Social Studies

Produced by 8th grade teacher Eric Langhorst, the "Speaking of History" podcast and blog is a mix of history education content that interests Eric personally, and which he understands will be appropriate and relevant for use as content with his students. By extension, many other students and teachers will find this material useful, as well. Eric offers his own reflections enhanced by sound clips he has recorded personally or acquired otherwise. He covers history, education, and technology through his combination blog and podcast.

Similarly, The Center for Teaching History with Technology, from which the bulleted list of teaching and learning applications at the beginning of this chapter was gleaned, offers serious social studies content in a way that takes advantage of podcasting technology. One well thought out example is part of the A Day in the Life of a Hobo project.

One type of learning product developed as part of this involves dramatic reenactment of historical events presented as a radio program of the day. A sample of these can be downloaded in MP3 format directly from this Web site. It is accompanied by a recording made by the teacher/designer of the project who describes the project and reflects on its pedagogy, success, and significance.

These are posted on the center's Web site as follows:

- Listen to an excerpt of our 1930s radio show: http://thwt.org/hoboexcerpt.mp3
- Listen to my comments about this activity: http://thwt.org/hobopodcast.mp3

Also given are links to background reading assignments and a link to the project blog in which the assignment was originally posted for students.

Taking oral histories from those directly involved in past events and processing them for reflection and understanding is an approach to social studies learning that is often aspired to, but not often achieved due to a wide variety of logistic considerations. In her article "Telling History," Diane Haugen (1996-2006) discusses various aspects of this.

> *While archivists have done an excellent job of organizing the oral histories as a whole and transcribing many of them, the primary problem remains that much of the story material exists in a form that is not readily available for classroom use. The archived oral histories provide a vast, untapped source of materials for creating interesting supplementations to existing history texts.*

Podcasting can be a powerful solution to this problem. Not only will it provide the material in an alternate mode (to text books), that will engage students, particularly those who do not find print material easily accessible, but it is easily stored, transferred and disseminated, and searchable, making it easy to align with traditional print materials.

A good example of how podcasting can be directed at oral history is the Teaching American History: Podcasting in Action podcast which can be found at the blog set up to support it. The header to this site states, "This is a collection of oral history podcasts created by participants in the Lane ESD Teaching American History Grant." The podcasts and blog are part of the Lane Education Service District's (Oregon) program developed under the grant (n.d.).

Another program that has used podcasting technology for a similar purpose is the University of West Florida's project to preserve the African American history of Pensacola. In an article in the UWF (University of West Florida) News titled "Public History Students Podcast Oral History," Patrick Moore, associate professor and director of the University of West Florida Public History Program explains:

> *Too many people overlook Pensacola's rich African-American heritage ... Pensacola was heavily influenced by Caribbean culture—not just slavery and civil rights like many other Southern cities. Once the people pass away,*

the history will be gone forever, so it's very important to capture it now. (Pedrazza, 2006, p. 2)

Arts

For a good number of years visual arts teachers have used the thumbnail gallery, a very popular form of Web authoring software, as a way to display student art work on the Web. Easy to use, it is a way of uploading a good deal of student artwork and offering it up in a browsable environment that is somewhat analogous in experience to wandering through a museum gallery and following one's nose as to what to look at and in what order.

The Mabry School in Cobb County, Georgia is one of a number of schools exploring an updated version of this that offers many compelling advantages. The practice involves a visually enhanced podcast, which essentially runs as a music accompanied slide show, the graphics being displayed in the iTunes graphics box.

Art is not only a discreet curriculum area of its own, but also a language in and of itself that is highly applicable across the curriculum; in this sense this style of enhanced podcast offers innovative opportunities for student communications in all subject areas.

The podcast "Your Art Teacher ... Emma Craib talks to her friends (of all ages)" is a podcast by an art teacher who offers art lessons through her podcast. This approach is especially valuable considering that the services of a full-time art teacher is something that so many schools apparently are forced to do without. This podcast might serve as professional development for non-art teachers interested in doing art with their classes. However, in format it is appropriate for an entire group to listen to together, teacher included. After episode class reflective discussions used as jumping off places to art activities are likely to be highly productive as teacher and class plan their follow up together. A great many teachers, particularly those on the elementary level, would like to include art or more art in their classes, but feel they need guidance.

Crafty Pod is a "how to" oriented podcast. This is very much narrative procedure, but mixed up with ongoing reflective conversation. There is entertainment value here, as well. One of the great challenges in teaching art is allowing large groups of students to choose among numerous direction intensive projects. Often a teacher can only manage one project for the entire group, if for no other reason than the mass and intricacy of directions and instructions given prevent more than one being handled. With the procedures presented in podcast form, students may listen in quietly on their own and listen over and over again as they glean the precise direction needed at the moment.

Visual art an area in which many podcasts from museums, artists, art educators, art advocacy groups and producers of artists' materials are available.

EdTech Musician is a podcast for music students and music aficionados that covers music history, trivia, news, and recorded music.

Musicians, professional and amateur, are often by personality type self-teachers who rely on materials produced to support them as they absorb ideas and techniques on their own. There is a wealth of music education oriented podcasts available, largely aimed at the self motivated, stick to it types who in the past might have worked from *teach yourself* booklets purchased at music stores. Flexible school music educators may find these useful as they free themselves up by having part of their class working independently with such podcasts. They also offer an avenue for diversifying what can be done within the context of a large class. Some examples are: The Horn Studio, The Folk Song of the Day, The Sax Tips Podcast, and The Daily Frail (banjo). There are many others.

Across the Curriculum

Podcasting will prove valuable in all those student activities for which the use of language is essential or can enrich the quality of learning. Obviously, this is true in instructional areas that are explicitly language oriented, like English language arts, English as a second language, or in the teaching of foreign languages. Podcasting offers similar opportunities in other subjects, as well.

Writing across the curriculum, a well established approach to enhancing learning in both ELA and subjects like math, science, and social studies sets a strong precedent for this. The spectrum of intellectual processes, like researching, discussing, communicating, and documenting, all of which must be carried out to foster learning, require language. Standards documents for *nonlanguage* subjects make broad use of terms like "demonstrate understanding," "identify," "argue," "critique," "represent," "recognize," "respond," "deliver," and "communicate."

For instance, the New York City Board of Educations performance standards document in science under Scientific Connections and Applications lists "Demonstrates understanding of big ideas and unifying concepts" and under Scientific Communication lists "Represents data and results in multiple ways" (New York City Department of Education, n.d.).

The Illinois Learning Standards for Mathematics under Communicating states

> *"Express and interpret information and ideas.*
>
> *Everyone must be able to read and write technical material to be competitive in the modern workplace. Mathematics provides students with opportunities to grow in the ability to read, write and talk about situations involving numbers, variables, equations, figures and graphs. The ability to shift between verbal, graphical, numerical and symbolic modes of representing a problem helps people formulate, understand, solve and communicate technical information. Students must have opportunities in mathematics classes to confront problems requiring them to translate between representations, both within mathematics and between mathematics and other areas; to communicate findings both orally and in writing; and to develop displays illustrating the relationships they have observed or constructed." (http://www.isbe.net/ils/math/standards.htm) (Illinois State Board of Education, n.d.b)*

Apart from these formal frameworks, podcasting is a vehicle to carry exciting student projects that draw context from the use of media students find in the world all around them. Good examples are the podcasts done as learning projects at the Ringwood North Primary School in Australia. Their projects that embrace writing, oral presentation, journalism, research, and large amounts of enthusiasm are good examples found at the program's Web site: http://www.ischool.net.au/.

TECH SKILLS AND TECH CURRICULUM AREA

In almost all localities, standards documents and curricula call for the integration of technology into the teaching and learning of almost every subject area. Podcasting creates a focused, embedded use of technology that fully supports instructional activities aligned to standards and that has a learning curve that can be described as just enough, just in time.

ISTE (International Society for Technology in Education) has developed a longstanding series of standards for technology in education. These provide an essential framework from which the teaching and learning of technology can be planned in conjunction with its alignment to teaching and learning across the content areas. http://cnets.iste.org/currstands/cstands-netss.html

Listed on ISTE's Web site, these technology foundation standards for all students are called the *NETS for Students.*

The current technology foundation standards for students are divided into six broad categories. Standards within each category are to be introduced, reinforced, and mastered by students. These categories provide a framework for linking performance indicators within the Profiles for

Technology Literate Students to the standards. With the revised ISTE standards the integration of critical thinking, project-based learning and authentic assessment are even more explicit (ISTE, 2007). Teachers can use these standards and profiles as guidelines for planning technology-based activities in which students achieve success in learning, communication, and life skills.

The ISTE NETS standards of 2007-2008 address the following areas: basic operations and concepts, social, ethical, and human issues, technology productivity tools, technology communications tools, technology research tools, and technology problem-solving and decision-making tools. Classroom podcasting involves all of them to one degree or another.

CONCLUSION

We have seen how podcasting has many natural connections to teaching and learning in the various subject areas both from a discipline-specific approach and from a multidisciplinary one. Furthermore, these connections are not tangential but provide solid, and in many cases highly relevant practices and resources for teaching and learning. Podcasting has very strong unifying characteristics, allowing subjects to be joined in a logical and seamless fashion. It can provide a basis from which technology may be effectively brought into the teaching of various curriculum areas where other aspects of its integration may have seemed contrived or excessively difficult to implement. This, in conjunction with its ability to provide valuable insights into technology, and in particular the way technology has changed communications, make it an especially valuable practice for education.

RESOURCES

A Day in the Life of a Hobo Project. http://thwt.org/tomslessons.html

Acorns. http://www.digitalpodcast.com/detail.php?id=3487

Book Discussion of Grandfather's Journey by Allen Say. http://opalpodcast.blogspot.com/2006/09/book-discussion-of-grandfathers.html

California State Board of Education: Grade Five English-language Arts Content Standards. http://www.cde.ca.gov/be/st/ss/enggrade5.asp

The Center for Teaching History with Technology: Podcasting in and out of the classroom. http://thwt.org/historypodcasts.html

Crafty Pod. http://www.podcastdirectory.com/podcasts/1689

Dan's MathCast. http://www.dansmath.com/pages/podpage.html

EdTech Musician. http://edtechmusician.libsyn.com/

Illinois Learning Standards for Math. http://www.isbe.net/ils/math/standards.htm
In Our Time. http://www.bbc.co.uk/radio4/history /inourtime/inourtime_science.shtml
ISTE. http://www.iste.org
ISTE NETS Standards. http://cnets.iste.org/currstands/cstands-netss.html
ISTE NETS Standards 2007-2008, http://www.iste.org/AM/Template .cfm?Section=NETS
Is All about Math (Video Podcast). http://www.zencast.com/channels /showchannel.asp?mc=2&cid=7933
Joseph H. Kerr School: Reducing a Fraction. http://www.archive.org/details/ JosephHKerrSchool_1
Keane, N: Booktalks Quick and Simple. http://nancykeane.com/rss.html
Let's Talk About Harry. http://www.scholastic.com/harrypotter/podcasttour /index.htm pp. 1
Mabry School Podcasts. http://mabryonline.org/podcasts/archives /student_podcasts/art/index.html
Math for America. http://mathforamerica.org
The Math Factor. http://www.podcast.net/show/83323
NASA: 21st Century Explorer Podcast Competition. http://www .explorationpodcast.com/about.php
New York State Core Curriculum in Mathematics. http://www.emsc.nysed.gov/ciai /mst/mathstandards/intro.html#The%20Five%20Process%20Strands
OPAL Podcast. http://opalpodcast.blogspot.com/
The Open Classroom—Podcasts for Revision. http://theopenclassroom.blogspot .com/2006_10_01_theopenclassroom_archive.html
Podcasting Math. http://techplan.edzone.net/ci2006/MathPodcasts.doc
Public History Students Podcast Oral History. http://uwf.edu/uwfMain/press /topstoryarch.cfm?emailID=16187
Reading Rockets. http://www.readingrockets.org/podcasts/
Science and Society. http://www.scienceandsociety.net/#stock
Science Friday—Making Science Radioactive. http://www.sciencefriday.com/feed
Speaking of History. http://speakingofhistory.blogspot.com
Teaching American History: Podcasting in Action. http:// tahpodcasts.blogspot.com/
Wild Chronicles. http://www.nationalgeographic.com/podcasts
Who Said Amy. http://www.whosaid.org/howtoplay.htm
Your Art Teacher ... Emma Craib talks to her friends (of all ages). http:// odeo.com/audio/1934741/vie

CHAPTER 15

PODCASTING AND PROFESSIONAL DEVELOPMENT

Simply stated, podcasting has the potential to transform professional development (PD) for teachers. This potential applies to a variety of professional development types and goals and the mechanisms by which they are implemented.

On the most accessible level, podcasting can provide more professional development to teachers by virtue of its capacity to increase the amount of time teachers have to spend on it. It also has the capability to provide better material for PD through its capacity to capture and integrate powerful, high-quality content. Furthermore, it allows for content to be stored, cataloged, retrieved, and distributed easily and conveniently, leveraging technology's sophisticated search and sort mechanisms.

On a deeper level, podcasting offers different types of PD, addressing different dimensions of the professional and intellectual lives of teachers, satisfying needs and intelligences that haven't much been addressed up until now.

In his book *A Whole New Mind*, author Dan Pink (2005) points out an important societal trend that indicates the direction our future will take. He states,

> The last few decades have belonged to a certain kind of person with a certain kind of mind—computer programmers who could crank code, lawyers who could craft contracts, MBAs who could crunch numbers. But the keys to

Podcasting for Teachers: Using a New Technology to Revolutionize Teaching and Learning, Revised Second Edition, pp. 231–244

> the kingdom are changing hands. The future belongs to a very different kind of person with a very different kind of mind—creators and empathizers, pattern recognizers and meaning makers. These people—artists, inventors, designers, storytellers, caregivers, consolers, big picture thinkers—will now reap society's richest rewards and share its greatest joys. (Pink, 2005)

Clearly, the purpose of professional development goes beyond simply providing teachers the skills and knowledge they need currently, or have needed up until now in order to perpetuate the status quo. As education attempts to meet the evolving needs of digital natives, professional development must impart new skills and understandings to teachers who are preparing students with a vastly changed relationship to what it means to be educated and function in society.

Podcasting, a technology and body of practice that is part and parcel of the new digital world, models the realities of that world as its riches are tapped to prepare teachers to do their job better within it. As is easy to apprehend from the review of instructional practices highlighted in this book, podcasting is highly aligned with the learning needs and styles of the creators, storytellers, and big picture thinkers to which Pink alludes.

NEW PRESENTERS, NEW AUDIENCES, NEW KINDS OF PROFESSIONAL DEVELOPMENT

An interesting podcast and one that provides some important insights into what podcasting can bring to PD is The Faculty Room, available at this show's blog which reads at the top of the page "The Faculty Room: Ramblings of a Second-year High School Teacher."

Most interestingly, through the advent of podcasting technology, this podcaster, a young teacher at the very beginning of a teaching career, has access to an audience. This is something that ordinarily is only available to highly experienced, "successful" teachers who have gone on to become staff developers. Generally, those with access to an audience are compliant souls who have earned the right to deliver PD by virtue of having become proponents of a school or district's party line.

This podcast, which appears to have been supported by the author himself, was only produced for a half dozen or so episodes. Clearly, it provides the sort of worthwhile observations about teaching that we might expect in a PD podcast. However, it also captures many of the unexpected dimensions of teaching that are so useful to focus on when providing PD for new teachers, including their sense of overwhelm with the job and confusion about seemingly unworkable conditions. One of the blog entries includes the following side note to the show notes

> One of my students attempted to hang herself last night. My school spent a good amount of time today trying to make people feel better. They had stations all over for distraught students and faculty to cry on each others shoulders. They made an announcement at the end of one of the later periods where they played a tape giving no information and spreading rumors everywhere. I know this is a tough situation to deal with from an administrative level, but I do not feel that it was handled as well as it could have. (The Faculty Room, 2006, p. 1)

Because this podcast captures so much of the reality of new teachers, it offers great value as a focus for teachers and those who supervise them. It is a good example of how podcasting can convey things that other, more traditional media can not. It offers levels of authenticity that are indicative of the power of the new technologies.

Another podcast that provides interesting counterpoint to the above is the John Merrow Education Podcast. Merrow is a well known and highly successful media commentator on education and educational reform. This podcast's blog states "John Merrow, an education reporter for over 30 years and correspondent for the *NewsHour* with Jim Lehrer on PBS, profiles significant issues in K-12 and higher education." The show notes entry for episode # 50 states

> Over the course of a school year, five NYC Teaching Fellows have tackled every classroom challenge that's come their way, including disruptive students, violence, high pressure testing, and the reality of becoming teachers with almost no training.
>
> We've watched them overcome the jitters of their first day of school and struggle to maintain control of their classrooms. Two of their colleagues at PS25 in Brooklyn quit early in the year and one of our rookies, Renee Cason, came close. She admits "I hate this year" but also promised she would not throw in the towel. In this NewsHour episode, the sixth of seven, you'll find out if she makes it and hear the rookies reflect on all they've faced. (McNeil/Lehrer Productions, 2006, Episode 50)

The high quality of this series reflects the budget, experience, and support behind it. Clearly, it illustrates the validity in Pink's statement about how "These people—artists, inventors, designers, storytellers, caregivers, consolers, big picture thinkers—will now reap society's richest rewards," as this work shows that Merrow is many of these types rolled into one. It is ironic, however, how in some ways the easy to use, low cost, accessible to all podcasting technology levels the playing field, and The Faculty Room, even in contrast to Merrow's work, comes off as having much to offer. That a teacher on a shoe string budget like the author of The Faculty Room can convey much of what a professional broadcaster does in this one, shows how the media, truly, is democratized and enables us to address dimensions of the lives of educators that were largely inaccessible previously.

Breaking the PD Time Barrier

Podcasting's virtue of facilitating "Time Shifting" for schedule stretched teachers represents perhaps its area of greatest potential to significantly impact PD for educators.

Many involved in PD for educators have come to the frustrated understanding that while motivated teachers in need of professional development abound, quality content with which to fuel it is available, and that adequate trainers and facilities with which to provide an experience for them are available as well, there is one factor remaining that stands in the way. Time! Teachers are simply too busy teaching in order to receive the professional development they need to maintain or improve their teaching practice. The time factor represents a very serious impediment to even the potentially best professional development programs.

Over the past decade, distance learning has been used with a good degree of success to address this time issue. By offering teachers the opportunity to utilize periods of time that would likely not otherwise be available for professional development, more time, in a sense, is created for them.

By offering teachers synchronous online courses (classes given at a set, mutually agreed on time) teachers can attend from the convenience of their own homes when they are not working. This yields more time for PD. There have also been many examples of efficiencies established by synchronous PD done during the work day, accomplished by allowing participants to save on travel time and expenses, and attending from their desks or school libraries without having to leave their workplace.

Taking this idea a step further, asynchronous, non-simultaneous, courses create a much greater opportunity as each individual can log on and spend as much time as desired at a stretch as he works through a course at his own pace and at his own convenience. Online PD has saved incalculable dollars and hours in travel and brick and mortar facilities expenses, making an educational experience possible for millions who would not have been able to have one otherwise.

But while online professional development offers great advantages, it has limitations imposed by technology devices and connections. Yes, time is reorganized to take advantage of periods that previously had to lie fallow, but they are still limited to only where and when participants have access to an Internet enabled computer. So called anywhere, anytime learning in reality only happens where and when one can be connected. Even with the advance of WiFi, PD participants are still tethered to the source of their signal. Consequently, a great deal of potentially available time and opportunity still can not be tapped.

Podcasting offers new potentials in this regard in several ways. First off, because the cost of MP3 players is low, many more devices can be put in many more hands at the prices required. And above all, a charged player loaded with content is truly mobile. It need not pick up any sort of enabling signal, making it freer than computers, cell phones, or satellite radios. Unlike predecessors like the Walkman or Discman though, it is also not dependent on static, expensively produced and limited content. Fresh content is easily and inexpensively produced (as other sections of this book illustrate) quickly and available in new supplies continually. When we bear in mind that we can access podcasts from connected computers, as well as from MP3 players, a picture of far great ubiquity achieved through technology flexibility is understood.

The RSS feed innovation makes this picture even rosier. Unlike other forms of on-demand content, podcasts are pushed to subscribers, reminding them of the availability of new content, and freeing them up to use it rather than search for and acquire it. The implications of all these advantages for the delivery of PD are very significant.

Repeated, On-Demand Access

PD content often needs to be revisited and reviewed in order for learners to get from it all that's there. A complex combination of learning processes is at work involving comprehension and cognition and repeated access to content allows learners to glean missing information and reflect on items not fully absorbed in previous encounters.

Unfortunately, professional development is most often provided in workshop format in which content is presented just once. This is due to economic and organizational reasons. It is often true that school districts offer this type of professional development because their organizational particulars and available resources make it the only practical option. Podcasting offers even these constricted PD situations flexibility and increased reach.

Through the recording of professional development content and its distribution via podcasting, practitioners are able to access content whenever they want, as often as they want. This can make the difference between "getting it" and struggling to absorb as much as can be learned in a single face to face session.

Course casting, an early application of podcasting developed on university campuses calls for making an audio recording of an event that is entirely conceived of as a traditional face-to-face lecture and podcasting it. A number of organizations have attempted to provide professional development to teachers using this approach. A microphone is set up in a live workshop and the unedited recording is disseminated in the hope that it will prove of value.

Unfortunately, the practice of course casting has largely proven to be unsatisfactory in several respects. First, typically, course casts are media resources of low value in respect to production quality and their ability to engage and hold an audience. A live lecture may hold class members' attention because of the weight of the real life presence of the instructor, but fall flat when they are recorded and played back.

Furthermore, confusion and problems may creep in when an interactive live presentation is reduced to an audio recording without preparation. For instance, while the material that was presented live is made available for review directly after class, instructors note that this produces a decrease in attendance at the original, face to face lectures. Apparently, in the minds of some students the podcast lecture and the lecture itself are essentially one and the same and they prefer to take in the lecture at their own preferred time and place via the podcast version.

A far better approach to the use of podcasting for instructors would be to provide ancillary materials that enhance and enrich the live session. These could be content items appropriated by the instructor, adapted by editing or enhancing, or produced outright by the instructor from scratch.

Above all, professional development content that is presented as a podcast should not be conceived of simply as recorded live sessions. The differences between the two approaches must be accounted for in the planning stages. Qualities like language and grammar—ordering and pacing of content—sound and voice quality, all play an important part in the way the listener accesses and assimilates the content. Creating professional development podcasts should be conceived of as a process of production rather than replication.

Good examples of podcasts that are carefully prepared for this type of purpose are made available by the professional development podcasting system of the Human Resources Development department of Broward County Public Schools (http://hrdpods.blogspot.com/). Also, the Ohio Treasure Chest of Technology Resources, which teachers certainly will want to revisit as it provides a record for them of highly useful items as well as providing new ones on a regular basis (http://www.ohiotreasurechest.org).

TYPES OF PODCAST PROFESSIONAL DEVELOPMENT

Understanding that podcasting increases teacher access to PD content brings us to reflecting on which types of PD it can be applied to effectively. Several categories and examples follow.

Reflective Discussions

One of the types of PD practices that works well in the podcast format is the reflective discussion. A great deal is added to understanding a field and its practices by listening to discussions between accomplished and experienced colleagues. These experiences are often hard to come by. Podcasting can offer new possibilities in informing educators about important issues by this approach.

Imagine a situation in which the state department of education has altered the way the essay writing portion of its eighth grade English language arts standardized performance test is to be graded. A new set of criteria has been developed for student performance, as has a new rubric for applying these criteria to establish a grade for each student. Of course, the state will send out a memorandum and instruction booklet explaining the test, essay question, criteria, and use of the rubric. All schools will mandate that those teachers assigned to administer and grade the test read these.

Many schools in attempting to provide a higher level of preparedness will hold meetings in which these staff members will be guided in going over the booklets and discussing their thoughts and concerns. In fact, the Metropolis school district, a large conglomeration of 100 schools, will classically host a districtwide institute a week ahead of these school-based meetings, at which a representative teacher from each of the schools with an eighth grade is to be trained in the scoring issues. These participants will then turnkey their colleagues back at their home schools during the school-site training.

However, in a neighboring district of the same size, the administration tries something different and to great effect. Elm School's Mrs. Clinton, a 35-year veteran of teaching eighth grade English, Lakeside School's Mr. Smith, a 19-year veteran of the same, and Ms. Colon, a vice principal with 27 years experience supervising and supporting eighth grade English language arts instruction, attend a meeting arranged at district headquarters with a representative from the State Education Department's Testing and Accountability Division. Their discussion, reflecting their highly informed and experienced perspectives on the test and how to handle it, is recorded and podcast for all teachers in the district. Teachers will be able to listen to this whenever and however often they feel the need, including commuting to school on the day of the test.

The above is a hypothetical application, but one with real world precedent already. The Mabry School in Georgia, in order to satisfy its need to inform staff about the details of how its students scored on a recently administered high stakes test, produced a graphically enhanced podcast that communicates this information to school community members. For this school podcasting was the most practical media with which to record the information and the most desirable manner of distributing it.

> *2006 CRCT Scores Released (VP)*
>
> *We have created this video podcast of Mabry's CRCT scores from May, 2006. Sometimes data can be confusing, so here is a simple way to understand what you're about to see: We want more purple and no yellow. Each bar graph shows the percentage of students below grade level (yellow), on grade level and meeting expectations (blue), and above grade level and exceeding expectations (purple).*
>
> *The first chart in each data set shows an overview of that grade level's performance in each subject. The next several charts show how our students compared to the students in Cobb County as a whole and the state of Georgia in each subject area.*
>
> *You will notice that, in some subject areas, the data looks significantly different than it has in the past. These tests were renormed last year. For a more detailed explanation of the data, you can visit these two posts as MabryOnline: CRCT Data from May, 2006, Posted and Student Achievement Data from May, 2006.*
>
> *If the data goes by too fast for you, simply click the Pause button. (Mabry School, 2006, pp. 1-4)*

More examples of reflective discussion podcasts can be found at the Collaborative Leadership in Education Web site of Oakland Universit.

Forum Style Podcasts

Imagine a radio show series just for third grade science teachers in the Seattle area. That's the kind of thing possible through podcasting. Such teachers would likely want to include in their instructional program guided observation activities for the youngsters. They might include things like the weather, the seasons, and wildlife and their migrations. These are specific to their local area, as are their pedagogical concerns influenced by policies, organizational considerations, and resources specific to their locality and school and district, as well. Many of the factors controlling their success are highly timely and fleeting. A weekly podcast, for instance, would provide hundreds of teachers with up to the moment local knowledge that would be invaluable in preparing them for their teaching assignments.

Are there new exhibits and things to see at any of the area's dozens of museums and parks? Are television shows scheduled for local viewing that are anticipated to mesh with the curriculum particularly well? Has there been an unfortunate incident in the district, like the passing away of a faculty member, an accident involving youngsters, or simply the loss of an important game? A forum-style podcast can help teachers prepare themselves to tackle difficult and out-of-the-ordinary tasks in guiding and instructing youngsters.

An example of this type of podcast is Soft Reset which can be accessed through its Web site. This podcast is produced for teachers who use palm type handheld computers in their classrooms. While those teachers involved with this instructional concern are spread out geographically, their interests are narrowly focused and highly specific to the subset of technology devices and applications common to their classrooms. The site's notes for a recent episode read

> *Episode #14: Science—Tony and Mike share probeware, spreadsheets, participatory simulations, and reference programs for Palm and Windows Mobile that help with science instruction. Your hosts also share applications that teachers use for other subjects, but can also be used for learning science. The episode ends with audio from the U.S. Virgin Islands. Be sure to listen for the harsh consequence if a student in Miss Prince's school loses a stylus. (Vincent, 2006, p. 12)*

Narrative Procedure

There are some PD and supervisory needs that call for access to an informing voice, but that do so at times when access to a computer or colleagues is difficult or impossible. Alternatively, an example of this might happen when the computer is in use for another purpose and is better used when freed from playing an audio file in order to handle other tasks.

A good example of this can be found on the K-12 Handhelds Podcast Sharing Page. The posted audio file titled "Page Design Options of School Center (MP3 audio)" is a detailed, step-by-step procedure in Web authoring for a specific purpose. The page description reads "This is a description of the options available to teachers creating their Web sites using the School Center Application. The author is Natalie Tolbert, staff member of Mansfield High School in North Little Rock, AR" (Tolbert, n.d., p. 12).

Guest Star Addresses

The school district has parted with a $1,000 to match the thousand raised by Oak Street Elementary students by washing cars, selling cupcakes, and saving pennies. The money is to be spent on a rare treat, an hour-long auditorium assembly appearance by Meg White Fawn, a famous Native American writer of young people's literature. For years her book *Flying with Eagles—Walking like Bears* has been a much loved staple of the early elementary literacy program. All the students know it by heart and quote it to one another. While Meg will dazzle the 400 students of Oak Street with her hour-long appearance, the students at the districts other 15 elementary schools will not be able to share in it. With Meg's permission, the district head of technology sets up some basic audio equipment in the auditorium and records the session, which he will later podcast for the benefit of all. Not only will the students of the other schools be able to share the experience soon after the big day, but all of them, including the students at Oak Street, will be able to download and listen to it again and again. This guest appearance will be a valuable resource for years to come when future classes read *Flying with Eagles*, too.

An example of this type of podcast can be accessed from the Web site of Robert Pottle, a well-known children's author who does many school assemblies. While intended to promote his performances, it conveys how the value of a live performance may be preserved by digital audio recording and disseminated by podcast technology (Pottle, n.d.).

PODCASTS AS PART OF AN EXTENDED PROFESSIONAL DEVELOPMENT RESOURCE PACKAGE

The podcast professional development experience can be made far richer if it accounts for interactivity between trainer, trainee, and peer colleagues. Because a podcast is a downloadable media item that does not exist in synchronous real time, this has to be approached differently than a conventional broadcast radio program that accepts phone calls on the air or that responds to emails on the fly as it broadcasts. Podcasts can function well in this context when they are part of a continuum of online communication resources. Kathy Schrock's Kaffeeklatsch is a blog that is used to support the teachers of Nauset Massachusetts public school district in their use of technology. The blog is part of a continuum of items that includes several other blogs, a conventional Web site, and the podcasts, all work together to get the job done (http://kathyschrock.net/blog, http://nausetschools.org/podcasts/index.htm and http://nausetpublicschools.blogspot.com, Shrock, 2006-2007; Nauset Schools, 2005-2006a; 2005-2006b).

One blog entry offers teachers in the district numerous links relating to their need for background information about interactive whiteboards. Additionally, there is a link to a podcast that is accessed through the district's separate podcasting blog that features an interview with one of the district's teachers talking about her experiences with this type of equipment.

Because podcasting is a new medium it is often thought of as an isolated, stand alone entity. However, as it comes to be used by more and more educational professionals it is often reconceived as one of several, related digital media tools. When used as a suite, there is a synergy created that offers important advantages for professional development.

MASTER CONVERSATIONS

Podcasting offers a new type of professional development offering something that has been hard to make available on a broad based basis previously. Among those experiences which can make a great difference to the evolving practice of teachers and other professionals is a conversation between master practitioners. Imagine lucking into a situation in which you can be a "fly on the wall" as a couple (or more) of highly experienced, articulate masters in your field let their hair down and trade insights. This is the type of thing that does indeed happen, but with no guarantee of regularity. A great example is Podchat with Gayle Manchin, First Lady of West Virginia (available from iTunes) in this series she does highly insightful interviews with some of the most important educational thought leaders.

The podcasting format encourages these informal, yet highly valuable conversations. Imagine listening in to a conversation between Oppenheimer and his staff as they kick back and think through the subtleties of the scientific process they experienced and contributed to during their tenure on the Manhattan Project. How would that move the understanding of nuclear physics beyond what's available in texts or through formal lectures?

In his article in *Information World Review* titled "Putting Feeling into Content," Tracey Caldwell, states:

> "Podcasts are adding the 'human touch' to previously dry corporate information. They are providing a fresh new learning tool for professional development and study in corporations and universities." This is decidedly different than simply providing more professional development, although that dimension is an advantage of podcasts as well as Caldwell states, too, that "They (podcasts) allow people to 'time shift' when they want to receive information into previously dead time so, for example, an executive can catch up on regulatory developments while driving in a car. (Caldwell, 2006, p. 2).

Talking about his interview with Timo Hannay, head of Web publishing for Nature Publishing Group (NPG), Caldwell states "he believes podcasting offers added-value to text-based journal papers" and quotes him as saying "Audio conveys personality, passions, interests—and you get the feeling behind the paper. The scientist talking about their work conveys the human side." (Caldwell, 2006, p. 11).

PODCAST FOR TEACHERS

The weekly show produced by the authors of this book, Podcast for Teachers, now succeeded by Teacher's Podcast (http://www.teacherspodcast.org), was and is both an effort to continue to evolve podcasting as a form of, and delivery mechanism for, professional development, as well as a source of important professional material to the many thousands of audience members who have found their way to it. It is described in detail in King and Gura's article "Professional Development as Podcast" that appeared in *Techlearning* in May, 2006.

> *By accessing our weekly podcast, teachers around the globe can "click into" timely, quality, and helpful professional development sessions on the uses of technology for teaching and learning. They can do this 24/7 based on their own schedule. What takes this beyond mere online courses though, is that this content can be listened to anywhere. Interested parties may download our Web-based broadcasts free of charge from the Fordham and Podcast for Teachers, Techpod sites (www.podcastforteachers.org) or from the numerous media/podcast directories, such as the original iTunes, Yahoo Podcasts, Podcast Alley (www.podcastalley.com), etc. Users will listen on any computer or transfer the material to any MP3 player, such as an iPod, a Sansa, iRiver, and so forth. Imagine professional development set free of fixed location and as mobile as music has become to the iPod generation.*
>
> *Our weekly* Podcast for Teachers, Techpod [now produced as the Teachers' Podcast] *offers interviews with educators, authors, and "ed techies;" curriculum ideas; news resources; technology tips; and research that educators can use in the classroom. It's available any time and any place: on the beach, in the supermarket, or while commuting to work. Teachers who want to be "in the know" can fit professional development into their schedules rather than having to make their schedules fit someone else's. (King & Gura, 2006).*

SOURCES

Another dimension that affects the nature and quality of the professional development offered teachers is the source of the talent involved in delivering it. Generally, PD is designed and delivered by either school district instructional experts or sometimes by a school's own resident expert, by independent service providers and university schools of education, and by the developers and publishers of instructional materials. This last category is important because often the PD content revolves around skills and techniques the teachers will use in implementing those materials in their classrooms. Alternatively, the PD may involve a philosophy or approach closely associated with publishers' materials. There may be crossover between these categories, particularly in presenting PD content about the use of published materials which, if not done by the publisher directly, will be done by a university or service provider who promotes their use, or by a school district employee offering insight into the use of materials acquired by the district. All of these efforts can be facilitated greatly by the production of podcasts which might be created by any of the parties involved. However, publisher generated podcasts are likely to be the most highly produced and in some respects effective. They represent a step forward in getting important information distributed that is timely, updateable by those most directly involved in producing the materials on which they are based, and conveniently distributed and consumed.

Stenhouse Publishers is an example of a publisher who moved into podcasting early on. It offers short PD-oriented podcasts to promote its books that give insight into the type of PD possible through podcasting. While the podcasts are clearly conceived to generate interest in book purchases, it does deliver worthwhile conceptual content with the added value that reviewing materials, something that has long been a part of PD, is greatly facilitated allowing prospective readers to get an overview from the authors directly.

Their Author Conversations: Podcasts web site reads "Welcome to Author Conversations, a new series of podcasts featuring Stenhouse authors discussing their books, their teaching lives, and their work beyond the classroom" (Stenhouse Publishers, 2007, p. 1)

Here's another example, this one of a school district attempting to provide a similar type of PD by podcast. This podcast also addresses the use of published material, but from the perspective of a district employee. Here, the Portland, Oregon school system produced a PD session on the use of a popular published curriculum piece which it made available through its Math Podcasts Web site which states: "Questioning Strategies in EDC by Andy Clark (37 minutes)—Andy Clark, former district math coordinator, gave this presentation to the Beach Elementary staff on questioning strategies in Every Day Counts, the calendar math program" (Portland Public Schools, n.d., p. 2).

Education is a field in which scarcity of essentials is a constant feature of the landscape. Although teaching has never been more sensitive to the need for professional development, PD remains an essential service that remains very scarce, a situation over which teachers have little or no personal control. Podcasting offers the possibility to change this, providing more PD in a wider variety of forms, and doing so in a way that allows more teachers to take advantage of it.

As podcasting has become more well known it has been adopted by some providers of professional information with a solid track record, but who embrace new vehicles as their potential becomes clear. The Today's Middle Level Educator, a podcast series produced by the National Middle School Association is an excellent example of how we may expect to see more and more quality professional development content provided as podcast in the future (http://www.nmsa.org/Publications/TodaysMiddle LevelEducator/tabid/1509/Default.aspx).

RESOURCES

Author Conversations: Podcasts. http://www.stenhouse.com/podcast.asp

The Faculty Room. http://jaion.libsyn.com

Kathy Schrock's Kaffeeklatsch. http://kathyschrock.net/blog

K-12 Handhelds Podcasting Sharing Page. http://www.k12handhelds.com /podcastshare.php

Mabry School Podcast Central. http://mabryonline.org/podcasts/archives /student_podcasts/art/index.html

The Online NewsHour. http://www.pbs.org/newshour/rss/media

Podcast for Teachers, Techpod. http://www.podcastforteachers.org

Podchat. http://www.wvgovedact.org/podcasts

Portland Public Schools Math Podcasts. http://www.kindergarten.pps.k12.or.us/ .docs/pg/10434

Soft Reset. http://www.learninginhand.com/softreset

The Teachers' Podcast. http://www.teacherspodcast.org

CHAPTER 16

BEYOND COURSE CASTING

Transforming and Expanding the Learning Platform

DOING THINGS BETTER AND DOING BETTER THINGS

As is the case with the adoption by educators of any new technology, determining podcasting's place in the educational landscape requires some probing and reflection. At times digital technologies are embraced by schools simply because educators want to *include* new items of significance that appear on the horizon. The impulse here is to keep schooling relevant by at least superficially making part of what's going on in the greater world, part of school.

Going a little deeper than this level of adoption is the understanding demonstrated by wise educators that they should *take advantage* of resources that evolve in the overall process of mankind's intellectual growth. If banking, healthcare, and military management have discovered, for instance, that maintaining e-mail lists facilitates communication among large groups of staff members, then logic would dictate that the staffs of schools can benefit this way as well.

In some ways the adoption of podcasting conforms to this second level of integrating established innovations within educational settings. How-

Podcasting for Teachers: Using a New Technology to Revolutionize Teaching and Learning,
Revised Second Edition, pp. 245–263

ever, there is a third and deeper level of technology adoption, one in which educators develop practices specifically for their own needs. This chapter will work its way toward this third level, one in which podcasting is adopted not simply to show that school is relevant, and not only to help educators do things a little bit better, but one in which they do *better things*. In other words, the ways podcasting expands and transforms the platform from which teaching and learning is carried out.

A WORD ABOUT "COURSE CASTING"

Often, when a new technology like podcasting emerges there is a period of time in which a limited understanding of its true significance directs how that technology is applied to the work of education. It is only natural and normal that in this initial, emergent time period that those motivated to begin using the new technology turn to established practices, and attempt to marry them to the new technology. This is particularly so in regard to communication technologies or media technologies. This phenomenon was in full effect when the World Wide Web emerged. In the beginning many early Web authors simply put text online and assumed that the reader would navigate this text in much the same way that print readers do. Over the years, the significance of having a Web presence was better understood and the habits of Web audiences studied and understood better, too. Consequently, a unique and very highly effective new form that we now recognize as the Web site emerged. It is not difficult to identify what is and what is not an effective Web site. Over the years we've come to develop a consciousness about how Web sites should look, feel, and function. It will likely be the same as podcasting matures.

A first, but unfortunately somewhat defining, attempt at establishing a solid educational application for podcasting was course casting. That this application would emerge is understandable when viewed within the context of emerging technologies and their evolution. Unfortunately, in the minds of many, this first application has shaped the entire understanding of podcasting's value and function in the world of education. This is not true, as is amply proven over and over again in this book. Still, understanding course casting is useful for those wanting a complete understanding of podcasting.

Course casting is most closely associated with the world of higher education. In the classrooms of a number of universities, some forward thinking professors decided that recording their lectures and then podcasting them would be an interesting and useful thing to do. Generally these course casts were unedited, presenting the class or lecture in its entirety—coughs, door slams, silent periods in which chair shuffling and page turning go on interminably, included. They frequently have very poor sound quality, basic audibility apparently being the overarching standard in their production. Because little effort was invested in the production of these podcasts, they represent little value. While the idea of capturing content from a well delivered course or lecture might have wide appeal course casts are so rough and "off the cuff" that their potential isn't realized. Of the many draw backs to this approach that have been noted, one of the most significant is that early on, many course casting professors noticed that a portion of their students had concluded that if the class could be downloaded in its entirety, there was little point in actually attending the class in the flesh.

Ironically, despite a general thumbs down about the educational significance and efficacy of course casting, a good number of universities, likely due to the initial attention paid to it in the press and a desire to be "cutting edge," have established course casting programs, encouraging faculty members to participate in this practice.

What's clear is that podcasting is best viewed as a way to add to what goes on in class and not simply to record or perhaps, replace it. Podcasting requires planning and production, especially editing.

PEDAGOGY OF DIGITAL AUDIO

> It is in our IQ testing that we have produced the greatest flood of misbegotten standards. Unaware of our typographic cultural bias, our testers assume that uniform and continuous habits are a sign of intelligence, thus eliminating the ear man and tactile man. *Understanding Media: The Extensions of Man (McLuhan cited in Alger, 2005, para. 2)*

> Reflecting on a quote from Marshal McLuhan, accomplished educational technologist and Marshall McLuhan Distinguished Educator Award winner, Brian Alger opines "today, we could easily replace 'I.Q. testing' in the above quote with 'standardized testing' and without any significant change in the validity of McLuhan's grievance." (Alger, 2005, para. 7-8)

In stating this he points out that our print dominated classrooms render education myopic, eschewing entire realms of thinking, knowing, and learning that are other than text-based. This would mean little if there were no viable alternatives and until recently this was largely the case. So called "audio visual" resources for instruction were cumbersome, hard to come by for most teachers, and represented a very paltry body of content. Educators could perhaps sense that a great deal of valuable content for learning might be produced by bringing media, particularly audio—the spoken word in all its varieties—into the classroom, but it simply was very far from possible to do so.

Recently, however, a spectrum of easy to use, inexpensive, easy to acquire, and highly practical digital technologies have emerged and converged to reverse this situation. Podcasting is perhaps the pinnacle of this set of innovations in terms of what it offers educators.

LISTENING AIDS READING

While standards and other well known instructional framework documents would indicate that "Speaking and Listening" is considered an essential area of literacy learning, it frequently takes a back seat to the other dimensions of reading and writing. These, more favored and stressed areas of the curriculum appear very prominently on the standardized tests that currently represent the impetus for what gets done in classrooms.

Furthermore, because the majority of teachers are individuals who have thrived in print dominant classrooms, they relate to print reading and writing as having the most importance in preparing students.

Ironically, there is evidence that supports the idea that the teaching of speaking and listening skills will produce better performance in text-based literacy skills, as well. In his paper "Reading With the Mind's Ear: Listening to Text as a Mental Action," Randy Bomer puts forth the idea that

> If reading is understood as consisting of multiple kinds of thinking, then listening is one of the most important forms of mental action in which readers engage. Readers must hear sentences in order to make sense of nested syntactic relationships. They also must hear sounds that occur within the text in order to participate in its world, and they must attend to the voice(s) of the text or narrator. (Bomer, 1996-2007, p. 1)

RETRIEVING SPEAKING AND LISTENING

The following document appears on the Web site of the prominent professional organization NCTE (National Council of Teachers of English) where it is identified as "an NCTE Position Statement—a statement on an education issue approved by the NCTE Board of Directors": Titled On Including Speaking and Listening in National Assessment of Educational Progress (NAEP) Assessments (1973 NCTE Annual Business Meeting in Philadelphia, Pennsylvania)" it states:

> Within the general areas of language arts, the present NAEP program stresses reading, written composition, and literature, with little stress on

> speaking and listening skills. Although over the years NAEP staff members have made informal assurances that more attention will be paid to listening and speaking, not enough has been done. At its meeting in Minneapolis in November, 1972, the NCTE Commission on the English Curriculum adopted a resolution supporting the inclusion of speaking and listening in NAEP. Be it therefore resolved, that the National Council of Teachers of English transmit a statement of its conviction to the Director of the National Assessment of Educational Progress that national assessment should include the evaluation of speaking and listening skills in a form consistent with their importance. (NCTE, 1998-2007, pp.1-2)

This was a serious indicator of what many hoped would be a trend. However, since 1973, when the report was issued, the prominence of speaking and listening as components of literacy taught has, many would argue, lost ground. For instance, the California Department of Education (2006) includes on its public Web site a page titled "Released test questions from the 2003, 2004, and 2005 California Standards Tests (CSTs)."

As an example of the diminished states of listening and speaking, a look at the Grade 4 English language arts test, a high stakes assessment instrument that many would point to as typical of this type of test administered currently, reveals that:

1. The skills tested include: word analysis, reading comprehension, literary response and analysis, writing strategies, and written conventions. "Listening and Speaking" do not even appear as strands to be tested.
2. The test features numerous print stories that the students are directed to read to themselves, reflect on, and answer in classic multiple choice a, b, c, or d fashion. There is no opportunity for students to use listening and speaking skills as a way of demonstrating their competencies. Print, in addition to representing the exclusive content format on which they are tested, represents the exclusive mode by which they are permitted to make responses for which they are held accountable (California Department of Education, 2006).

In so many ways this represents a serious educational disconnect. For instance, the U.S. Department of Labor, in its book *Skills and Tasks for Jobs—A SCANS report for America 2000* lists the following as "basic skills": Reading, Writing, Arithmetic & Mathematics, Listening, and Speaking. (U.S. Department of Labor, 2000, p. 19, para. 1).

As is becoming increasingly apparent, digital media is asserting itself as perhaps equal to print in our current media immersed world. To avoid making this phenomenon part and parcel of the overall instructional program being implemented in our classrooms is to abdicate our responsibility to prepare youngsters for success in the world they surely will enter after school. It behooves responsible educators to identify and assimilate into the instructional program approaches and practices to make speaking and listening a prominent part of the educational program. Podcasting is one with high potential.

PODCASTING AND PROJECTS

In her article "Start with the Pyramid," Diane Curtis explains

> In a growing number of schools, educators are echoing (Seymour) Papert's assertion that engaging students by starting with the concrete and solving hands-on, real-world problems is a great motivator. Ultimately, they say, such project-based learning that freely crosses disciplines provides an education superior to the traditional "algebra at 9, Civil War at 10, *Great Expectations* at 11" structure. (Curtis, 2001)

Project-based learning is an established approach to structuring learning activities for students that provides an obvious connection to podcasting. A concept closely related to learning projects is authentic activities. Authentic activities have been a goal of educators for a considerable time. In essence, authentic activities are those that have students learning things for real reasons, those beyond simply satisfying arbitrary requirements of school.

Standards by which the authenticity of an activity assigned to students may be understood and rated are listed by Fred M. Newman and Gary G. Wehlage in their article "Five Standards of Authentic Instruction." They include:

1. Higher Order Thinking,
2. Depth of Knowledge,
3. Connectedness to the World Beyond the Classroom,
4. Substantive Conversation, and
5. Social Support for Student Achievement (Newman & Wehlage, 1993, pp. 8-12).

Podcasting offers a vehicle by which a range of activities that would be considered authentic by these standards can be developed and implemented.

Number 3, in particular, Connectedness to the World Beyond the Classroom, is difficult to achieve in a traditional classroom. It is simply very challenging to find ways within the structure of school, an institution that by design functions away from the real world, to reverse that situation. Technology, particularly podcasting, offers a way to surmount this easily and effectively. Podcasts adapt to traditional instructional goals and practices easily and by nature are one of the most successful technologies to connect people yet developed.

Q: WHAT MAKES AN AUTHENTIC ACTIVITY AUTHENTIC? A: AN AUDIENCE!

In the article "Podcasts Offer the Audience Pupils Crave" which appeared in the U.K. publication *The Guardian* (10/4/05), Reporter Stephen O'Hear writes "children at the East Lothian comprehensive aged 12-13 together with the help of older pupils and teachers write and produce MGS Podcast, an entertainment and information show for the school and wider community." The co-coordinator of this project, Ewan McIntosh states "the students are highly motivated to podcast because the skills required are relevant and the process is not a simulation.... There are often bogus initiatives that touch the surface but don't get the kids really working on a meaningful product in the long term. These kids see themselves as podcasters till they leave school, and probably beyond" (O'Hear, 2005, para 3-4).

In the same article Educational Technology advisor, David Baugh states "I go into schools and work with young people and we record things... It isn't just mucking around. Somebody's going to listen to this and it's got to be good. And people are listening. Musselburgh grammar school's podcast has over 1,000 hits per show" (O'Hear, 2005, para. 10).

This is just one dimension of how podcasting expands the platform on which education is staged.

EXPANDING THE PLATFORM

The learning platform can be described as the combination of factors, such as time, available instructional manpower, resources, the learning environment, and practices that define and impact the quantity and quality of learning achieved. Podcasting, when embraced in a focused and visionary manner, can change this equation to the advantage of teachers and learners. The result is a transformed and expanded platform for learning.

Time

Podcasting adds time to the learning platform. The traditional platform is comprised of school time; generally, 6 hours and 20 minutes of instructional time—less, of course, time for attendance taking in each class, opening books and turning in papers, home room, travel from class to class, lunch, bus, and all sorts of other administrivia, leaving perhaps 3 hours of actual instructional time.

Traditionally this is extended by the addition of homework. Podcasting, like other forms of Internet-based or -related learning makes homework far more viable than simple review or slight advancement of in-school learning as it vastly enriches the resources and content available for learning. In fact, in many cases connected learning may only happen or primarily happen away from school.

By making it possible to learn in a great variety of environments, particularly in those which are not supported by infrastructure specifically set up to accommodate traditional instruction, podcasting can help learning happen in places not associated with it previously. The result of this is that learning can happen more often.

Similarly, podcasting can help learners make more use of time that is taken up with other activities. The portable and easily transportable character of MP3 playing devices enables learners to absorb content while walking, driving, shopping, and a host of other time-consuming activities that do not demand the full attention. The net effect of these two dimensions of podcasting's relationship to personal time is that more time can be devoted to learning without any significant trade off.

RESOURCES

Content Resources

Content for Different Learners. Podcasting offers variety in pedagogy and instructional materials, allowing educators to better accommodate the full range of multiple intelligences and learning styles evidenced by their students. According to BBC NI (North Ireland) Schools, a Web-based resource to inform teachers about student learning and

> By discovering how pupils learn, educators can provide opportunities for pupils to capitalize on their strengths and improve their employability skills.... Auditory learners relate best to the spoken word. They listen to a lesson and may write notes later. They are happy to rely on printed notes. Often auditory learners will not understand written information until they

have heard it. Auditory learners tend to be sophisticated speakers. (BBC NI, 2003, para 1, 3)

Classrooms are still very heavily oriented toward primarily supporting the learning of those individuals who relate well to text-based content. Podcasts represent an abundant source of audio-based content that can make instruction more accessible and satisfying for auditory learners. As a result of this, learning strands long considered to be an important part of literacy, namely listening and speaking, are being given a new look and new ways to reclaim the attention they have lost over the years as they have been eclipsed by written and text-based activities.

The Business Studies content area is one that is highly dominated by print text. Using audio-based content and activities in business courses, therefore, can offer students, who are auditory learners, and others, a welcome bit of variety. Podcasts like the following examples illustrate the viability of this approach.

The first example Learn Business English on Your Terms, a podcast series, addresses the theme of business English, a content subset that is of importance to both native and nonnative English-speaking business students. The show notes for the episode Trends read

> In today's podcast lesson we will be looking at how to describe trends in English. In business a trend is the general direction of things such as the prices of goods or sales volumes. Trends can be thought of in varying lengths including short, intermediate and long term. If one can identify a trend, it can be highly profitable, as you can read and predict where a market might be heading. (OnDemand Training Ltd., 2005-2006, para 1)

The second example moves the practice of podcasting to the other end of the spectrum in which students, having been exposed to podcast models, take on the production of podcasts directly and produce content that can be used by others. An example of student work done on the theme of economics is done by two graduate students at George Mason University is The MISEScreants: An Ongoing Narrative of Graduate School by Two Austrians. The show notes for Episode 5 read

> "Episode 5: An interview with Roderick Long.
> Roderick Long professor at Auburn University talks philosophy, anarcho-capitalism, and updates on his think tank The Molinari Institute with the MISEScreants. Podcasting provides an ever increasing body of quality, easy to use, FREE content. (D'Amico & Martin, p. 8)

Acquiring sufficient content to satisfy the demands of young learners hungry to follow their interests can be challenging for teachers, particularly in the upper elementary grades where books are conceived and produced as relatively short-term experiences. Current approaches that center on youngsters selecting their own books from a variety of choices further increases the need for ever growing libraries of titles.

StoryNory is a British group that publishes original and traditional childrens' stories, offering them free as podcasts through their Web site and a variety of podcast directories. They produce a new story roughly once a week. There is a continuity of characters and types of stories, which are very accessible.

The StoryNory podcasts are downloadable from the Web site or by RSS subscription. A recent Web site post illustrates the appeal to young listeners,

> Warning: This a rather scary story, particularly if you are a very small tadpole. Halloween is the most frightening night the year, or it is the most scrummy night of the year, depending on whether you are on the right end of a trick or a treat. Prince Bertie the Frog, Colin the Carp and friends are in search of fun and things to eat, but they encounter a real wicked witch in the form of Princess Beatrice's Stepmother. Bertie makes a wish, and then wishes that he hadn't. (Blog Relations Limited, 2007)

Customized and Current Content. The above is also an example of a further dimension of podcasting's impact on learning, the availability of content to support customized and individualized learning. By searching the assortment of podcasts posted on the Internet, students can acquire content more truly suited to their individual needs and tastes than is common in classes where the practice is for all students to use identical content materials.

Yet another way podcasting transforms the body of content available is by providing frequently updated material. Some areas of study, social studies for instance, require a steady influx of content that is updated. This is particularly important for time sensitive content, like news and commentary—content is no longer static and dated as soon as it is consumed. Through the RSS syndication function, fresh content is pushed to learners as soon as it is created and posted. This creates new dimensions for the class experience. Class is no longer where one brings the news or discusses it, it becomes one of the more important places where one goes to get the news and share the experience of getting it fresh continually.

A good example of this is the NewsHour Podcast offered through the Public Broadcasting System, the Web site of which describes it as providing "The latest updates, in-depth reports, interviews and analysis from The NewsHour with Jim Lehrer (Updated every weeknight)." The Web site offers a link titled News for Students, which has a detailed lesson plan on Podcasting titled "Featured Lesson Plan: Podcasting—Sharing Your Ideas About Featured Topics and Issues." This extended unit of study gives students background information on podcasting technology and its dimensions as a medium, an overview of podcasting's potential and role in reporting the news, an understanding of how students and others can use podcasts as a learning resource, and a guided experience in creating their own podcasts, that culminates with the sharing of their own podcast with peers beyond their immediate local.

Manpower and Talent Resources

Podcasting Brings Additional Voices Into The Learning Space. Recordings of famous speeches are available for download and use as instructional content. Original documents and primary sources need not be found exclusively in the province of print, as a variety of essential sound documents have been uploaded for podcasting. Items like John F. Kennedy's inaugural speech and John Glenn speaking from Friendship 7 are available as podcasts from Speeches and Historical Audio Podcasts, a Web resource that states "The speeches and sounds that helped define our world, in convenient podcast form. From Cronkite to Churchill, "Ich bein ein Berliner" to "Mr. Gorbachev, tear down this wall."

Similarly, podcasts of history in the making, speeches by prominent people of a more recent nature are available from resources like the University of California Television's *Conversations with History* (2003) podcasts. Recent episodes include: The Struggle for Human Rights in Iran, with Shirin Ebadi, Intellectual Journey: Challenging the Conventional Wisdom, with John Kenneth Galbraith, and Activism, Anarchism, and Power, with Noam Chomsky.

These podcasts can be reviewed in class or listened to as homework when experiencing an authentic, primary source in audio format is needed to enhance a unit of study. Other items that can be accessed this way include interviews with famous graphic artists speaking about their work. Such podcasts can be found at WordBalloon. "Wordballon: The Comic Creators Interview Show" the Web site describe it states,

> WORDBALLOON features one on one interviews with the writers and artists behind today's pop culture favorites. The creative minds behind today's hottest comics, films, and Television, tell behind the scene stories providing a DVD like commentary on their works, without spoiling the stories. Hosted by Chicago Radio Host John Siuntres, Wordballoon covers the cult entertainment scene, like no other podcast. (Siuntries, 2006, pp. 9-10)

Similarly, a variety of the world's foremost scientists talk about their research and discoveries on the BBC podcast show Naked Scientists. The show Web site states

> WHAT IS "THE NAKED SCIENTISTS"? The Naked Scientists are a media-savvy group of physicians and researchers from Cambridge University who use radio, live lectures, and the Internet to strip science down to its bare essentials, and promote it to the general public ...
>
> ... Each edition of the hour-long radio show comprises a carefully-researched digest of the preceding week's top science news stories followed by interviews with guest scientists who usually join the team in the studio to answer questions about their subject directly from the listening public. (Naked Scientists, 2001-2005, pp. 1-6)

MOBILE LEARNING

Podcasting makes learning mobile, enabling content to be accessed by students virtually anywhere and anytime. Podcasts are content that is hyper portable. A loaded and charged MP3 player can play back any downloaded content without connection to the Internet or a personal computer, with the need of being within range or line of sight of WiFi, BlueTooth, broadcast, or satellite radio waves.

Procedures, Directions, and Instructions

Procedural narratives is an application of podcasting that has not evidenced a great deal of activity as yet, but which has great potential. Whether it be directions in using a data probe to collect pH information from a pond, a procedure to mix paints of a desired color and texture for a mural, or making a batch of chili or chocolate chip cookies, digital audio and podcasting can make these valuable activities work smoother.

Performing such data collection activities in the field away from the school and the infrastructure that supports it is a type of science activity that many teachers would like to make more extensive use of. However, data collection procedures are involved and the reassuring voice of the teacher is crucial in supporting newcomers to this type of activity. With a podcast played through a battery powered handheld, the student can have the benefit of this, hands free, and repeated on demand as often as needed. A good example might be a trip to a body of water in order to measure ph, collect samples, test for temperature, clarity, salinity, and other properties. Manipulating materials, making notes, and completing tasks can be greatly facilitated by the use of audio played through personal head phones.

Guided Experiences

Rather than have students simply read and discuss an important chapter in history that happened locally, a narrated walking tour can be the richest possible way to convey the context that goes with content. However, while it is possible for teachers to take students on field trips personally, doing so involves getting permissions from administrators and parents, getting classes covered during one's absence, and preparing students for the outing. And of course, often one or two students will be absent on the day of the trip and having them make up the experience is difficult as well. All of these elements represent a serious set of limitations and at best such an undertaking can be done only once or twice a school year.

Alternatively, recording the field trip narrative and posting it as a podcast that is downloadable to portable MP3 players will allow students to do the excursion, perhaps with their parents or peers, at their own pace and on numerous occasions. teachers to invest the time saved in the creation of other experiences for their students.

An example of this type of podcast can be found at the Web site of iToors Podcasts.

An interesting episode is listed as

> London. The city that inspired some of literature's heaviest hitters is also the city that nurtured a large array of controversial writers, those writers whose writings—or life caused scandal and revolution around the world. Walk in the footsteps of writers whose influence is still felt around the world today—Lenin, Marx, Wilde, and Burroughs to name a few. (iToors, 2007, p. 8)

PODCASTING TRANSFORMS INSTRUCTION

Podcasting impacts instruction in several ways. On its most basic level it offers fresh and highly motivational activities with which the standard curriculum can be addressed. For instance, if the traditional curriculum calls for students to prepare and perform a dramatic reading of a work of literature, a classic assignment in the English language arts syllabus, having students prepare and present their work as a podcast instead of a live oral presentation will accomplish that goal exceptionally.

A very worthwhile example of how this type of activity can be effectively implemented can be found at the *ReadWriteThink* online curriculum resource which offers an extended unit of instruction titled "Audio Broadcasts and Podcasts: Oral Storytelling and Dramatization" at the Web site: http://www.readwritethink.org/lessons/lesson_views.asp?id=901.

This unit calls for students to review the form of dramatic readings, like the famous "War of the Worlds" piece done by Orson Wells, work their way through a series of activities to analyze and familiarize themselves with dramatic readings as performances, and ultimately create their own, which may be podcast. The unit's plan states student objectives as follows

Students will

- listen to (and read) an audio broadcast.
- explore the historical and cultural context of an audio broadcast.
- establish criteria for effective audio storytelling and dramatizations.
- compose a dramatization of a scene from a recent reading. (Read Write Think, 2007, p. 4)

In addition to providing an enhanced and enriched English language learning experience, the dividend to the above activity is that in doing this podcast or audio report, students out of necessity learn a variety of media and technology skills. For instance, students will need to learn: audio recording, audio editing, and perhaps some of the online production/management aspects of posting podcasts. Furthermore, their writing skills will be sharpened. In order to do a podcast they'll need to outline, write some sections completely, read or perform some of the written material, and perhaps involve themselves in interviewing or other oral history related skills. They may also need to do some post production writing chores. Some of these are aspects of writing that are not often addressed by hard copy dominated instruction.

SERENDIPITIES: PODCASTING EXPANDS THE PLATFORM IN WAYS BEYOND EXPECTATION

Podcasting Increases the School–Parent Connection

"At some schools, the rules are clear: Kids can chill out to downloaded music on portable players, but once they're inside, iPods and other learning distractions must be stowed in backpacks or lockers and kept there" relates *Washington Post* reporter, Fern Shen in her article "IPods Fast Becoming New Teacher's Pet." (2005, p. 2)

> At Jamestown Elementary School in Arlington, Camilla Gagliolo took another approach. Rather than fighting the fad, she's capitalizing on it by giving students iPods and re-imagining them as a learning tool.
>
> Podcasting, it turns out, is also well-suited for keeping busy parents in touch with the world their children inhabit all day at school.
>
> All they have to do is program their computers to capture the broadcasts—which could range from school announcements to plays to basketball games—and they can then listen to them on their desktop computer or download them to a portable player.
>
> "This idea is so great: I can hear what my daughter is doing and we can tell her grandparents, and they can hear it where they are," said Alison Pascale of Arlington, whose daughter Kalyn McNulty, 10, is one of the Jamestown podcasters. (Shen, 2005, pp. 3-5)

The above anecdote points to an unanticipated, but potentially, highly valuable asset that podcasting brings to the educational platform. While "published" items, like podcasts, are generally considered authentic activities in the sense that they provide structure, focus, motivation, and valuable feedback to students who produce them as learning products, vehicles by which learning is made to happen, it turns out that podcasts have value to their "audience" as well. Giving parents a glimpse into what their children are doing in school, not solely through periodic formal report card assessments, but rather in an easily accessible and engaging manner in which the day-to-day results of school work are presented as formative tools, is, as can be seen from the parent quoted above, a highly valued interaction between parent and school.

Ms. Gagliolo, media director of Jamestown Elementary school participated with the Smithsonian institution to produce several podcasts based on the school's visits to the museum. The Smithsonian Web site offers a page that describes the project, detailing how the students produced a podcast as a result of their visit from which the following quotes are taken.

> **Before the Visit**
> In preparation for the trips, each student filled out answers to worksheet questions: *What do you really want to see and why? What do you hope to learn about and why?* Their answers were the basis for the Pre-Visit episodes. They used iPods equipped with microphones to record predictions of what they would discover on the visits and the questions about mammals that they hoped to have answered.
>
> **During the Visit**
> A focused assignment is always a good idea for class museum visits. Museums can be overwhelming places, and students can feel lost in the jumble of attractions. The Jamestown students had an additional focus in this project.

> They would be going after the answers to specific questions, not only for themselves, but also for their podcast audience.
>
> At the National Museum of Natural History, they recorded descriptions of what they were seeing and thinking. They then met with one of the museum's experts on marine mammals and recorded an interview. In addition, they took digital photos, shot video footage, made drawings, and wrote journal entries. These "visuals" would be posted on the school Web site to accompany the podcast. (Shen, 2005, pp. 17, 18)

Not only did the students have an exceptional learning experience, but the podcasts they produced stand to inform their parents and peers about it. The podcasts also serve as a model for replication by other classes in other schools and as a tool for the museum to use in educating teachers. It is evident form this example how podcasting transforms the learning platform by establishing a vehicle to foster creativity in students.

The *Washington Post* article previously cited quotes the podcasting educator as saying "It just makes so much sense. They are so drawn to this technology. They are so excited by it. They're comfortable with it," said Gagliolo, the school's technology coordinator. Quoting Gagliolo and a student, Shen further points out

> Using little more than an iPod and a school computer, Gagliolo and her students have been making podcasts—online radio shows that can be downloaded to an iPod or other portable MP3 player. Avidly discussing their favorite iPod colors and models while they made recordings of their poems and book reports the other day, the fifth graders bubbled with ideas for future subjects.
>
> "We could read parts of books to show why we like them. We could do interviews. If there's a field trip, we could make a recording of it and post it," said Mohamed El-Sayed, 10. "Kids anywhere will like to hear about us." (Shen, 2005, pp. 4, 5)

Recently, however podcasts more specifically directed at the subject of strengthening relationships between schools and parents have emerged. Episode 21 of the Intercultural Development and Research Association's Classnotes podcast series titled Engaging Parents in Education is a good example (http://www.idra.org/Podcasts/Resources/Engaging_Parents_in_Education/).

Podcasting and Assessment

Performance assessment has been an area of interest of educators for a significant amount of time. While content standards list what students should learn and know, performance standards aid in measuring how well they have learned the content. Implementing a program to assess student growth by measuring learning reflected in performances, however, is considerably more challenging than administering standardized tests that require students only to fill in bubble sheets as a way to select multiple choice answers.

Podcasting is a way of structuring learning activities to produce a product, which in the case of a podcast may also be viewed as the result of a performance. Furthermore, podcasts (and related digital audio products) are easily storable, portable, and retrievable. Most importantly, they capture a snapshot of learning that is useful not only for summative assessment, but as a formative assessment resource to inform continuing teaching and learning, analyzing performances and targeting how to improve them.

An interesting example of student audio performances that may be seen in this light are the "What I know about Seeds—Mr. Gates' 2nd Grade Class" podcasts posted on Mr. Gates' teacher blog (Gates, 2006). These oral reports are done by individual students, but on a single standardized theme, something quite different than the practice of having a few students produce podcasts periodically as an extra, special, or alternative assignment. This is an important aspect of structuring podcast-based activities to perform the function of focused student assignments, in much the same way that traditional assignments and projects do. Such assignments state clear, consistent expectations defined by a set of criteria by which projects are to be done and evaluated. The social nature of the classroom learning environment dictates that all students be held to the same standards, often implying a single consistent assignment.

One educator who has created a more complete podcasting-based program of instruction is Jenny Ashby, founder of the Bendigo Education Apple Users' Team (BEAUT), and staff member at Epsom Primary School in Victoria, Australia. That Epson has made podcasting a prominent feature of its instructional program can be inferred from its Web site titled Our Prep 1/Podcast which reads "Welcome to our Podcast—Our podcasts tell about our learning. We hope you enjoy them" (Ashby, n.d.a, p.1).

In "Thinking beyond pen and paper: An interview with Jenny Ashby" an article appearing in The Knowledge Tree: An e-Journal of Learning Innovation put out by a consortium of Australian educators called the Australian Flexible Learning Framework, Ms. Ashby states

> we are wanting to see what happens when we use podcasting in the classroom with children, whether the children become more engaged, and basically enjoy what they're doing more then with pen and paper. The project that's involved at my school is a "living history" project—the children are interviewing past students, pupils, and teachers, and other people who've worked at the school over many years—and they are creating podcasts that

will be on in our Web site, eventually—later in the year for our 125th anniversary. (Murray, 2006, p. 8)

The results of that project can be reviewed on the Living History Podcasts Web site which states, "In 2006 students from Epsom Primary school interviewed past and present students, parents, teachers and staff from Epsom Primary school. There are 13 interviews. You can listen to them as podcasts" (Epsom Primary School, 2006, p. 1)

Assessment is seen by many as an essential element of educational programs. Formative assessment completes the cycle of the ongoing learning process, informing the next round of learning activity. Ms. Ashby has consequently created a rubric by which students' podcasts may be analyzed and evaluated. This rubric, downloadable at http://www.beaut.org.au/podcastrubric3.pdf, comprehensively rates student performance in creating the podcast, assigning one of three levels of achievement for each of seven elements involved in their creation, like: audio/music, information, interviews, and group/partner work. That this program is well structured as one that promotes twenty-first century learning is clear, as the rubric values collaboration, an important aspect of it. This, as well as the formative intention of this instrument is made apparent through its closing statement "Remember this is not the only podcast you will do so everyone will get to have a turn at the different jobs. The best podcast will be made by the group who gets along the best. You need to give and not always have things your way for the sake of the group" (Ashby, n.d.b., p. 2).

CONCLUSION

The above is a clear illustration of how podcasting embraces what is new and inspiring in education, while remaining grounded in solid core curriculum-based instruction. As technology continues to assume more and more of the basic intellectual chores that used to represent the value of learning, calculators and spreadsheets handling complex computational and record keeping, for instance, the more human skills of effective communication, collaboration, strategizing and problem solving will continue to emerge as highly important areas for education to address. Podcasting is a sterling example of a practice that fits squarely into this shift of emphasis, providing a practical set of activities with which to engage New Millennial students as education adjusts to the realities of the technology age.

RESOURCES

California Department of Education: 2003, 2004, and 2005 CST Released Test Questions. http://www.cde.ca.gov/ta/tg/sr/css05rtq.asp

Conversations with History. http://www.uctv.tv/podcasts/subscriptions.asp?feed=conversations
Epsom Primary Podcasts. http://www.epsomps.vic.edu.au/podcasting/Prep1/Prep1/Podcast/Podcast.html
iToors Podcasts. http://www.itoors.com
Learn Business English on Your Terms. http://www.ondemand-english.com/podcast/tag/economics
Naked Scientists. http://www.thenakedscientists.com/
MISEScreants. http://www.mises.org/classroom/misescreants.asp
ReadWriteThink. http://www.readwritethink.org/lessons/
Speeches and Historical Audio Podcasts. http://web.mac.com/johnkfisher/iWeb/JohnnyPodcast/Welcome%20Page.htm
StoryNory. http://storynory.com/2006/10/23/halloween-on-the-pond/
What I know about seeds. http://lms.saisd.net/cblog/index.php?blog=6&cat=84
Wordballoon: The Comic Creators Interview Show. http://feeds.feedburner.com/WordballoonPodcasts

REFERENCES

Alger, B. (2005). *Learning the medium is the message.* Retrieved January 15, 2007, from http://www.experiencedesignernetwork.com/archives/000663.html

Andersen, C. (2006). *The long tail: Why the future of business is selling less of more.* New York: Hyperion.

Andreatta, D. (2006, January 23). *Podcasting 101: Kids get professors' lectures to go. New York Post.* Retrieved August 30, 2006, from http://pqarchiver.nypost.com/nypost/results.html?num=25&st=basic&QryTxt=Podcasting%

Arnold, T. (2006, May 16). Panic! Juggling! YouTube! *USA Today,* p. D8. Retrieved August 30, 2006, from ProQuest at http://proquest.umi.com /pqdweb?did=1038067301&sid=1&Fmt=3&clien-tId=9148&RQT=309&VName=PQD

Ashby, J. (n.d.a). *"Epsom Primary Podcasts" Our Prep/1 Podcast.* Retrieved January 15, 2007, from http://www.epsomps.vic.edu.au/podcasting/Prep1/Prep1/Podcast/Podcast.html

Ashby, J. (n.d.b). *Podcastingrubricc.* Retrieved January 15, 2007, from http://www.beaut.org.au/podcastrubric3.pdf

Baylor School. (2006). *Baylor School podcasts: Jamy Wheless '82.* Retrieved January 9, 2007, from http://www.baylorschool.org/podcasts/061020_jamy_wheless.asp

BBC NI (North Ireland) Schools. (2003). *Teachers: Learning styles.* Retrieved January 15, 2007, from http://www.bbc.co.uk/northernireland/schools/11_16/gogetit/teachers/learning.shtml

Bennett, S., Salmi, H., & Myton, D. (n.d.). *Michigan Department of Education technology enhanced lesson plan.* Retrieved January 11, 2007, from http://techplan.edzone.net/ci2006/MathPodcasts.doc

Blog Relations Limited (2007). *Storynory: Halloween on the pond.* Retrieved January 15, 2007, from http://storynory.com/2006/10/23/halloween-on-the-pond/

Bomer, R. (1996-2007). *Reading with the mind ear: Listening to text as a mental action.* Retrieved January 15, 2007, from http://www.reading.org/publications /journals/jaal/v49/i6/abstracts/JAAL-49-6-Bomer.html

Bradley, J. (2006a). *Slauson podShow.* Retrieved September 15, 2006, from http://www.Slauson-PodShow.com

Bradley, J. (2006b). *Wise guy podcast.* Retrieved September 15, 2006, from http://www.WiseGise.com

Caldwell, T. (2006). Putting feeling into content. Retrieved January 16, 2007, from http://www.iwr.co.uk/information-world-review/featrues/2165853/putting-feeling-content

California Department of Education. (2006). *2003, 2004, and 2005 CST Released Test Questions*. Retrieved January 15, 2007, from http://www.cde.ca.gov/ta/tg/sr/css05rtq.asp

California State Board of Education. (n.d.). *Grade 5: English-Language Arts Contents Standards.* Retrieved January 11, 2007, from http://www.cde.ca.gov/be/st/ss/enggrade5.asp

The Center for Teaching History with Technology. (n.d.). *Podcasting in and out of the classroom.* Retrieved January 11, 2007, from http://thwt.org/historypodcasts.html

Creative Commons. (2006). *Podcasting legal guide.* Retrieved January 10, 2007, from http://wiki.creativecommons.org/Podcasting_Legal_Guide

CUNY Matters. (2006, Summer). Professors using podcasts as one of their newest technology tools. CUNY Matters. Retrieved September 5, 2006, http://www.podcastforteachers.org/TechpodArchives.html

Curtis, D. (2001). Start with the pyramid. Retrieved January 15, 2007, from http://www.edutopia.org/php/article.php?id=Art_884&key=037

D'Amico, D. & Martin, A. (n.d.). *Misescreants: An ongoing narrative of graduate school by two Austrians.* Retrieved January 15, 2007, from http://www.mises.org/classroom/misescreants.asp

Dunlap, E., McInnis, J., Wiggins, S. & McCarthy, M. (n.d.). *Project-based learning.* Retrieved January 8, 2007, from http://www.ncpublicschools.org/schoolimprovement/support/briefs/project

Edutopia. (2006). *Project-based learning.* Retrieved January 8, 2007, from http://www.edutopia.org/php/keyword.php?id=037

Electronic Frontier Foundation. (2006). *EFF: Legal guide for bloggers.* Retrieved January 10, 2007, from http://www.eff.org/bloggers/lg/

Eley, S. (2006, September 9). *Escape POD Episode 70: Squonk the Dragon. Escape Pod: The Science Fiction Podcast Magazine.* Retrieved September 13, 2006, from http://www.escapepod.org

Epsom Primary Podcasts. (n.d.) *Our Prep/1 Podcast.* Retrieved January 15, 2007, from http://www.epsomps.vic.edu.au/podcasting/Prep1/Prep1/Podcast/Podcast.html

Escape Pod. (2006). *Escape Pod: The Science Fiction Podcast Magazine.* Retrieved on September 13, 2006, from http://www.escapepod.org

ESLPOD. (2005). *About us, ESLPOD*. Retrieved January 9, 2007, from http://www.eslpod.com/website/about_us.php?PHPSESSID=9488bbf6e586413e512382246fadb4f6

ESLPOD. (2006). *ESLPOD.* Retrieved September 10, 2006, from http://eslpod.com

Evans, L. (2006, Sept. 25). Academic commons. Retrieved January 11, 2007, from http://www.academiccommons.org/ctfl/vignette /using-student-podcasts-inliterature-classes

The Faculty Room. (2006). *Home page*. Retrieved January 16, 2007, from http:// jaion.libsyn.com

Farlex, Inc. (2007a). *Computing dictionary of the free dictionary.* Huntingdon Valley, PA. Retrieved January 11, 2007, from http://computing-dictionary .thefreedictionary.com/MP3

Farlex, Inc. (2007b). *Computing dictionary of the free dictionary.* Huntingdon Valley, PA. Retrieved January 11, 2007, from http://computing-dictionary .thefreedictionary.com/XML

Federal Communications Commission. (2006). *Children's Internet Protection Act (CIPA) of 2001.* Retrieved on January 10, 2007, from http://www.fcc.gov/cgb/ consumerfacts/cipa.html

Feedburner.com. (2006). *Podcasts and videocasts.* Retrieved September 13, 2006, from http://www.feedburner.com/fb/a /podcasts;jsessionid=F3CC0C8011E030B770852992F

Feeley, J. (2006, May). *Lights! Camera! Vodcast! Wired Magazine, 14*(5). Retrieved on September 2, 2006, http://www.wired.com/wired/archive/14.05/howto.html

Felix, L., & Stolarz, D. (2006). *Hands-on guide to video blogging and podcasting.* New York: Elsevier.

FOOcast. (2006). *FOOcast home page*. Retrieved January 9, 2007, from http:// podcastnz.com/ index.php?main_page=product_music_info&cPath=4&products_id=27

Friess, S. (2006, June 28). *Podcasting after iTunes.* Retrieved June 16, 2008, from http://www.wired.com/techbiz/media/news/2006/06/71257

Gates. (2006). *What I know about seeds.* Retrieved January 15, 2007, from http:// lms.saisd.net/cblog/index.php?blog=6&cat=84

Geoghegan, M. W., & Klass, D. (2005). *Podcast solutions: The complete guide to podcasting.* New York: Friends of Fred.

Gura, M., & King, K. P. (2007). *Classroom robotics: Case stories of 21st century instruction for millennial students.* Charlotte, NC: Information Age.

Gura, M., & Percy, B. (2005). *Recapturing technology for education: Keeping tomorrow in today's classrooms.* Lanham, MD: Scarecrow Education.

Harel, I., & Papert, S. (1991). *Constructionism*. Westport, CT: Ablex.

Haugen, D. (n.d.). *Telling history.* Retrieved January 10, 2007, from http:// www.wcdd.com/wc/proposals/proplist.html

Haugen, D. (1996-2003). *The importance of storytelling in learning.* Retrieved January 10, 2007, from http://www.wcdd.com/wc/proposals/thprop/thscope.html

History in Our Time. (n.d.). *Science archive.* Retrieved January 11, 2007 from http: //www.bbc.co.uk/radio4/history/inourtime/inourtime_science.shtml

Illinois State Board (n.d.a). *Illinois learning standards in science.* Retrieved January 12, 2007, from http://www.isbe.state.il.us/ils/science/standards.htm

Illinois State Board (n.d.b). *Illinois learning standards for math.* Retrieved January 12, 2007, from http://www.isbe.net/ils/math/standards.htm

Institute of Learning (n.d.). *The principles of learning.* Retrieved January 8, 2007, from http://www.instituteforlearning.org/develop.html

International Society for Technology in Education (ISTE). (2006). *ISTE NETS standards*. Retrieved January 10, 2007, from http://cnets.iste.org/currstands/cstands-netss.html

International Society for Technology in Education (ISTE). (2007). *ISTE home page*. Retrieved February 15, 2007, from http://www.iste.org/

iToors Podcasts. (2007). *Home page*. Retrieved January 15, 2007, from http://www.itoors.com/iToors/index.php?option=com_content&task=category§ionid=9&id=20&Itemid=56

Jonassen, D. (1995). *Computers in the classroom: Mindtools for critical thinking* (1st ed.). Upper Saddle River, NJ: Merrill Prentice Hall.

King, K. P. (2002). *Keeping pace with technology: Educational technology that transforms: Vol. 1. The challenge and promise for K-12 educators*. Cresskill, NJ: Hampton Press.

King, K. P. (2003). *Keeping pace with technology: Educational technology that transforms: Vol. 2. The challenge and promise for higher education faculty*. Cresskill, NJ: Hampton Press.

King, K. P. (2005). *Bringing transformative learning to life*. Malabar, FL: Krieger.

King, K. P., & Eissinger, P. (2008). *Transformationed Education LIVE!* Retrieved September 1, 2008, from http://www.transformationed.com/podcast

King, K. P., & Griggs, J. K. (Eds.). (2006). *Harnessing innovative technology for higher education*. Madison, WI: Atwood.

King, K. P., & Gura, M. (2005, October 17). *Podcast for Teachers, Techpod: Episode 8: Exploring new dimensions! Conversations about educational innovations*. Retrieved September 10, 2006, from http://www.podcastforteachers.org/TechpodArchives.html

King, K. P., & Gura, M. (2005, October 31). *Podcast for Teachers, Techpod: Episode 10: We've gone global!* Retrieved September 10, 2006, from http://www.podcastforteachers.org/TechpodArchives.html

King, K. P., & Gura, M. (2006). *Professional development as podcast*. Retrieved January 16, 2007, from http://www.techlearning.com/showArticle.php?articleID=185303670

King, K. P., & Gura, M. (2006, February 6). *Podcast for Teachers, Techpod: Episode 24: Engaging, enraging and empowering!* Retrieved September 10, 2006, from http://www.podcastforteachers.org/TechpodArchives.html

King, K. P., & Gura, M. (2006, April 10). *Podcast for Teachers, Techpod: Episode 33: Tech 2 GO V: Keycast panel cast blast cast!* Retrieved September 10, 2006, from http://www.podcastforteachers.org/TechpodArchives.html

King, K. P., & Gura, M. (2006, September 11). *Podcast for Teachers, Techpod. Episode 54: Media literacy, blips to fakes, books, wikis and art history*. Retrieved September 11, 2006, from http://www.podcastforteachers.org/TechpodArchives.html

King, K. P., & Gura, M. (2007). *Podcast for Teachers, Techpod*. Retrieved January 9, 2007, from http://www.podcastforteachers.org

King, K., & Gura, M. (2008, June 2). *Episode 18-Education bridges: Transparency, learning and disruption*. Retrieved June 16, 2008, from http://www.teacherspodcast.org

King, K. P., & Gura, M. (2008). *The Teachers Podcast*. Retrieved September 1, 2008, from http://www.teacherspodcast.org

King, K. P. & Heuer, B. (2006). *Adventures in transformative learning.* Retrieved September, 15, 2006, from http://www.podcastforteachers.org/atl

King, K. P., & Wang, V. (Eds.). (2007). *Comparative adult education around the globe.* Hangzhou, PR China: Zhejiang University Press. Worldwide distribution: Transformation Education, LLC, www.transformationed.com

Lafferty, M., & Walch, R. (2006). *Tricks of the podcasting masters.* Indianapolis, IN: Que.

Lane Education Service District. (n.d.) *Teaching American History: A Lane County Grant Project, Teaching resources from the technology sessions.* Retrieved January 11, 2007, from http://www.lane.k12.or.us/CSD/ushistory/resources.html

Langhorst, E. (2005-2007). *Speaking of history.* Retrieved January 12, 2007, from http://speakingofhistory.blogspot.com

Lawler, P. A., & King, K. P. (2000). *Planning for effective faculty development: Using adult learning strategies.* Malabar, FL: Krieger.

Level Playing Field Institute. (2006). *Smashcast.org smashing science and technology into your brain.* Retrieved September 3, 2006, from http://www.lpfi.org /education/smashcasting.shtml

Lewin, J. (2008, May 5). *New media is now mainstream media; Podcasting growth is "massive."* Retrieved June 16, 2008, from http://www.podcastingnews.com/ 2008/05/05/media-mainstream-media/

Lo, H. (2006). *The ADHD podcaster.* Retrieved on January 9, 2007, from http:// www.theadhdspecialist.com/adhdblog/podcast.html

Lofting, H. (1920). *The story of Dr. Doolittle.* New York: Dell.

Mabry School. (2006). *Podcast Central: 2006 CRCT scores released (VP).* Retrieved January 16, 2007, from http://mabryonline.org/podcasts/archives/2006/09/ 2006_crct_score.html

McLeary, J. (2006). *The open classroom—podcasts for revision.* Retrieved January 12, 2007, from http://theopenclassroom.blogspot.com/2006_10_01_ theopenclassroom_archive.html

McNeil/Lehrer Productions. (1996-2006). *The Online NewsHour, Episode 50.* Retrieved January 15, 2007, from http://pbs.org/newshour/rss/media

Murray, J. (2006). *Thinking beyond pen and paper: an interview with Jenny Ashby.* Retrieved January 15, 2007, from http://kt.flexiblelearning.net.au /edition-11-editorial/thinking-beyond-pen-and-paper-an-interview-with-jenny-ashby

Naked Scientists. (2001-2005). *What is the Naked Scientists?* Retrieved January 15, 2007, from http://www.thenakedscientists.com/HTML/Background /background.htm

National Council of Teachers of English. (1998-2007). *On including speaking and listening in National Assessment of Educational Progress (NAEP) Assessments.* Retrieved January 15, 2007, from http://www.ncte.org/about/over/positions/ category/assess/107382.htm

National Public Radio. (2005). *Science Friday—Making science radioactive.* Retrieved January 12, 2007, from http://www.sciencefriday.com/feed

National School Boards Association. (n.d.). *Authentic learning.* Retrieved January 8, 2007, from http://www.nsba.org/sbot/toolkit/authlrn.htm

National Space and Aeronautics Administration (NASA). (n.d). *NASA 21st century explorer podcast competition.* Retrieved January 12, 2007, from http://www.explorationpodcast.com/about.php

Nauset Schools. (2005-2006a). *Nauset Schools podcasts.* Retrieved January 16, 2007, from http://nausetschools.org/podcasts/index.htm

Nauset Schools. (2005-2006b). *Nauset Schools blogs.* Retrieved January 16, 2007, from http://nausetpublicschools.blogspot.com

Newman, F. M., & Wehlage, G. G. (1993). *Five standards of authentic instruction. Authentic Learning, 50*(7). Retrieved on January 18, 2007, from http://pdonline.ascd.org/pd_online/diffinstr/el199304_newmann.html

New York State Education Department. (n.d.). *New York State Core Curriculum in Mathematics: Every teacher of mathematics. (2005).* Retrieved January 12, 2007, from http://www.emsc.nysed.gov/ciai/mst/mathstandards/intro.html#The%20Five%20Process%20Strands

New York City Department of Education (n.d.). *New standards performance standards science.* Retrieved January 12, 2007, from http://schools.nyc.gov/offices/teachlearn/documents/standards/science/ms/66overview.html

North Central Regional Educational Laboratories (NCREL). (2004). *Authentic learning.* Retrieved January 8, 2007, from http://www.ncrel.org/engauge/framewk/efp/rel/efprelra.htm

O'Hear, S. (2005, April 10). *The guardian.* Retrieved January 18, 2007 from http://www.ohear.net/full_publication.php?publicationID=23

Pedraza, J. (2006, July 15). *History Students Podcast Oral History, University Marketing Communications.* Retrieved January 11, 2007, from http://uwf.edu/uwfMain/press/topstoryarch.cfm?emailID=16187

Pink, D. (2005). *A whole new mind.* Retrieved January 16, 2007, from http://www.danpink.com/excerptwnm.php

Read, B. (2005, September 9). *Lectures on the go. The Chronicle of Higher Education, 52*(10), A39. Retrieved August 30, 2006, from http://chronicle.com/free/v52/i10/10a03901.htm

Reader's Digest. (2007a). *What is RD Outloud?* Retrieved February 18, 2007, from http://www.rd.com/openContentCategory.do?contentCategoryId=685

Reader's Digest. (2007b). *What is RD Outloud?* Retrieved February 18, 2007, from http://www.rd.com/content/openContent.do?contentId=30478&pageIndex=0

ReadWriteThink. (2007). *Audio broadcasts and podcasts: Oral storytelling and dramatization.* Retrieved January 15, 2007, from http://www.readwritethink.org/lessons/lesson_view.asp?id=901

Ruthmann, A. (2005). *Cranbrook Composer's Podcasts.* Retrieved January 9, 2007, from http://cranbrookcomposers.blogspot.com

Sacramento City Unified School District (n.d.) *What is Differentiated Instruction?* Retrieved January 8, 2007, from http:// www.scusd.edu/gate_ext_learning/differentiated.htm

Scholastic. (2007). *Let's talk about Harry.* Retrieved January 11, 2007, from http://www.scholastic.com/harrypotter/podcasttour/index.htm

Schön, D. (1983). *The reflective practitioner.* New York: Basic Books.

School Library Journal, SLJ.com. (n.d.). *School Library Journal podcast.* Retrieved January 9, 2007, from http://www.schoollibraryjournal.com/noclamp/CA6389459.html

Shields, K. (2007a). *Small voices, episode 1.* Retrieved January 9, 2007, from http://kinderteacher.podomatic.com/entry/2006-07-10T06_30_33-07_00

Shields, K. (2007b.) *Small voices, episode 4.* Retrieved January 9, 2007, from http://kinderteacher.podomatic.com/entry/2006-07-12T10_38_06-07_00

Schrock, K. (2006-2007). *Kathy Schrock's kaffeeklatsch.* Retrieved January 16, 2007, from http://kathyschrock.net/blog

Shen, F. (2005, October 19). iPods fast becoming new teachers pets. *Washington Post,* p. B01. Retrieved January 15, 2007, from http://www.washingtonpost.com/wp-dyn/content/article/2005/10/18/AR2005101801670.html?nav=hcmodule

Silverstein, S. (2006, January 23). More undergrads playing hooky when class notes go online. *Chicago Tribune,* p. 9. Retrieved August 30, 2006, from Proquest Database http://proquest.umi.com/pqdweb?did=974184141&sid=2&Fmt=3&clientId=9148&RQT=309&VName=PQD

Siuntres, J. (2006). *Wordballoon the comic creators interview show.* Retrieved January 15, 2007, from http://feeds.feedburner.com/WordballoonPodcasts

Smithsonian Education. (2007). *Podcasting with your students.* Retrieved January 15, 2007, from http://www.smithsonianeducation.org/educators/lesson_plans/podcast/jamestown.html

Stenhouse Publishers. (n.d.) *Author conversations: Podcasts.* Retrieved January 16, 2007, from http://www.stenhouse.com/podcast.asp

Technorati.com (2008). *About us.* Retrieved June 16, 2008, from http://technorati.com/about/

Tennessee State Department of Education. (2001). Social Studies K-12 Process Standards. Retrieved January 11, 2007, from http://www.tennessee.gov/education/ci/cistandards2001/ss/cissprocessstandards.htm

Thornburg, D. (1999). *Technology in K-12 education: Envisioning a new future.* Retrieved January 5, 2007, from http://www.air.org/forum/Thornburg.pdf

Tolbert, N. (n.d.). *Podcasting share page.* Retrieved January 16, 2007, from http://www.k12handhelds.com/podcastshare.php

Tricom Podcasts. (n.d.). *Authors in your pocket.* Retrieved January 9, 2007, from http://www.tricompodcast.com/site/welcome

Umbach, G. (2006). *Department of History, John Jay College of Criminal Justice.* Retrieved Ocotber 15, 2006, from http://web.jjay.cuny.edu/~history/umbach/worldspring06/

U.S. Department of Education. (2000). *White Papers on the Future of Technology in Education.* Retrieved January 12, 2007, from http://www.air.org/forum/wpapers.htm

U.S. Department of Education, Office of Special Education Programs. (2006). *Readingrockets.* Retrieved January 11, 2007, from http://www.readingrockets.org/about

U.S. Department of Labor. (2000). *Skills and tasks for jobs—A SCANS report for America.* Retrieved January 15, 2007, from http://wdr.doleta.gov/opr/FULLTEXT/1999_35.pdf

Vincent, T. (2006). *Soft reset.* Retrieved January 16, 2007, from http://www.learninginhand.com/softreset

Walch, R. (2006.) *Podcast 411 directory of directories.* Retrieved September 10, 2006, http://www.podcast411.com/page2.html

Warlick, D. (2006). *Connected learning.* Retrieved September 10, 2006, from http://davidwarlick.com/connectlearning/

Wikipedia. (2006). *School radio.* Retrieved January 9, 2007, from http://en.wikipedia.org/wiki/High_school_radio

Wired. (2006, May) A guide to the online video explosion. *Wired Magazine, 14*(5). Retrieved on September 2, 2006, from http://www.wired.com/wired/archive/14.05/guide.html

Yerrick, R. (2006, October 19). Globalizing education one podcast at a time. *THE Journal.* Retrieved January 10, 2007, from http://www.thejournal.com/the/newsletters/smartclassroom/archives/?aid=19444

ABOUT THE AUTHORS

Dr. Kathleen P. King is a professor of education at Fordham University's Graduate School of Education in New York City. Mark Gura is also affiliated with Fordham University and Transformation Education LLC as well. They are both frequent presenters and keynote speakers for teacher professional development conferences and seminars. Among them they published 20 educational books and hundreds of articles, and earned numerous awards for their contribution to the field. In addition to their many years of experience in the classroom as educators in K-12 classrooms (Mark), adult education and higher education (Kathy), and instructional technology design and professional development across all grades (both), they are also the creators, producers and cohosts of the first educational technology professional development podcast for K-12 and higher education educators hosted by a major university, Podcast for Teachers (http://www.podcastforteachers.org) and now independently as Teachers' Podcast (http://www.teacherspodcast.org)

DR. KATHLEEN P. KING

Dr. King has been a professor of education at Fordham University's Graduate School of Education since 1997. She was director of the university's RETC Center for Professional Development (2003-2007) and coordinated many grants including New York City Department of Education Title IID grants and a U.S. Department of Education FIPSE/LAAP grant that serves teachers across the nation via online technologies, Anytime Anywhere Learning Professional Development School (AALPDS). Her work provides a dynamic base for many initiatives in professional development services, partnerships, and research.

She has planned, designed, conducted, and researched faculty and staff development in educational technology for K-12 schools, higher education institutions, and other organizations. Her background is distinct in that although she is an educator and academic, she also has been a "techie" as a private computer and engineering consultant for hardware and software purchasing and troubleshooting and training for many years.

Dr. King has authored, coauthored, and edited several books including: Innovations in Career and Technical Education (2008); *Classroom Robotics in the Innovative Instructions Series* (2007); *Comparative Adult Education Around the Globe* (2006); *Harnessing Innovative Technologies in Higher Education* (2006); *Bringing Transformative Learning to Life* (2005); *Keeping Pace with Technology* (2002, 2003); and *A Model for Planning for Effective Faculty Development* (2000). In addition, King is founding editor of an education journal. She has published 12 books, 30 book chapters, and more than 100 articles and papers. Her grant writing has resulted in over $15 million in external funding and contracts for Fordham University (1998-2007).

King is a frequent presenter and keynoter at local, national, and international research and professional conferences on the topics of faculty development, transformational learning, and educational technology. Her research has been widely recognized through refereed presentations at conferences including EDUCAUSE, ACHE, AERA, AERC, International Learning Conference, Professional and Organizational Development Conference, and Sloan E-Learning Conference.

MARK GURA

Mark has been an educator for more than 3 decades. A former director of instructional technology for the New York City public school system, he has also been outreach coordinator for Fordham University's Graduate School of Education. In his additional outreach consulting work for educational technology and school change he and Kathy work with a team of professionals at Transformation Education LLC (www.transformationed.com). Through TELLC, they serve the educational technology needs of administrations, teachers, schools, and organizations both nationally and internationally. This work focuses on fostering the use of educational applications of technology for instruction across the content areas, including the exploration of emerging forms of digital media and distance learning, as well as supporting the planning, and development of technology innovations that will affect change and support educational leaders at all levels. Mr. Gura draws on his extensive background as a literacy, science, and arts educator in promoting the creative use of technology to provide highly motivating, relevant activities for students. He has done extensive work in preparing teachers to be effective instructors in the digital age, designing and implementing professional development for many thousands of teachers.

Mr. Gura is author of *Visual Arts Units* (2008), coeditor of *Classroom Robotics* (2007) and coauthor of *Making Literacy Magic Happen: The Best of Learning & Leading with Technology* (2001) and *Recapturing Technology for Education: Keeping Tomorrow in Today's Classroom* (2005), as well as numerous articles on instructional technology, educational policy and reform, and arts education. He has given numerous keynotes and presentations throughout the country and is widely known in not only education circles but also the computer hardware and software field because of his work in the New York City Department of Education and his commitment and understanding to innovative uses of technology in education.

Mark and Kathy also cohost the internationally distributed Web-based broadcast The Teachers' Podcast, previously known as Podcast for Teachers; this is a podcast about educational technology innovation which is hosted by Transformation Education LLC. The Teachers' Podcast features valuable resources, insights, and lively conversations about technology with leading educators. Mark and Kathy share the latest in educational technology updates, news, views, interviews and research for practical use for teachers and learners of all ages. The Teachers' Podcast (TTPOD) is distributed freely via the Web and listed in iTunes, podcastalley.com, podcast411.com, odeo.com and many other podcast databases. PFT has won international awards for technology innovation in professional development of educators and has served more than 4.3 million listeners to date (8/05-10/08). More information about the podcast may be found at http://www.teacherspodcast.org

The work with podcasting has extended much further so that Dr. King has developed many additional podcasts and online, virtual workshops. Additional podcasts include: Adventures in Transformative Learning (www.podcastforteachers.org/atl), Talking Financial Literacy Podcast (http://www.talkingfinlit.org) funded in part by The McGraw Hill Companies, and produces the District Leader's Podcast (http://www.districtleaderspodcast.org) as an outreach of McGraw Hill Education, and Podcast for Professors (http://www.podcastforprofessors.org). Online, virtual workshops are offered in a virtual environment which includes two-way audio, presentations, and text chat; topics include podcasting in education, twenty-first century learning, and Web site development.

INDEX

LaVergne, TN USA
22 April 2010
180236LV00002B/26/P